Stockdog
Savvy

Just a Stockdog Story

by Gary Bogy

Do you remember when I was just a little tyke,
and you bought that hot new colt named Ike.
He was the color of new fallen snow
I ran right down to say hello.
Then he kicked a mighty blow,
he nearly hit me, but I ducked low.

I got mad and heeled him hard,
we fought all over the yard.
And when the storm's end was near,
you were pullin' on my ear.
Then I knew I had done wrong,
and sang out a sad song.

You said it would be all right,
it was just a kid fight.
Back then you were just a boss
to a young pup and a green broke hoss.
We made the rounds the three of us,
gathered stock and lots of dust.

That was how it all began,
we all became working friends.
Remember that steer we penned out West,
his horns were longer than the rest.
He was aiming to run me thru,
if it had not been for Ike and you.

Dropped a loop around his neck,
then I really gave him heck.
The you meet that darned old girl,
left me and Ike in a swirl.
We could not find you for a while,
then you brought her home with a smile.

She was really neat,
I loved to lay there by her feet.
One day we got a place of our own,
you and her called it a home.
You remember that brindle bull named Prince,
he had you pinned against the fence.

I told him to let you go and bit him very hard,
he must have kicked me from the yard.
Now I found a place to rest,
like those mountain meadows out West.
But the flowers here stay year-round,
and nobody ever mentions a dog pound.

All the animals here are friends,
it's the way it should have always been.
I sure missed you there at first,
and knew it could not have been worse.
The say it never, never ends,
and I keep making more good friends.

I wanted you to know I am okay,
And I hope to see you here someday.

Ty Taylor and his Aussie, Poco, at the end of a working day on the Lazy 3 Mill Iron Y Ranch.

For Tyler (Oty) and Katy Lynn —
the fourth generation to carry on.

Stockdog Savvy

By Jeanne Joy Hartnagle-Taylor and Ty Taylor

Stockdog Savvy

ISBN 13: 978-1-57779-106-5
ISBN 10: 1-57779-106-1

Library of Congress Cataloging-in-Publication Data

Hartnagle-Taylor, Jeanne Joy, 1955-
  Stockdog savvy / by Jeanne Joy Hartnagle-Taylor and Ty Taylor
     p. cm.
  ISBN-13: 978-1-57779-106-5 (pb : alk. paper)
  ISBN-10: 1-57779-106-1 (pb : alk. paper)
1. Herding dogs. I. Taylor, Ty, 1956- II. Title
  SF428.6.H35 2009
  636.737—dc22
                                  2009039438

Cover Design: B. J. McKinney
Cover Photo: Jeanne Joy Hartnagle-Taylor
Editing by: Sheila Dolan
Interior Design by: Dianne Nelson, Shadow Canyon Graphics

4 5 6 7 8 9 0
PRINTED IN THE UNITED STATES OF AMERICA

Contents

Preface

Early stockdog training came out of the need to get a job done. As a boy, my father's job was to gather the cows and bring them to the barn for milking. They were often in the lush grass on the pastures on the other side of Boulder Creek—which ran through the lower half of the family farm—he had to take off his shoes and wade across the water to get them.

He figured out if he tossed rocks across the creek, he could coax Buster, a three-legged bobtail dog, to the other side and then persuade him to bring the cows, so he wouldn't have to get them himself.

After that, all he had to do was tell Buster to "go get the cows," and Buster would swim across the creek and gather the herd. He dutifully brought the cows, and if any one lagged behind, he would duck down and gently nip it on the heels.

As a child, I saw my father tell Jinx, a little blue Australian Shepherd, to "bring the sheep." She took off across the pasture to gather the entire flock and bring them down the lane to the corrals at night. He didn't train her how to do this, it was natural for her. The pups learned as they went along, doing chores.

In the 1960s, my parents gave me the *Purina Farm Dog Book*. It had delightful pictures of Carl Bradford, who was the Ohio State University Research Center Shepherd, working his beautiful Border Collies. *National Geographic Book of Dogs* also had some wonderful pictures of his dogs herding sheep and ducks around miniature white fence obstacles. From that point forth it was my dream to teach my dogs to do the things I saw in the book. In those early days there really were no training books to speak of, and we did not have the luxury of training videos or DVDs.

When I started training I didn't know how to make the sheep stand quietly in the middle of a field so I could teach the dog to circle around them. That was a mystery to me. The *Purina Farm Dog Book* described a mechanical method of using pulleys to teach the dogs to move to the right or left, but that was highly impractical, so I put my mother's imported Manx cats in a crate and taught the dogs to circle around them. It seemed to work fine. I didn't discover the flaw of that idea until one day I had gathered a small group of cattle from a pasture, and while bringing them into a corral to load them into a stock trailer—a barnyard cat ran through the corral—and away went the dog.

I decided to start using the goats that were grazing in the pasture with the horses. They found refuge by staying with the horses, so I put halters on the horses and then it was easy to keep the goats in a quiet bunch. It seemed like we were making progress. I was training a keen little cowdog at the time. The first time I worked her from horseback was when we were trying to drive a herd of cows across a creek with rushing water. Naturally, the cattle were reluctant to move off the banks into the water, so I asked her to "skit 'em up," she did. When the horse felt the sting on his heels he plunged into the creek. The cows were still standing on the creek bank . . . another lesson learned.

It wasn't until we met Lewis Pence, a sheep shearer and Border Collie trainer from Ohio, that we really learned how to teach. He was a gracious man who was willing to share his knowledge. Lewis was also one of the few men at that time who actually trained his own dogs, unlike many of the others who were importing trained Border Collies from Scotland. We also met other men who were competing in open sheepdog trials, but who were reluctant to teach the art to others. We discovered they were unable to handle upright, close working breeds because they didn't respond like their Border Collies. Through our friendship with Lewis we learned how to teach a dog the skills necessary to nurture successful trial dogs. Those skills also helped us foster efficient, useful ranch dogs.

Ty—my husband and co-author—learned the value of a good cowdog and how to handle them while working with Cletus Hulling, a world-class cutting horse trainer. From that point on, he used his dogs to move livestock in the sale yards and for ranch work. When we got married, he didn't know that much about sheep, but it didn't take him long to gain an appreciation for them. At the time we were touring throughout the western United States and Canada with his country music band. To unwind after weeks on the road, he'd come home and saddle up his horse to take the flock out to graze in the open grass land. It was one of the most relaxing, peaceful experiences he's ever known.

We collaborated on our experiences in *Stockdog Savvy* to help others get the most out of their own herding dogs—whether for farm and ranch work or just for pure enjoyment. Gratitude to my parents, Ernie and Elaine Hartnagle, for breeding talented stockdogs, a bloodline of distinction. They are to Australian Shepherds what the King Ranch is to Quarter Horses. Special recognition goes to the friends and family who have always been there for us and have helped us along the way. Most of all, the final credit goes to Jesus, the greatest Shepherd who ever walked the face of the earth.

Jeanne Joy Hartnagle-Taylor

Foreword

There is no one that I know who is more qualified to write a book on training the many herding breeds than Jeanne Joy. From the time she was a little girl, her main interest was herding dogs.

To detail her many credentials would fill an entire book of its own. I will attempt to only list a few of her major achievements. For a number of years, Jeanne held a position of trainer and instructor for the Stockdog Fanciers of Colorado, an all-breed herding club that encompassed the major breeds; and many of the lesser known breeds. She never saw a dog that she didn't like, and worked with them with enthusiasm and understanding. Simultaneously, Jeanne developed her own unique family of working Australian Shepherds. In 1983, the first stockdog futurity was held in Waxahatchie, Texas. Her dogs placed first, second, and fifth in an outstanding field of fourteen entries.

During the coarse of her career, she worked with local ranchers and the United States Department of Agriculture moving cattle to and from various locations with her dogs. Joe D. Taylor of the huge Taylor ranch headquartered in Moab, Utah, became her mentor as they worked the different areas, from the summer grazing grounds in the high mountain ranges to the winter desert grounds. Jeanne also worked wild bison for the Department of Interior.

She spent four years handling and managing the Corriente roping stock at the Thacker arena, a training and contest facility. She, with her eight especially trained Aussies, after each run, cleared the arena, and in bunches of ten to twenty drove them to the back to the roping chutes. This fast moving facility ran from one hundred to several hundred runs on any given performance.

Jeanne Joy became the youngest ever person to be approved by the Australian Shepherd Club of America to judge conformation and stockdog trials. In this facet of her life, she adjudicated in most of the lower forty-eight states and Alaska. Her travels took her throughout North America and Europe, judging and lecturing. One of the highlights includes performing with her dogs in Mexico by invitation from the Governor of Jalisco.

In the literary world, Jeanne Joy became a published author, writing an untold number of articles for dog magazines. In 1986, she authored the book, *All About Aussies* that is now in it's fourth edition. She is recognized world-wide as the breed's foremost authority and historian.

As you read thru the pages of this wonderful book, you will feel her keenness, her credibility, gained thru her many personal experiences in her unique literary style, bringing into play incidents that are generally overlooked by too many authors in this particular discipline. To sum it up, Jeanne Joy "has been there, done that." And she now extends her knowledge for you to read, learn and enjoy.

Ernie Hartnagle
July, 7, 2009

Introduction

Using herding dogs can be useful and extremely satisfying. However without proper training they can be frustrating. The dog needs to be able to outmaneuver and rate livestock. In order to teach these skills the trainer needs to have an understanding of the animals—sheep, cattle, ducks, geese, goats or turkeys—and the way they think and move.

It is important to keep in mind, no two dogs are alike. Each trainer must be flexible and willing to adapt or modify the teaching process to the individual dog's unique ability in order to develop him to his highest potential. The techniques described in *Stockdog Savvy* are based on a lifetime of practical experiences. It was written to educate and equip owners with the knowledge and skills necessary to maximize their dog's natural talent on different types of stock. The book outlines a methodology—teaching herding skills through play training to working ranch dogs in the real world—for working successfully with all breeds of herding dogs.

Chapter 1

HERDING DOGS

It has been said, "Most of the footprints in the sands of time were made by working shoes." By the side of those footprints are paw prints.

HERDING DOG CHARACTERISTICS

Herding dogs work because it's natural for them. The inclination to circle stock in an attempt to round up the animals and keep them bunched in a group is inherent in dogs whose ancestors were cultivated for their working abilities. This instinct is obvious even in young dogs of these breeds as they encircle their littermates or try to round up children, sometimes nipping at their heels.

All of the fundamental herding traits possessed by working dogs are derived from the hunting instincts of their remote ancestors, behavior that

Instinct to herd is innate, and without stock to work, dogs will attempt to use their skills on other moving objects, including the family cat.

1

Working Trial Champion Twin Oaks Winslow Breeze heading a steer.
PHOTO BY GARY R. ANDERSON.

is still seen in wolves, coyotes, and other wild dogs. In approaching their prey, the fastest members (the headers) of the pack come out from behind and run to the front of the herd, cutting off their quarry. When the prey turns back to flee, the driving members (heelers), who are generally the slower members of the pack, prevent them from escaping, allowing the pack to circle in for the kill. Through selective breeding, humans have cultivated dogs with the traits that are the most useful in tending livestock— and bred out the desire to kill.

Heading and driving are the two distinct behaviors displayed by herding dogs when working with stock. When one animal breaks away from the group, the heading instinct causes the dog to get ahead of the runaway to block its escape. (In fact, without training and supervision, some dogs may head and then re-head the escapee, preventing its return to the herd or flock.) A natural driving dog, on the other hand, has an inherited tendency to wear behind the stock (sweep back and forth in semicircles) to keep the animals moving. A driving dog won't instinctively race to the head of escaping stock.

While many breeds were developed to have a stronger inclination toward one working style or the other, the most versatile stock dogs are those capable of both heading and driving. Headers can be taught to stay behind stock and drive, and some driving dogs can be taught to swing out to the front of the animals to change their direction or turn back a runaway.

Herding dogs from working bloodlines possess an internal power and presence that help them gain the upper hand over their charges in a deliberate, authoritative manner. A dog that is working sheep must be able to demonstrate the same degree of power and authority as a cowdog, but without using the same kind of force. Even on cattle operations, where grip (use of the teeth in an inhibited bite) is often necessary, severe, uncontrolled biting can be detrimental.

HERDING INSTINCTS DEFINED

When dogs gather and drive a herd or flock of animals, specific behaviors that result from herding instincts are necessary to manage the livestock.

Powder River Strawboss wearing behind cattle. PHOTO COURTESY JIM AND SUE FOSTER.

Balance, bark, concentration, eye, grip, power, and stock savvy are inherited traits that are needed for a dog to herd livestock effectively. The ideal dog can get the job done without unnecessary force or getting stuck with too much eye. Herding instincts can be enhanced through experience, but only to the degree that the dog has inherited the trait.

Balance is the dog's ability to find the appropriate distance and position (in front, behind, or off to the side) to control livestock. The dog's balance changes according to the flightiness of the animals being handled. Herding dogs lacking good natural balance require more instruction from their trainer to control livestock effectively and move them in the desired direction.

Bark is the dog's use of voice to move stock without biting. When faced with a challenging animal, a forceful bark or growl at the right time is desirable. However, a dog that yaps constantly can upset animals, even causing them to fight back or challenge the dog. Continual barking can indicate an inexperienced dog or a lack of power or confidence. A young dog in the early stages of training may overuse his voice, but should be able to learn with experience when and how to use it most effectively.

Concentration is the amount of attention the dog gives to the stock. Obviously, herders with good concentration are more successful than less attentive dogs. This natural behavior can either be improved through proper handling or impaired through improper handling. But even though dogs that are easily distracted may be trained to improve their focus, they will never be as successful as dogs that are born with good focus.

Tazz, a Belgian Tervuren (ABTC HTCH/ASCA WTCH/AKC Champion Winjammer's Spit In Yer Eye) using eye. COURTESY PAT MORGAN.

Heeling. PHOTO BY GARY R. ANDERSON.

Eye is the ability of the dog to control an animal by staring fixedly at it to influence its movement. Border Collies and Australian Kelpies are considered "strong-eyed" breeds, and strong-eyed individuals may possibly appear from time to time in other breeds. Different breeds use eye to some extent; individual dogs within a breed will vary in the degree of eye that they use. The correct amount of eye helps the dog to concentrate and behave in a steady manner that doesn't upset the flock. A loose-eyed dog has a greater tendency to use voice and body movements (e.g., wearing, shouldering), which may be less useful when working small groups of flighty stock. Loose-eyed dogs typically are more suitable for working large groups of animals.

An overly strong eye, on the other hand, can cause a dog to be sticky or hesitant in his approach; he may even become so mesmerized by the animals that he is unable to work effectively. The ideal stock dog exhibits necessary eye when confronting defiant or stubborn livestock, but will relax and return to watching the entire flock once the confrontation is over.

Grip refers to the use of bite. As with any herding instinct, the dog's ability to use grip sensibly is developed through experience. Grip is acceptable on the head (the nose or poll) or on the lower leg or foot (front or hind). Nipping at the heels or hocks is referred to as *heeling*. Grip is important in handling obstinate livestock, but it's not effective unless it's backed by confidence. Sometimes a young or inexperienced dog grips or may even bite out of lack of confidence. (*See* Power *below.*) However, dogs that chase and demonstrate predatory biting (going for the throat or hamstring with the purpose of bringing animals down) may not possess enough true herding ability to warrant training—and they can't be trusted to work alone and out of sight.

Power (or force) is the dog's ability to exert its authority or influence over livestock. This requires good stock savvy (*see* Stock Savvy *below*). In herding dogs, power usually indicates strength of working character. There are degrees of power: A dog that lacks herding instincts can exhibit force toward livestock but may not have the ability to control them. Upright, close-working dogs with moderate eye generally have more power than wide-running dogs. (The term "upright" refers to the dog's working posture—he doesn't crouch low like a predator stalking prey.) Wide-running dogs may do well on a few head of livestock in a trial competition, but don't usually have the power to move a large flock of sheep at a distance.

Stock savvy is the dog's instinctive ability to outthink the livestock. In other words, if an animal is trying to break away from the group, the dog moves into position to prevent the escape before the animal is able to get

Chippa, a reindeer herding dog owned by Silja Jonsson, demonstrating the upright, close-working style. PHOTO COURTESY JONSSON STOCKDOGS.

XP Snap, a Border Collie owned by Michelle Brothers, demonstrating the type of eye and body posture the breed is distinguished for. PHOTO BY LORI HERBEL OF XP RANCH PHOTOGRAPHY.

away. For a dog to use stock savvy, he must have good balance. In real working situations, an intuitive dog will usually pick up the animal's intention before the trainer does. If the dog has to rely on the handler to tell him when to make each move, he may miss the opportunity to prevent a problem from arising. Some breeds, such as Border Collies, Aussies, Kelpies, English Shepherds, and McNabs, tend to be naturally more stock savvy than a lot of others.

Style encompasses the amount of eye, natural working distance, force, use of bark, and grip used by a dog. Many of these traits are inbred and cannot be taught. Dogs can be trained to use grip appropriately, for example, but they cannot be made to "low heel"—nip the heel of the cow's weight-bearing leg and then duck low enough to avoid the resulting kick—any more than dogs with little or no inborn eye can be made to use strong eye.

HERDING DOGS TODAY

At present, Australian Cattle Dogs, Australian Shepherds, Border Collies, English Shepherds, Kelpies, and McNabs are still the breeds most frequently found on farms and ranches in North America, but with fewer ranch jobs

Las Rocosa Charlie Brown, owned by Mindy Bower and Kevin Hall, working steers on the Uh Oh Ranch on the High Plains in Kiowa, Colorado. COURTESY MINDY BOWER.

available for dogs, more herding dogs have found their way into urban and suburban homes. Many urban owners are fascinated by their herding breed's innate ability to work stock, which has resulted in the rise in herding testing and stockdog competitions. In rural and suburban areas, dogs are sometimes kept to work small herds of animals or poultry, or conversely, the livestock is kept so the family's companion dog can be trained to work.

New opportunities, such as patrolling geese, are opening up for herding dogs in the modern world. A gaggle of geese can create large amounts of goose droppings and burn the grass, resulting in thousands of dollars of damage annually. While geese are a nuisance at parks and golf courses, they present a major hazard on airport runways. Herding dogs are the most effective non-lethal solution for these goose problems.

Mitigation (brush control) is another way herding dogs are being utilized in traditional ways. Sheep and goats have long been recognized as an effective alternative to herbicides to reduce woody plants and brush and to control weeds that provide fuel for fire in potential fire zones. They are eco-friendly in wetlands and along stream banks. They work faster and are more cost-effective than human crews who manually clear off wild blackberry

Tanya Wheeler's dog herding geese off a lake in Thunder Bay, Ontario, Canada. COURTESY TANYA WHEELER.

vines, other briars, and unwanted foliage from steep inclines. However, it still takes the resolve of good herding dogs to manage them.

For all these reasons, or just for the pure enjoyment of watching a dog do the work for which he was bred over many centuries, interest in herding and stock dog training is alive and well.

A PROFILE OF

Diana Waibel — A New Set of Legs

 For over thirty-five years, Diana Waibel has raised purebred, registered Border Leicester sheep. She started raising her quality flock of long wool sheep with bloodlines from New Zealand. Waibel is a director for the American Border Leicester Association and has been a member of the organization for just about as long as it has been in existence.

Di was raised in the Willamette Valley about sixty miles south of Portland, Oregon. She has been wheelchair bound for the last 25 years due to a fall with a jumping horse when she was around forty years old. Border Collies are an enormously important part of her Mist O Morn Farm. "The dogs allow me to continue raising my sheep, which also keeps me active and healthy," she states.

Di is a fiercely independent, dynamic person. After the accident she was determined she was not going to give up her farm or the way of life she loved so dearly. Nor was she going to resign herself to sit on the sidelines. Even though she had lost the use of her legs, she figured she still had the use of her arms, a sound mind, and her magnificent Border Collies.

She also credits a lot of thoughtful friends and family for helping her to create a wheelchair accessible farm. They helped her build ramps in and out of the barn and a concrete runway from the house to the barn. She has a lot of little pastures that feed into the barn, the center of the operation. She is able to handle the flock from one location at the hub where the gates swing in either direction. "I have to work my dogs different than a lot of people," she said. "I have a lot of little pastures that feed back into the barn. I can send my dogs and they bring the sheep in. They help me load sheep into the stock trailers, move sheep in and out of the barn pens, push between the sheep and the walls, and just about do the majority of the work."

When Di picks a puppy, she starts with proven working bloodlines. That is the key element in the success of her ability to train and work sheepdogs. She wants to know that both the parents are really good working dogs. Then, she takes the time to teach the dog necessary obedience commands prior to ever training them on sheep. "Especially for me in a wheelchair, I can't run the dog down." When the dog is about a year old she starts their education on sheep, working them for about five minutes a day, sometimes twice a day. Before long, the dogs obey willingly, which allows her to give them plenty of opportunity to think and use their natural ability.

Di has even competed in sheepdog trials in a wheelchair. At one trial, the judge from Scotland wanted to buy her dog. He said, "It is a wee fine dog you have there." Di responded, "She might be a wee fine dog, but she's my legs, plus my buddy."

Chapter 2

WHAT TO LOOK FOR IN A HERDING DOG

CHOOSING THE RIGHT BREED FOR YOUR NEEDS

Whether your herds are cattle, sheep, reindeer, geese, hogs (dogs have even been used to herd fish into shallow waters for easier netting!), choosing the right breed requires research. Over the last century, herding breeds have been bred for conformation and companionship or for performance. This practice has resulted in two distinct varieties — working dogs and show dogs. Until the beginning of the American Kennel Club's herding program in 1989, most herding dogs were bred for the show ring and as attractive companion animals, with the emphasis on form rather than function. Their forerunners had been used to work livestock, but herding ability was rarely one of the criteria used to breed show dogs.

Correct basic structure for each breed is all important. The influence of the conformation shows promoting the long, flowing stride produced by greater front angulation and flatter pelvic angles has sacrificed the agility so crucial for herding dogs to make quick turns and abrupt stops at full speeds while working livestock. It is extremely important to buy from a breeder who produces dogs with stock handling ability rather than pet or show dogs. Puppies from champion bloodlines may or may not have the appropriate aptitude for actual stock work, regardless of herding instinct certificates that may have been awarded by breed associations. Even then, some bloodlines in breeds such as the Belgian Sheepdogs are extremely fast, tough dogs with an intense prey drive—making it difficult for inexperienced and junior handlers to work with.

ALL BREEDS ARE NOT CREATED EQUAL

The contrast between the German Shepherd Dog—trotting along a perimeter to keep determined sheep grazing within a boundary of an unfenced

A Kelpie with power and purpose, developed for working huge flocks in the harsh conditions of the Australian Outback. PHOTO BY LORI HERBEL OF XP RANCH PHOTOGRAPHY.

field, and the Kelpie sprinting across the backs of sheep in tightly packed sorting chute—is remarkable. Herding extremes around the world are amazing, but no more so than Nordic dogs in the Northern latitudes driving domestic caribou from the tundra to the forests to graze on lichen (reindeer moss).

Breeds had to be hardy to withstand the weather extremes of their native country. They differ because each was produced for specific conditions. Border Collies, for example, work at a greater distance from their stock than most breeds do, and they use a lot of eye—methods suitable for handling nimble Scottish blackface sheep in the Highlands. Less responsive sheep in other parts of Europe required a closer-working dog breed, such as the Briard or Mudi.

Cowdogs, such as the Catahoula Leopard of the American South, were developed for taking wild cattle out of swamps and for handling feral hogs, rather than the less aggressive English Shepherd needed to work a variety of farm animals from dairy cattle to turkeys.

The Bouvier, Rottweiler and Swiss Mountain Sennenhunds are also cattle-working breeds, but were developed to calmly herd dairy cattle to the milking barn and yet be sturdy enough to pull a cart. Their stature and working style, therefore, reflects some of the traits of a draft animal. These large, heavy dogs aren't built to stop or accelerate suddenly. While they have the

Echtenhof Django, a working type Bouvier (Roeselare Cowdog), bringing the dairy herd in for morning milking. PHOTO COURTESY ECHTENHOF KENNEL OF BELGIUM.

A red Australian Cattle Dog illustrates how the breed gained the nickname "Heeler." PHOTO BY JEFF JAQUISH AT ZINGPIX.COM.

Above: An athletic Australian Shepherd built to outmaneuver cattle on the open range. Below: An Aussie sprinting to head off a steer. PHOTOS BY GARY R. ANDERSON.

agility to leap up and grip the noses of fairly tame cows if necessary—they are not built for low heeling, which calls for a quick dog with a lower center of gravity, such as the rugged Australian Cattle Dog.

On the other hand, Corgis are low heelers, but they lack the sufficient leg length necessary to outmaneuver untamed cattle over long distances on

A plucky little Lancashire Heeler working cows in his native countryside.
PHOTO BY TRAFFORDPHOTOS.COM.

the open range, whereas Australian Shepherds and Stumpy Tail Cattle Dogs are well suited for that kind of work—built for the sudden bursts of speed needed for outrunning and turning an unruly critter or for responding to abrupt changes of direction.

CHARACTER, INTELLIGENCE, AND TRAINABILITY

Herding dogs in general are clever, easily taught and quickly trained. A sensible worker has a good balance of herding instincts and trainability, as well as a "want-to-please" attitude, and is highly desirable. The ideal herding dog of any breed is self-assured and determined—not easily discouraged by a stubborn stock animal.

Intelligence is reflected in their inquisitive expression. They also have the ability to think for themselves. There are numerous anecdotes of a dog responding to a situation such as a lost lamb that his master was unaware of. They are also intensely loyal and bond closely with their handlers. A herding dog, for instance, may use his nose to nudge his owner's hand or to bump his leg to get his attention. He would never consider using his teeth, except perhaps in a gentle pinch to show affection. When out for a walk, he may keep his owner in sight, running ahead, checking back continually. In the house, the dog may quietly follow him as he goes from one room to another.

One night, my father sent Ritchie, one of his ranch dogs, out to gather the sheep. Ritchie raced off into the pasture and gathered the flock and brought them into the corrals. He took off again. When my father called him, he responded out of obedience, but started barking at him and running in the direction he had come from. When my father followed him, Ritchie took him to a little lamb that had gotten stuck in a fence and was unable to get out. Had it not been for Ritchie, the coyotes would have killed the lamb that night.

Las Rocosa Ritchie, a working ranch dog, watching over his charges.

Herding dogs are able to think independently. Their ancestors were often required to work out of sight of the shepherd. If a lamb strayed from the flock, the dog had to gather it up without waiting for his master to tell him.

As natural guardians, they might take a child's small hands gently into their mouths or use their shoulders to direct a child away from a street. They have been known to place themselves between a child and a parent who is losing patience. At the end of the day, their work is not finished. The herding dog will not settle down until his people (his flock) are safely in bed, and then he may sleep by the doorway to guard against intruders. Courage is tightly woven into the fabric of temperament in herding breeds. These tendencies spring from their heritage as keepers of the flock, home, and heart.

Some herding breeds, such as Bouviers and German Shepherds, for example, are very territorial. Forceful-natured breeds like the talented Rottweiler are not for everyone. They can be dominant and headstrong. They require an assertive owner who is able and willing to provide good canine leadership skills. Add their size and strength, and it's obvious that they carry a much greater ownership responsibility than the average breed does. If your home is a busy one, a breed with strong protective instincts may not be a good choice for you. These dogs may view drop-in neighbors and children running in and out as intruders.

The Swiss family of Mountain Dogs (also known as Sennenhunds) offer some of the qualities of the Rottweiler, but are milder and more tolerant of the type of pushing, wrestling, and quick movements that come with kids in the home. In the same way, Rough and Smooth Collies are laid-back. They can be wonderful with children and good family dogs, although they may view the neighbor's rambunctious children as part of their flock and may possibly nip while attempting to round them up.

Noise Sensitivity

Herding dogs that are sensitive to noise may become intimidated by loud, harsh commands, the crack of a bullwhip, the clanging of chute gates, and other loud noises. A dog that cowers at sounds may be too sensitive for stock work. They will require a much gentler approach in training and quiet handling. Most important, however, is the individual's ability to recover quickly from such a shock. Puppies that are insensitive to the noise will hardly take any notice, and are not going to be as responsive and alert in training.

Outgoing, but Assertive Dogs

An assertive dog with an outgoing temperament will tend to be friendly but strong-willed. He will take advantage of a shy or passive handler, who will have a difficult time becoming the pack leader of a dominant dog. This type of dog has the potential to be a good herding prospect—with an experienced handler—but is headstrong and probably not the ideal dog as a trial candidate. He definitely is not a good fit for first-time or junior handlers.

Gentle Dogs with Biddable Character

A dog of this nature is fairly submissive, adaptable, and easily controlled. He requires thoughtful handling and responds well to motivational training by handlers who are willing to give much-needed praise and confidence building. He will look to his handler for leadership. He must be trained with firm but kind handling and positive reinforcement. He is gentle and affectionate, easy to train, and reliable with novice and junior handlers. While this dog is easy to train, he can be easily intimidated and ruined by rough handling or by a compulsion-based trainer who may lose patience with a softer dog.

Soft or Timid Dogs

If the dog lacks in self-confidence, he can become shy and fearful if he is not handled properly. The dog will require careful socialization and much positive reinforcement. A dog of this nature won't likely be a good trial candidate.

Dominant or Hard Dogs

A highly dominant dog will want to be the boss. This pup's nature will resist human leadership. In order to succeed with this type of dog you will have to show him that you, the pack leader, mean what you say. This type of dog may make a good farm or ranch dog, but will be very stressful as a trial dog. This type of dog is especially difficult for an inexperienced or passive handler, and most certainly a junior handler. In the hands of a knowledgeable, experienced trainer, this dog might make a good farm or ranch dog, but is not a good trial prospect. Forceful males are more inclined to seek out dominant animals and confront them.

Dogs That Are Independent or Indifferent

Independent dogs are not particularly affectionate and don't particularly enjoy petting. A dog with these traits has little desire to please. A dog with a marked degree of independence may be difficult for the average handler to train and work. If the dog is lacking confidence he may be shy or antisocial and does not make a good trial prospect.

Male or Female

The testosterone in males can benefit them as far as increased strength and stamina. In breeds like the Rottweiler and Nordic breeds experts indicate

Stir, a Rottweiler female owned by Phyllis Clark, fending off the charge of a mother cow. PHOTO BY DEB CONROY.

there is a marked difference between the character of males and females—males are generally harder and less sensitive. Females, on the other hand, are more biddable and receptive to discipline.

PUPPY TESTING FOR INSTINCT

You cannot accurately determine the working style completely until the dog is older (perhaps a year or more, depending on breed and bloodlines). A good example is the Puli. A number of Puli puppies and young adults show good promise when tested on stock. Yet, as they mature they become weighted down by heavy show coats, which may hinder them and cause them to lose interest, or they lack the determination needed for working.

Probably the best indicators of potential herding ability are the traits of the dog's ancestry; examine the pedigree for proven working bloodlines. An established breeder will serve as a valuable source of information. He knows the bloodline and should be familiar with characteristics of the puppy's ancestors. He has also viewed the puppies on many occasions in different situations—both apart and in the company of their siblings.

However, it may be possible to observe young puppies to get a ball-park estimate about their potential herding ability. Between six and seven weeks, puppies may be tested on ducks. Begin by placing four or more ducks in a round pen. The round pen is useful here because the puppies are unable to corner a duck. However, if a puppy acts too rough with a duck you must not hesitate to rescue it. Don't scold the puppy, but quietly step in and pick up the puppy so the duck can get away.

You can test each puppy separately, but it is preferable to test the litter first as a unit, as they have developed together as a pack. Walk quietly towards the ducks or let the mother start moving them. The movement should set the puppies' instincts in motion. When one puppy reacts, it will trigger the others to take notice.

No two puppies will react the same way toward the flock each day. Their interest or curiosity may be exhibited by watching, following, or chasing the ducks. Some puppies will even take hold of a duck's tail feathers, which may be an indicator of the heeling instinct; other puppies will move to the head of the flock. Some puppies will use varying degrees of eye, which you may recognize when the puppy drops his head slightly and stares at the ducks. It is often apparent even at this early age that the working instinct is present. However, some dogs won't display herding instincts until later, perhaps between month 12 and month 18.

Pay attention to how they work together. Some puppies will follow, while others will attempt to keep the flock grouped together and go to the

Australian Shepherd introducing her puppy to ducks.

Many years ago, we rescued a delightful Bearded Collie named Podger from a family who lived in town. They didn't have a fenced yard and couldn't keep him in any longer. He was very friendly and loved children. His herding instincts were so strong he would race around the neighborhood and round up the children walking to and from school. He never attempted to nip or harm them in any way, but he would just continuously circle them. He needed a job. We were able to re-home Podger on a large sheep farm where his talent was utilized in a practical way.

head to block them from escaping. Even at this young age, it will be evident that some puppies will exhibit more natural distance responding to the pressure of the ducks. Some puppies may be hesitant and watchful. Catalog these traits and compare them to the working characteristics of the ancestry.

Herding traits must be evaluated in context of the breed. An adult Sheltie with assertive traits will not be as powerful as a mature Beauceron, for instance. Also, a puppy with hard-hitting herding behaviors, such as the Pumi, may be much too forceful for someone aspiring to herd ducks and sheep.

Chapter 3

PREPARING YOUR PUPPY

Your dog should be self-confident in any environment and have a strong bond with you, his handler, before his formal stockdog education begins. He won't be able to give his full attention to learning if he's missing either of these two positive elements.

Socialization from an early age is important for sociability. This is the time during which character and attitudes will be greatly influenced by what they are taught. Exposure to pleasant people in safe, friendly environments is critical. If dogs don't have it, they may have difficulty adjusting later to new situations and surroundings.

Your dog's trust in you will be deepened when you take care that he is safe from harm in unfamiliar surroundings or while you are exposing him to new situations. Keep him with you as much as you can to enhance the bond between you. This will lead to your dog's recognition of you as the leader of his pack and a trusted companion. With this kind of conditioning, new places and situations soon lose their frightening dimension and the dog becomes eager to explore them. This is the good time to introduce short car rides.

GETTING YOUR DOG READY TO WORK THROUGH PLAY

Play training is an excellent method for introducing a young dog to some of the skills and tools of his trade before he's ready for serious training, or when stock is unavailable. It has the added benefit of providing light physical conditioning, helping to maintain his level of fitness before he starts real stock work—or later, to keep him fit between herding sessions.

▼

These games are supposed to be fun, but don't overdo it during
hot weather, and remember to give your dog a drink of water
when he needs it.

▲

HERDING GAMES AND COMMANDS

These games help you to learn the commands, too, minimizing confusion
when you add the third element—the livestock. Later, these exercises can
be used to let an extremely exuberant dog run off extra energy prior to an
actual training session with stock. Any dog can enjoy these games at almost
any time or place. You can begin with a toy or ball fastened to a fishing
pole with a string.

Katy Lynn, the authors' daughter, having fun teaching her dog herding
commands with a ball fastened to the end of a fishing pole.

1. Toss the toy, letting it drop onto the ground. As you lure the puppy
    with the toy on the pole, make sounds and wiggle the toy to stimulate
    his interest.
2. Let your dog catch the toy in this cat-and-mouse game often enough
    to give him a continued incentive to play.
3. To get the toy back, go to your dog and say, "That'll do," then ask him
    to "give," and gently take the toy from his mouth.

4. Follow with praise so that there's a reward for giving up the toy.
    This game will set the groundwork for most of the basic herding com-
    mands that he will need to learn. These commands include "walk up,"
    "steady," "skit 'em up," "away to me, "come bye," "back out," and
    "look back."

Walk Up

Teaching your dog to go to the stock can be turned into a game. You will
need a toy or ball that your dog is very attracted to. Tying the object to a
pole or stick with a length of string gives you more flexibility, because you
can use the toy at a distance from your body.

Using a ball to teach "walk up."

1. Lower the ball or toy to interest your dog in going after it.
2. You can pull the toy toward yourself as you walk backward or move it
    from side to side.
3. As he follows it, instruct him to "walk up."

Your dog should follow the incentive (the toy). If he doesn't, you
might step up the energy you put into teasing him with the wiggly, darting toy.

Steady (Take Time)
Here's another directive that can be taught in game format.

1. Hold the toy or ball in front of your dog, above his head.
2. Lower the lure; if your dog rushes to get it, raise it out of his reach.
3. While raising the lure, he will hesitate; name the behavior by saying the word "steady."
4. As he concentrates on the lure, lower it gradually only as your dog walks toward it in a steady, deliberate manner.

You will be able to notice in this game if the young dog has eye. This technique can be used to develop a certain degree of eye, too, in dogs that have the genetic tendency for it.

"Steady."

If he rushes in, raise the ball and repeat the command, "Steady."

Skit Ahold (Skit 'Em Up)

You will encounter situations in which you want your dog to use stronger force on the stock, such as when the stock decide that they will not be moved. This skill, too, can be learned by way of a game.

Using play to teach the dog to grip.

1. Use a hissing sound, "tsss," to focus his attention on the toy. The hiss stirs a positive response from the dog. Lower it or drop it to the ground where he can take hold of the toy and tell him to "skit 'em up" (get 'em up) and allow him to grab the toy.
2. When he has the toy, let him shake it and play a gentle game of tug-of-war. Ultimately, this activity teaches the dog to move in and use whatever force is necessary to move the stock.
3. Tell your dog "that'll do," then ask him to "give," and gently take the toy from his mouth. Reward him for giving up the toy.

Away to Me and Come Bye

This game introduces side or directional commands for circling the stock to the right or left; "come bye" is for clockwise movement and "away to me" for counterclockwise movement.

1. "Come bye" is taught by pulling the lure clockwise with your dog in pursuit. As the dog is engaging in the action, name the behavior. The dog will soon associate the action with the term.
2. To change direction, flip the toy to the other side of your dog and use "away to me."

Above and below: Luring the dog clockwise to teach "come bye."

Back Out

The "back out" command, which alerts the dog that he is too close to the stock and must back away, can be introduced with this game.

1. Step toward your dog and make him give ground to you. As he does, instruct him to "back out." If necessary, raise the toy out of reach.
2. Start with requiring just a few steps' worth of backing up, and then reward with a game of ball or tug and lots of praise.
3. Gradually increase the distance you're asking him to back away. Continue the rewards and keep his spirits high.

Dog responding to "back out."

Look Back

One more command that your dog can learn through play is "look back." This alerts your dog that he must leave one group of stock, turn back, and look for the next one.

1. While your dog's attention is focused on a toy or ball, toss a different object behind him and instruct him to "look back."

"Look back."

2. Your dog should turn his attention to the second object. If necessary, direct the dog to the toy by pointing to it while walking towards it and repeat the command "look back."
3. If your dog seems confused or doesn't turn around, guide him by the collar and turn him in the direction of the second toy. Repeat the "look back" command.
4. When your dog retrieves the object, congratulate him and reward him with a game. Even if he doesn't fetch the toy but just moves toward it, encourage him with praise.

These games, as well as your more directed training, help create an eminently satisfying relationship between you and your dog. Your dog senses that he is well loved, and he will exhibit confidence and loyalty. You experience the rich reward of watching your dog perform successfully, and you gain a devoted companion. If he cowers or sulks at any time during play training, you'll want to examine your methods—and work to make play training enjoyable for both of you.

INTRODUCTION TO STOCK

Herding instinct has to be present in order for you to develop it. No amount of training will instill the natural responses of a well-bred dog. In addition to instinct, the dog must demonstrate a sustained desire to work, although you should not assume that because puppies are eager to work, they are mentally mature enough to start training.

It cannot be stressed enough that a pup shouldn't be started on stock too young. If a pup isn't physically able to outrun the training animals, he may get into a habit of nipping, trying to prevent the animal from escaping. The ideal time to start training is after the dog has passed adolescence and is nearing a year of age. It isn't until this age that a dog is mentally and physically ready to handle the rigors of herding training. Keep in mind that each dog is an individual.

Before training begins, it is helpful if the puppy is being raised around stock and can see and smell the animals while you are doing chores. You can allow younger pups to investigate gentle, non-threatening stock in a round pen. Walk around the animals with the dog at your side so he can become acquainted with them. If the puppy shows interest, you can allow him to go in among dog-broke animals to see how he responds. (*See* "Starting a Dog on Stock.")

If the herding instinct is present, you can build it slowly. As soon as the puppy starts to move toward the stock, tell him "walk up" so that he learns to move in the direction of the stock. If the animals move away and the puppy goes to the head, making an effort to stop them, tell him "good dog," and step back from the stock so the puppy can turn them and bring them back to you. Lots of praise will help him learn quickly to associate commands with actions. Repeatedly setting up successful experiences will enhance good instinct and instill good habits.

You can also expose the puppy to stock by letting him occasionally watch other dogs being trained and worked on stock from the outside of the pen or corral. Do not let the puppy chase the animals or play with them; if he causes them to split and run, he will learn bad habits before you are able to establish good habits. Unless a puppy with heading instincts is mature enough to outrun and block an escaping animal, he may learn to inappropriately bite the animal on the side in trying to stop it. This shouldn't be confused with prey-driven aggression. This behavior is more of a manifestation of an inexperienced dog's frustration. A good trainer's job is to set up this situation in such a way that the young dog meets with success. Working in a round pen, or better yet, using some easygoing sheep that are conditioned to go to the trainer, can be very effective.

If a young dog lacks interest, there is not much that you can do until he *turns on*. Some dogs are interested in stock from a very early age, while others do not turn on until later (perhaps between 9 and 18 months), even with repeated exposure to stock.

It isn't fair to assume that all dogs that come from "herding breeds" are going to want to herd. Herding instinct cannot be taken for granted. If the young dog has some good instinct, an experienced handler can do a lot to bring out the best in that individual.

Safety Concerns

Some dogs, especially larger breeds, are not ready to start herding until 12 to 18 months. Serious training should not begin until the dog's growth plates have closed. These are the soft, spongy, non-calcified cells near the ends of the long bones, where new bone forms. They are the weakest part of the bone and are easily damaged. Fractures to the growth plates can result in limb deformities and osteoarthritis. The upper front leg (the humerus) and the thigh bone (the femur) are particularly susceptible to injury. The growth plates close at approximately month 10 in smaller breeds and month 14 in larger breeds.

Eight to 10 weeks is a critical period during which puppies are most susceptible to the influence of frightening or upsetting experiences—such as being butted by a ewe, or attacked by a hissing goose. Such incidents during this period can have a lasting effect on them.

Between four to six months of age, the pup's adult teeth will come in. His bite may shift during this period, as the muzzle lengthens and the jaw grows into adult proportions. Some dogs may be reluctant to retrieve and pick up balls or toys because of teething discomfort, which subsides around the time a dog is a year old.

PROBLEM SOLVING:
Dog acts like he's forgotten what he's been taught

Hormonal changes can affect personality as a dog goes through puberty. Females experience their first estrus, and males may start lifting their legs. Helping to build self-assurance is important during this time. Don't be surprised if your dog seems to forget all you have taught him, even if he has been obedient until now. You may need to start using a leash to reinforce simple commands such as coming when called.

PROBLEM SOLVING:
Dog chases cats, bicycles, and other moving objects

Running after animals or other moving things, like cars, for example, stems from prey drive. Chasing can also be related to the territorial instincts, such as chasing a strange dog off to protect his master's property. In either case, the dog must not be allowed to roam at large. He needs to be adequately contained so he doesn't endanger himself or anyone else. Prey drive can be effectively channeled into teaching herding commands through play training as described above.

WHISTLE COMMANDS

There are many times when you are working a dog at a distance or in adverse conditions that he may have difficulty hearing your voice commands. This is when a shepherd's whistle is helpful. It makes the command understandable to the dog and without conveying emotion (anger or frustration).

Blowing a shepherd's whistle takes practice, but it is not difficult to use. Place the solid edge of the whistle back against your tongue. Gently bite down on the whistle with the open side facing forward, toward your lips. To give commands, blow air down and through the hole on the top side (whichever side happens to be facing up—it doesn't matter because both sides have holes). It produces the same effect as blowing air across a pop bottle. You can produce various tones by using your tongue to regulate the air flow across the whistle.

To teach the whistle commands, blow the whistle as the dog is engaging in the correct action. Here are a few more suggested commands:

One long blast, "wheet," is effective in telling the dog to "stand" or "lie down." To call the dog to "come here," "whee whoo wheet" should attract its attention. Several long blasts, "wheeooo" might indicate "steady." Flanking commands are easily mastered by literally whistling the words. For example, "who wheeoo" sounds close to "come bye" or "go by," and "wheeooo wheeooo" sounds something like "away to me." A couple of short blasts, "wheet wheet," can indicate "walk up." "Wheet wheeoo" tells the dog "look back."

If you are unsure of your commands, you can practice by playing them into a tape recorder to see how they sound. This way, you won't confuse yourself or the dog.

Whistle commands can be easily incorporated in training. Use whistle signals just as you would use vocal commands. If the dog has been started with vocal commands, first give the vocal command, followed by the appropriate whistle signal as the dog is performing the correct behavior. The dog will quickly make the association with the whistle signals and the action.

A PROFILE OF

The Carrillo Family — No Dumb Dogs

Joan Carrillo manages beef cattle on her ranch in Chiloquin, Oregon, but she was raised on a 9,000-acre dairy ranch in Marin County, California, located on very rough coastal terrain. The land, Cabeza de Santa Rosa, belonged to her ancestor, Maria Ignacia López Carrillo, and was the first land grant deeded by the newly independent Mexico.

Joan's parents, Bob and Jean Carrillo, raised a beautiful herd of purebred Guernsey cattle. Guernsey milk has been long known for its high butterfat content, high protein, and concentration of beta carotene, which gives the milk a distinctive golden color and rich flavor. Joan was six years old when her parents entered into a business partnership and bought a herd of Holsteins. As part of the deal, they acquired their first herding dog, a blue Australian Shepherd they named Cookie. She soon became an invaluable part of the operation as she demonstrated her ability to bring the cattle off the rolling hills and find lost calves in the steep ravines and wooded canyons.

Once, she saved seventeen heifers from the Laguna (de Santa Rosa) River, the largest tributary of the Russian River, during a winter flood. The group of yearlings was stranded on a small island, so the dog swam through the raging floodwaters to bring the cattle to higher ground.

In the spring the Carrillos would start bringing the cows in for the morning milking before dawn. In order to locate the cattle in the dark, Joan's father put bells on some of the lead cows. He gave the dog the command, "Find the bell," and away she would go.

Since the Guernsey milk was being shipped under the Golden Guernsey trademark seal, it was necessary to sort the fawn and white Guernsey from the black and white Holstein cows to keep the milk from being mixed at milking time. Nobody knows how she was able to do it, but Cookie could separate the two different breeds of cattle, apparently by color.

This was a trait that she passed on—her granddaughter Tammy once surprised a group of trademark milk inspectors by separating the two breeds. As the inspectors were leaving, Bob Carrillo commented, "I am sorry, gentlemen, but I have never been able to teach these 'dumb' dogs to close the gate."

Chapter 4

LAYING THE FOUNDATION

CHARACTER TRAITS TO CONSIDER WHEN TRAINING

Taking time to know your dog is the number one requirement for developing a good working partnership. You will want to assess his degree of sensitivity. The average Collie (Smooth or Rough) or Shetland Sheepdog, for example, will not tolerate rough handling and may shut down completely. In contrast, the average Australian Cattle Dog, Rottweiler or Catahoula may require a firmer hand. However, compulsion as a training method—especially if the dog has aggressive tendencies and perceives unfair correction—can cause this type of dog to become more aggressive and to fight back. Even a submissive dog lacking in confidence may bite out of fear, to protect himself, when placed in a stressful situation or when physically dominated. On the contrary, some dogs learn well with just voice corrections.

The authors' son Tyler, also known as Oty, enjoying a buddy at the Uh Oh Ranch in Kiowa, Colorado.

Being Firm but Fair

Males generally begin to assert their dominance between about six and eight months. This is also the period when dogs may attempt to dominate their owners. It is important to establish your authority with your dog, but be fair. A severe correction isn't a shortcut for clear, consistent training. Corrections should not be thought of as punishment, but as instruction. Your corrections teach the dog that he has responded to your command incorrectly. Once corrected, the dog needs to be instructed what to do—and then rewarded for doing the correct thing.

One effective correction is worth ten thousand ineffective ones—but again, *effectiveness* varies, depending on the sensitivity of the dog. A dog's nervous responses (to noise and touch) can have a significant effect in the training and handling of dogs. A dog lacking sensitivity to touch or noise will require more persuasive training techniques. On the other hand, a highly sensitive dog can become overly stimulated, which may set off defense reflexes.

Ineffective corrections are no better than nagging and produce little or no result except resentment—and perhaps a dull and uninspired performance. On the other hand, improper, harsh, and injurious corrections are abusive. Abuse produces fear, which should not be confused with respect. Fear can also provoke a dog to bite.

Timing is the key to effective, efficient handling. Poorly timed rewards and corrections produce bewilderment, not understanding. Perfectly timed rewards and corrections produce black-and-white clarity in the dog. Always reinforce wanted behavior with praise and reward. True is the old saying, "You catch more flies with honey than you do with vinegar."

Border Collies that are confident and eager to go to work. PHOTO BY LORI HERBEL OF XP RANCH PHOTOGRAPHY.

LEASH TRAINING

Between 7 to 12 weeks puppies are in a period of rapid learning. They are ready to learn simple commands. This is an ideal time to begin house and leash training. Your first step is to fit your puppy with a nylon or leather flat-buckle collar. It should fit snugly enough so that it won't slip off if the puppy pulls back against it, but not so tightly that it is uncomfortable. You should be able to slide one or two fingers easily underneath the collar.

1. Take the puppy for a short walk around the house or yard. Talk kindly and calmly to him.
2. If he balks or resists or jumps around wildly, ignore him.
3. Don't scold him or jerk and yank on the leash. This might cause panic, and you don't want to trigger a fearful response. Keep in mind, puppies have a short attention span, are very impressionable, and learn by association.
4. Allow the lead to go slightly slack so that the puppy doesn't learn that a taut leash is normal. Give a gentle tug in your direction, and then immediately release the pressure and keep walking.
5. Kneel down frequently at first and call the puppy to you. You can reward him by petting him and telling him he's a "good boy," or offering a little food treat or a toy, depending on which your puppy values more.

THE THREE BASIC COMMANDS

Three basic commands are necessary for all stock dogs: "come here," "stand" (or "lie down"), and "stay." Your dog must come to you when he's called; this critical piece of basic obedience forms the basis of much advanced training, including the successful handling of livestock. You must also be able to stop your dog wherever he is and then direct him to remain in that spot until commanded otherwise.

You will do well to teach the basic commands *before* you work with stock. Train these elementary commands away from stock; it's too distracting to teach basic obedience and stock work at the same time. It lifts a lot of pressure from you and your dog if you have taken the time to teach your dog basic obedience first. Training takes patience; your dog won't be able to learn these commands overnight. Practice and repetition over a period of several weeks will be needed for the dog to become consistent, especially under distracting conditions.

Teaching the Recall (*Come Here*)

"Come here" is one of the most important commands you will teach your dog. Begin teaching your dog to come at a very early age. Between 7 to 12 weeks puppies may have a short attention span, but respond readily to their names and will come when called from short distances. During 12 to 16 weeks puppies go through a period when they may be more hesitant. They require much positive handling to create a good attitude toward training. Begin by demonstrating to your puppy that obeying the recall leads to good things. You begin training your dog to come every time you call him by name. When he reaches you, praise him to reinforce the behavior of coming to you. Never call him to you and then punish him for anything, such as slow compliance, because this only associates the recall with disapproval.

1. Teach him first on a long line (at least 12 feet [3.7 m]), then off lead. The lead is important to reinforce the follow through if your dog is less than compliant (and sometimes finds more interesting things to do than obey the recall, like playing "keep away." If you have any doubt that he'll obey, never call the dog during the teaching phase unless you can reinforce the command with a long line.
2. When he returns to you, give him lots of praise. The occasional food reward is a good way to further reinforce his response.
3. After he consistently returns to you on lead, you can start working from a greater distance, but always take it one step at a time. Do not release the dog in a large area until he responds off lead in a small, enclosed area.
4. If he fails to come when called, put him back on lead and let him drag the long line so you can grab it and reel him in if he doesn't respond right away.

Your dog's hearing is seventeen times better than yours. So why doesn't he listen? Between four to eight months of age, puppies test their wings and begin to assert dominance. Many young dogs will test their handlers when they are out of arm's reach or off leash. They require thoughtful and gentle discipline. When this occurs:

1. Calmly—no matter how frustrated you may be—catch the dog. Work in a small enough area that he doesn't get the idea you are playing a game of chase. Don't punish him, but do put on his lead and collar so you can go back a step and reinforce the correct behavior.
2. Call his name in an upbeat happy voice and instruct him to "come here." If he doesn't respond automatically, give a leash correction (a quick tug and release to get his attention).

3. Take several quick steps backward and reel the dog to you. You can also turn the encounter into a fun game. When you tell him to "come here," turn (180 degrees) and run away from the dog a short distance and let him chase you. He will be anxious to catch up to his escaping trainer. Let him know what a good dog he is for responding. He'll soon be eager to come to you whenever you call.

Above and below: Katy Lynn, the authors' daughter, inviting her dog Effy to "come."

Always praise and reward him when he offers the wanted behavior. It's much more effective than punishing behavior you don't want. The only way to gain reliability is to be consistent and persistent and by practicing this exercise at unexpected times in a variety of situations, such as while you are doing everyday chores around the house or yard. Your dog doesn't "know" the command until he knows it at different times and in different places.

Teaching *Stay*

When your dog will *stay* whenever and wherever commanded, you have achieved another of the fundamental exercises that underlies all types of training. This command is the basis for many stock-related exercises. Like the recall, the *stay* can be taught while doing everyday chores.

1. While you are walking with the dog next to you on a leash, stop moving.
2. When the dog is at a standstill, instruct him to "stay." If he moves forward, step into him so that he backs up, yielding to you.
3. Repeat the "stay" command.
4. Praise him for holding his position for a few seconds before you release him.
5. Any time he breaks the command, have him yield to you and back up to the original position.
6. Slowly start making him stay for longer and longer periods of time before you release him.

You can also use a long line to reinforce the "stay" command. Using a long line (at least 12 feet [3.7 m]), attach one end to the dog's collar and run the other end through a D-ring attached to a sturdy stationary object or around a fence post or a tree, keeping the free end in your hand with only a little slack in it.

1. Standing in front of the dog, give the command "stay" in a calm, firm tone, and walk away. As you walk away, the dog will probably follow.
2. If he attempts to move forward, pull the slack out of the line to keep him in his original position and repeat the "stay" command.
3. Move a few feet away, and leave him only for a few seconds. Return to him and praise him.
4. Repeat this in different places and for varying lengths of time, gradually lengthening the time that he's required to stay.

During this teaching stage, the only thing that you have requested from your dog is that he remain in a stationary position. As long as he

The author using a stationary object to teach the "stay" command.

does, it makes no difference for our purposes whether he chooses to stand quietly and watch or to sit or lie down. This method of introducing the "stay" can be practiced almost anywhere and at different and unexpected times. When he has learned to "stay" patiently for short periods, you can begin to leave him for longer periods.

When your dog's response to "stay" is reliable, you can introduce "stand."

Using a toy or food reward is a great incentive to keep the puppy
focused and eager to perform the wanted behavior.

Teaching Stand

There are times when it is necessary to stop your dog in his tracks. I prefer that the dog stop on his feet with the "stand" or "stop" command rather than respond to "lie down" or "down," because it allows him to maintain contact with the stock. Sometimes if you drop the dog and then bring him back to his feet, he has momentarily lost contact with his charges. Losing

Katy Lynn Taylor teaching her dog Kaylee to "stand."

that contact can be critical in tight situations where every movement counts.

The "stand" command can be taught from any position but is probably easiest to teach while your dog is walking along by your side.

1. While you are walking along with your dog on your left side, reach down with your left hand and place it under his body, next to the stifle, to bring about a standstill.
2. Give the command "stand" to label the behavior.
3. Holding the dog's collar with your right hand, praise him when he stops moving.
4. When the dog clearly understands that "stand" means to stop and stand, you won't have to use your hand to place him into position.
5. The next step is to give the command at different times, first with the dog at your side, then when you are in front of him.
6. Gradually lengthen the distance by using a long line and eventually having him off lead.

Proper Use of On-Leash Corrections

When teaching commands such as "come here," "stand," and "stay," you will most likely be using a leash and collar. You'll probably encounter situations where you need to give a leash correction. When properly given, the leash correction will get your dog's attention and guide him in the desired direction. A well-executed leash correction is a quick tug and immediate release, administered at the exact second the incorrect behavior takes place. For example, if you are working on "come here" and you give the command but your dog turns away from you to look at a squirrel, a quick pop of the leash against the collar informs the dog that this behavior is not acceptable. Some dogs may need one hefty tug, others may need two quick little tugs: tug and release, tug and release.

The basic foundation of manners described above, taught patiently and with fairness, will result in a youngster that has been brought along correctly through proper handling and that will look forward eagerly to the next phase. If, however, your dog slinks away when you take out the leash, then something is drastically wrong, and you must analyze your methods. Are you demanding too much or being too harsh? Are you correcting before the dog fully understands a command? If so, it is time to modify your approach.

Remember, timing, consistency, and encouragement for wanted behaviors—rather than a lot of nagging corrections for unwanted behaviors—will result in a dog that has a solid basis in obedience and is eager to move forward.

Once the dog has been taught the basic commands, practice them in a variety of different places and situations. Tyler Taylor practicing the basic commands such as "stand" and "stay" with his dog Gabe.

A PROFILE OF

Cletus Hulling — Good Dog Saves a Lot of Work

For most of his adult life, Cletus Hulling Jr. has trained and used stockdogs. He stresses, "Cattle really challenge a dog, so they have to be tougher and more aggressive to hold up. Some dogs just can't take the hard knocks of cattle." During a period of time when he didn't have a dog to work, he quickly discovered it took three or four people to accomplish the jobs that he and his dog had done together daily.

Hulling is a familiar name in cutting horse circles. In 1983, he gained recognition as a world class horse trainer by winning the Non-Pro Division at the National Cutting Horse Futurity on his beautiful mare, Miss Doc Hollywood. Since then he has trained and competed professionally at the Eastern National Finals.

Clete had seen cowdogs work and wanted one. He was in his late teens when he acquired his first stockdog, an Australian Shepherd he named J. B. Hulling used him to handle all the cattle necessary for training cow horses. He could ride to any gate on the place and tell the dog "get around." Like a bullet, J. B. would race out to fetch the cattle grazing in that field. When Clete was finished for the day, all he had to do was send J. B. to push them back out to pasture.

Since then Clete has moved to Wappingers Falls, New York, but stockdogs are still an indispensable part of his horse training operation. The dog he's using now is a 6-year-old Border Collie, dubbed Cap. "Once he gathers the cows, I can sort them into different pens," says Hulling. "All I have to do is open the gates and the dog will put them in the pens." When Cletus works a horse on a herd in the center of the arena, the dog will help him hold them together. Or if he separates a cow from however many are in the bunch, the dog will move that cow back at him, containing it so the horse can work it.

Hulling's dogs are basically his companions, working right by his side all day long. He insists a good dog saves you a lot of work. Cletus feeds them a high performance diet with a good joint supplement. "When I have two dogs, I try to work each one only a half a day or every other day because they work so hard," he says.

Border Collies as a whole are natural and fairly easy to train, because they learn a lot of things by instinct and repetition. Working is their preferred reward. The breed is also social and fairly friendly, which is important to Cletus since he has to deal with the public. In selecting an individual, he wants a dog with natural stock savvy, one that doesn't have to be told every move to make. He prefers muscular, well-built dogs with short hair to help them stay cooler in the summer. He advises that the quality of a dog's parents is an important consideration. Lastly, he doesn't work his dogs on cattle until they are a year old. Until that time he just lets the dog be his buddy and spends time getting a good handle on them.

Chapter 5

GETTING READY

Young stock dogs with a strong desire to herd or work tend to become very eager around livestock. Their instincts tell them that they should do something, but they are not always sure what or how.

THE HANDLER'S ROLE

It is the trainer's job to:

- Cultivate the dog's raw instincts (this comes from the dog's ability to hunt cooperatively).
- Establish and enforce the rules (this comes from the dog's willingness to accept leadership within its social structure).
- Help the dog succeed (this is the part where the human can think ahead and create successful experiences).

The trainer steps in to assist as needed, just as a parent guides a toddler who's learning to walk. Pushy dogs need guidance in learning how to apply the appropriate amount of force, while dogs lacking confidence need leadership in learning how to handle challenging animals. For example, when an animal faces a dog to confront him and test his authority, that is an opportunity for the trainer to step in and turn the aggressor's head away from the pup. This helps the young dog to gain self-assurance.

If you take the time to build a strong foundation at the beginning, there will be less opportunity for it to crumble under challenging circumstances. Take care to set the dog up to do the correct thing. Training is never an overnight success! Most stock dogs take four to five years of training before reaching the advanced levels in trial competition.

Persistence, patience, and common sense will reward you for your effort. Treating your dog kindly will teach him to trust you; keep in mind that your voice can project either calmness or anxiety. Even when things get chaotic, speak to the dog with calm authority.

Learn to read your dog as well as the stock. Give him a chance to act on his instincts and make his own decisions. Don't impair his ability as a self-thinker or make him so dependent on your command that at a critical moment, such as when an animal splits away from the bunch, he waits for you to tell him to bring it back.

Lastly, at times you will be required to walk backwards. It is helpful if you practice walking backwards prior to training the dog on stock so you will be able to keep pace in training and won't feel so awkward when the time comes.

HERDING ATTIRE

Clothing for herding activities should be comfortable and appropriate for weather conditions in different environments and terrain. Layers work well. A hat and long pants are suggested. Athletic, closed-toe shoes are an absolute necessity.

Fleetwood, a Border Collie working ducks at an ASCA trial in Texas after a rainstorm.

SETTING UP YOUR TRAINING AREA

To start the basics of herding training, you need at least four head of calm, gentle sheep, animals that will flock easily and readily move away from your dog. In a study of flocking behavior in sheep, it was determined that it takes a minimum of four sheep to make a flock; two or three sheep are less likely to stay in a group. When working with an inexperienced dog, you need sheep that are "dog-broke"—that is, sheep that are tame and used to being worked by a dog and will respond predictably. Avoid using stock that have become sour and offensive about being worked.

Since your dog may ignore even the basic commands when he is first introduced to stock, a controlled environment such as a circular pen is needed to contain the animals and keep them from getting too far away. A smaller area allows you to be on top of most situations that may occur, so you can prevent your dog from developing bad habits. The stock will also be less stressed if they are not being chased over a big field or arena. Once the basic building blocks of training have been laid, you can move your sessions into a larger area.

An enclosed space of about 90 feet (27 m) in diameter with a circumference of approximately 283 feet (86 m) or slightly larger is a good size for keeping the dog and livestock under control, while still allowing the stock to move away easily when your dog approaches them. A smaller size pen will also help keep a softer, more hesitant dog in contact with stock. If the training area is too small, your dog cannot stay far enough back from the stock to sufficiently balance them. Livestock can jump, so the training pen should be 4 feet (1.2 m) high for sheep or goats and 5 feet (1.5 m) high for cattle. Ideally, gates should swing in both directions.

A square or rectangular paddock can be transformed easily into a suitable training enclosure by placing panels across the corners to eliminate them. The panels can be opened up to teach a dog to work stock out of corners and for other exercises as necessary.

TRAINING AIDS AND EQUIPMENT

Your voice and position (in relationship to the dog and around the animals) and your training stick are your main training tools. As far as your voice—the first element—is concerned, what you say matters less than *how* you say it, or the tone of your voice. Anger and frustration will be reflected in your voice and will affect your dog's response. The second element of training is your movement and where you place your body to influence the movement of the dog and stock (pressure and release).

The training stick—a light sorting stick or shepherds crook—is the third element. Your training stick should be used only as an extension of your body, and only as needed to reinforce verbal commands—never to punish your dog. Use it as a visual aid to block the direction you *don't* want him to go rather than to point out the direction you do want. Otherwise, the dog becomes focused on the stick and not the stock. Used improperly, the stick can be a major distraction and hindrance to the dog, especially if he becomes fearful of it. When you get to the stage of teaching him how to pen or sort stock and need to use the stick to influence the movement of the animals, your dog may be reluctant to move in as directed.

Susie Banchak-Long using a training stick as an extension of her body to block Aja, her German Shepherd. PHOTO BY BECKY PARKER OF DALLY UP PHOTOGRAPHY.

Too often, unnecessarily harsh training methods are substituted for the steps that establish a strong foundation. Negative reinforcement and punishment are less effective methods in the long run in developing a confident, independent dog that understands the job at hand.

THE ROLE OF CLICKER TRAINING IN HERDING

Dogs form an association between actions and consequences (positive or negative). The more quickly the dog associates the behavior to the result, the faster he will learn. This is the premise behind both classical and operant conditioning.

Clicker training is a subset of operant conditioning. It involves a clicker (toy noisemaker) to "mark" or signal the dog—communicating in an unemotional way—the exact moment he is performing a desirable behavior. It is followed by a reward (treat, toy or game) to reinforce the action. This technique can be applied to developing focus in some dogs, and teaching basic obedience and some herding commands in play training. In actual herding, the clicker can also be used to indicate when the dog is performing an action such as flanking the stock correctly.

However, the technique of altering unwanted behavior in the click and treat method is to ignore it (no clicking or consequence), with the suggestion that unwelcome behavior will disappear through lack of reinforcement. Sorry to say, this ideology has been proven ineffective in stockdog training. Disregarding a dog splitting and running after and biting stock is not an option. Not only can it have devastating effects, but the prey drive reinforces the negative behavior and chase instincts.

COMMONLY USED COMMANDS

It makes little difference which commands you choose as long as you are consistent in always using the same words for the desired actions. The most common flanking or side commands are *come bye* or *go by* and *away to me* or *way to me*, although some trainers have varied them to *by* and *way to*, respectively. Some stockmen prefer *gee* for left and *haw* for right.

Too many commands will just confuse your dog, and in a tense situation may even confuse you. For most jobs, nine basic commands will enable you to take stock just about anywhere. You must be able to instruct your dog to stop moving (*stand, whoa* or *lie down*) and if necessary to remain stationary (*stay*). You must be able to call him to you (*come here*) and to move farther away (*back out*). You must be able to send him directly up to the stock from any direction (*walk up*), to slow down (*steady*), and to counterclockwise (*away to me*) or clockwise (*come bye*). Finally, you need a signal that the job is finished and he needs to come off the stock completely (*that'll do*).

When choosing commands, keep in mind if you use "come bye," for example, you may not want to use "come here." The dog can become con-

Cathy Balliu has instructed her Tervuren to "stand" so she can give the next instruction. PHOTO BY BECKY PARKER OF DALLY UP PHOTOGRAPHY.

fused. Instead, you may decide to use the flanking command "go by." Otherwise, you can use "here" or "that'll do" to call the dog to you. Also, if you are working a male dog, "go by" might sound like "good boy."

Commonly Used Herding Commands

Away to me or *way to me*—Flanks the dog counterclockwise.

Back out or *keep out* or *get out*—Moves the dog farther away from the stock and tells him to work with more space or distance from the animals.

Come here, come, or *here*—Calls the dog back to the handler.

Come bye or *go by*—Flanks the dog clockwise.

Steady or *take time* or *easy*—Regulates the dog's speed, maintains a steady approach, or slows his movement.

Get back or *get behind*—Used to send dog back behind the animals.

Commonly Used Herding Commands (continued)

Get em up—See "Skit 'em up."

Go by or *come bye*—Flanks the dog clockwise.

Go on—Sends the dog along a boundary.

Here, come in—pulls or draws the dog closer.

Keep out—Similar to back out, used also when dog trespasses perimeter in boundary work.

Lie down—Drops the dog in a stationary position.

Look back—Tells the dog to turn back to gather more stock.

No, nooo, or *ahhh*—Indicates a wrong action or wrong direction.

Skit 'em, skit 'em up, skit ahold—Tells the dog to make a controlled bite.

Stand or *stop* or *whoa*—Brings the dog to a standstill.

Stay—Tells the dog to remain stationary (don't move until told).

That'll do—Signals the job is finished, return to the handler.

There—When the dog is flanking, "there" indicates he is to turn in and move directly toward the stock.

Walk on or *Walk up*—Moves the dog to the livestock.

Way to me—See "Away to me."

Mick, an Aussie, flanking clockwise in response to a "come bye" command.
PHOTO BY LORI HERBEL OF XP RANCH PHOTOGRAPHY.

Herding Terms

Backing—Jumping on the backs of sheep packed tightly in a chute or alleyway to move them along.

Blind outrun—Dog follows a path to retrieve stock that is out of sight, maybe over a hill or behind natural or other obstacles.

Boundary work—Containing livestock within an unfenced perimeter.

Driving—Moving stock away from the handler.

Fetching—Bringing stock to the handler.

Flanking—Circling around the flock. On an inside flank, the dog is between the handler and the sheep; on an outside flank, the dog is on the far side of the sheep.

Heavy side—The side with most amount of pressure.

Holding a line—When dog is taking stock directly from point A to B without deviating from it.

Inside flanks—Flanks made between trainer and stock, as when driving.

Lift—The first contact the dog makes as he picks up stock in the gather process before bringing them to the trainer.

Light side—The side with least amount of pressure.

Outrun—The path the dog takes to move out and around to the backside of stock to get into the correct position to bring them to the trainer.

Pressure—Physical pressure caused by the trainer's position or force from stock movement and obstacles, as well as psychological pressure (mental and emotional).

Pulling—Another term for fetching.

Side commands—Directional flanking commands.

Square flanking—The dog changes his proximity off the flight zone—turning 90 degrees away—so as not to pressure the animals until he is in the correct position to move them in the desired direction.

Herding Terms (continued)

Walkabout—A walk that takes place over longer distances while the dog calmly fetches the sheep to the trainer; the dog gains experience bringing the sheep in a straight line.

Watch 'em—Tells the dog to focus on the stock.

Wearing—A natural action that occurs as the dog moves from side to side behind a group of stock to keep them moving forward. Sometimes wearing is used to describe the dog fetching or bringing stock to the handler who is in the lead position.

Luki, a German Shepherd from true herding bloodlines, gently eases the lambs under his care back into their boundary with the rest of the flock. COURTESY ELLEN NICKELSBERG.

A PROFILE OF

Bruce Fogt — From Novice to Champion

 Bruce Fogt grew up on a farm in Ohio and was involved with the local 4-H program. His neighbor, Lewis Pence, raised sheep and trained sheepdogs. One day Lewis suggested to Bruce that he needed to have Sparky, one of his Border Collie pups. Bruce replied that he wouldn't know how to train it, but Lewis promised to help him. Bruce wasn't sure he could afford to buy the dog, so Lewis asked him what he might have to trade instead. Bruce offered a Hampshire ram, and the direction of his life was changed forever.

Bruce recalls how he felt as a beginner: "Training was not as simple as I thought it would be. It was more like reciting the alphabet backwards while dancing the jitterbug." However, as he began to gain control of his young dog and the sheep were becoming more cooperative, he gradually came to understand how it was supposed to work.

Although Bruce's dog was moving around and bringing the sheep to him, the dog was still working too close. One morning Bruce asked Lewis, "How do I keep him backed off?" Lewis showed Bruce how to position himself near the sheep when he sent the dog, and as Sparky started to circle, Lewis taught Bruce how to move into the dog to force him to move out wider.

He cautioned Bruce to keep an eye on the dog, because after the handler moved away from the correction, the dog would try to slice in again. In order to counter the dog's actions, Lewis told him to back toward the sheep to get into position to give another correction. He also told him that dogs usually go about a third of the way around before trying to cut in, and noted, "You have to move fast to stay ahead of the dog." Sparky soon learned to stay out at the appropriate distance.

Bruce has become one of the most respected trainers in North America. He is a two-time national champion and at one time or another has won many of the most prestigious trials in the country. He publishes *The Working Border Collie* magazine and has authored a book, *Lessons From a Stock Dog*, based on his experiences in training and trialing, including his sessions with Lewis.

Chapter 6

Starting a Dog on Stock

INTRODUCTION AND THE FIRST LESSON

Young dogs are often inconsistent. When your puppy first encounters livestock, he may try to chase the animals; bark at them; rush straight through the middle of the group and scatter them; pull wool; or keep them in a tight bunch against the fence. He may also demonstrate little or no interest in the animals, instead sniffing the ground and eating animal dung or grass.

One of Tanya Wheeler's Tucker Creek young puppies' first exposure to sheep and showing playful interest, but not yet ready for serious training. PHOTO BY DEB CONROY.

The goals of the introduction and first lesson are:

- Develop confidence and sustained interest.
- Instill calmness through quiet handling.
- Teach the dog how to respond to pressure.

Working with tame, gentle stock is important at this stage of training. Furthermore, handling them in a relaxed way is part of fostering a calm and confident herding dog.

When you first introduce a dog to stock, enter the pen with the dog on a slip cord for quick release. Encircle the flock, walking between them and the dog, but staying nearer to the stock. Once the dog gets up his nerve, he may make a wild move and charge the flock. The natural heading dog will be anxious to position himself in front of the animals to block or stop them and turn them back. When he gets to the head and turns in, step back away from the flock, so he can send them in your direction. Ask him to pause briefly with the "stand" command and quietly praise him—"good dog." To get the dog to stop or turn and change direction, move in front of his shoulder towards his head.

Warning! Never leave your pup unattended with the stock; the situation worries the animals, and the dog can pick up bad or incorrigible habits. In addition, either the dog or the stock could be injured.

Joe Schneider holding the training stick, so his puppy Zelda has an open door to get around the sheep. PHOTO BY DEB CONROY.

Zelda is moving to "head off" the animals, while her owner, the pack leader, starts stepping away so she can turn them back to him. PHOTO BY DEB CONROY.

Encourage him to circle the flock again. It doesn't matter which direction the dog chooses to circle. Ideally, he will move freely in either direction. As he does, keep walking between the sheep and dog (following in a position just slightly behind the dog's shoulder) in an imaginary circle around the flock.

As a general rule, Border Collies and dogs of similar type respond fairly easily to pressure and body position. However, many large-flock dogs and cattle-working breeds are close working and not as sensitive to it. They tend to circle tightly, putting stock on the edge with unnecessary pressure. Gently push the dog out to a more comfortable working distance by walking towards his shoulder. As he yields, tell him "back out." When he does, ask him to "stand." Quietly praise him—"good dog." Now, release him and continue to move around the outer edge of the flock, *constantly making adjustments according to his response.*

If the dog is unresponsive to the pressure and doesn't back away, step into his shoulder more forcefully. When necessary, swat the ground with the training stick while you step towards the dog, causing him to give way. If that doesn't work, direct your training stick—with a small plastic beverage bottle taped to the end—toward his shoulder, and then gently push him away. If he doesn't respond to the mild pressure, then you will have to push him out more forcefully. If you bump the dog, the bottle will

Satin, an Australian Shepherd, is responding to mild pressure and body language from her trainer, Greta Krause. PHOTO BY DEB CONROY.

Jewell responding to increased pressure from her trainer, Jo Thompson, while the flock is contained along a fence line. PHOTO BY DEB CONROY.

Ace, a Border Collie, responding to the pressure from his trainer, who is directing her training stick at his shoulder. PHOTO BY BECKY PARKER OF DALLY UP PHOTOGRAPHY.

Becky Parker is flanking her young dog Rein in a semicircle to head the sheep to turn them 180 degrees, sending them in the opposite direction along the fence line. PHOTO BY GARRETT PARKER OF DALLY UP PHOTOGRAPHY.

prevent him from getting hurt. Do *not* overcorrect. As soon as the dog gives ground, release the pressure by stepping back towards the flock.

A technique that works well for strong, pushy dogs is to contain the stock along a fence. Step towards one side of the flock—bringing the dog around your body in an arc—and allow him to move in a half circle (from six o'clock to twelve o'clock, or twelve o'clock to six o'clock) on the open side (away from the fence) to turn the animals 180 degrees in the opposite direction down the fence. In doing so, he is learning to block and control the head of the stock. When they turn, stop him with a temporary halt—"stand." Praise him.

If the dog tries to cut in, split, or stampede the animals, instruct him to "back out." Every now and then, pause with "stand" and then "stay." This gives him a chance to settle and think—as well as relaxes the stock, which is significant to communicate calmness.

Keep the sessions short—no more than 5 to 10 minutes every few days or every other week, or even once a month until the dog is around a year of age. When the dog freely circles the stock and turns them, that is a good indication he is ready to move to the next level of training.

HOW TO USE THE TRAINING STICK CORRECTLY

As you circle the dog, the end of the training stick should be following behind (trailing) him. The only time it should be directed at him is when asking him to *back away,* or when you flip it in front of him to block him and change directions.

PROBLEM SOLVING:
Handler can't coordinate where to be or what to do in the bedlam
between the dog and stock

In most dog sports the handler is dealing with three elements; himself, the dog, and a fairly consistent, inanimate object such as a ball (or Frisbee) or an obstacle, as in Agility. In herding, the third element—the livestock—though controllable to some degree is animate, and can be highly variable. Moreover, when things get chaotic, there is the possibility of tripping, getting knocked down, stepped on, hit, or risking a knee injury.

A small circular pen about 16 feet (5 m) in circumference and three or four foot tall—pet exercise pens work well for this application—can be used to put a few ducks or geese in. The dog is able to stay in contact with the ducks while circling around the outside of the pen, while they are free to move about inside the pen. If necessary you can always step in the pen and move them yourself.

With the stock safely contained, you can now concentrate on controlling the dog. It gives you time to think and practice where you need to be, how to hold the training stick to get the dog to stop with a

Years ago, we sold a delightful little black tri male to a large sheep ranch in Wyoming. In the spring, when the pup was 14 months old, the owners brought him back to me for training. He was sired by Ch. Just Jake of Las Rocosa CD, ATD-d, STDcs and out of Ch. Las Rocosa Justa Sinner. Both his parents were proven ranch dogs. Yet, when I took him to stock, he didn't show any interest at all. He could have cared less.

For the first week or so, I taught him the basic commands. He was so responsive and really wanted to please me. Then, we went to sheep. For several weeks I tried just about everything I could think of, but he just didn't turn on. When we worked cattle—which was three to four times a week—I let him trail along with the other dogs. When we worked sheep—which was six days a week—I would encourage him to watch the sheep. Sometimes, I would let him follow along while I worked other dogs. At other times I took him by himself for short sessions with the sheep (maybe 5 or 10 minutes, no more). He was more interested in playing. He would jump up and give me a happy little grin, even if I was standing in the middle of the flock. I didn't scold him at all. Instead, I ignored him, but I always treated him kindly.

I gave him several weeks off—away from stock. When I brought him back I let him trail along while I worked other dogs, but I didn't ask him to do anything. I gave him plenty of opportunity, but never tried to force him to do anything. Nearly a month went by and one day out of the blue, he sparked and went to work. It was as if he had been working all along. That fall, in October, I received a picture of Scooter (Las Rocosa Scooter of TTT) herding 2,000 head of sheep. They told me he had moved the flock over 60 miles.

"stand," change directions, "back out," and "walk up" in a very positive manner.

Note: Keep upbeat, but calm and quiet. Do not allow the dog to race wildly around the pen. While he may release some pent-up energy, it can also wind him up!

PROBLEM SOLVING:
Instead of giving ground, the dog runs faster and cuts in
If the dog darts past you and cuts in instead of giving ground, you are not in the correct position. It may also be due to where you are

directing your pressure—i.e., at the dog's hip. Walking into the dog's hip instead of just behind the shoulder encourages him to rush and opens the door for him to cut in. If the dog is switching directions and cutting in, it may be that you are getting ahead of the dog's shoulder.

PROBLEM SOLVING:
Dog runs wide to avoid being caught

When the dog is racing wildly, running wide to dodge any attempt to stop him, back up to a fence so he cannot circle behind you. Step in front of the flock. While the dog moves back and forth in a semicircle trying to get to the sheep, stay near the sheep. To get him to stop, cross over in front of his shoulder towards his head and then step boldly in his face. Extend both arms outward in a v-shape toward the dog. Your training stick should be used to block him. This should cause him to hesitate, but if he ducks and goes the other way, head him off. Continue crossing over in front of his face—forcing him to change directions—until he stops.

PROBLEM SOLVING:
Aggression, biting, nipping (gripping) or wool pulling

Biting can be due to a lack of confidence, fear, excitable stock, untimely corrections, confusion, or frustration. When you are first introducing a dog to stock, don't be anxious if the dog occasionally nips or grabs a little wool. Help the dog maintain adequate working distance. If the dog lunges in and grabs one of the animals, growl at him and tell him "back out." Apply the same techniques described above to push the dog back out when he runs in close and circles too tightly. Remain calm with the dog to help him work through the problem. Some distance from the stock will help the dog settle down and will allow you to have better control.

Quiet training animals are essential. Dogs can get very excited and tend to grip when introduced to stock that is inclined to bolt. Anxiety in a dog is often indicated by the dog's tail. A calm dog carries his tail in a relaxed position, but when he is wound up, he will often carry it higher. Be alert to the earliest signs of anxiety.

It is important not to confuse predatory instincts with herding instincts. A dog that consistently singles one animal off from the flock or goes for the animal's throat (or hamstrings) is displaying hunting behaviors, not herding—and may not be suitable for herding. Some dogs are extremely aggressive, displaying excessive roughness. Exceptionally dominant dogs with hard temperaments and predatory instincts are less responsive to pressure as they mature and are more inclined to bully stock without provocation.

Forceful biting—biting and hanging on (with full, hard bites)—is not uncommon in dogs from bloodlines bred for Ring Sport. They tend to be very bite oriented due to the focus breeders place on aggressive instincts. Some dogs are predatory and can be injurious to stock, especially sheep. The handler must protect the stock from injury. If the dog attacks one of the animals, scold the dog with a gruff "No." A rattle bottle (empty plastic beverage bottle with a few pennies or pebbles inside) can be fastened with tape to the end of the training stick and swatted in front of the dog's face to interrupt the current behavior. Tell him in a strong, growling voice to "back out." You don't want to discourage the dog to the point of quitting, but you do want him to yield. You can't progress in training until he is ready to listen. If aggressive biting is a constant problem, you can put a muzzle on your dog until he settles down. This gives you the opportunity to teach and develop your timing without constant worry about injury to your livestock.

If a dog like this loses interest when corrected, see "Problem Solving: Dog looses interest, quits working." However, there is always the possibility he wasn't as interested in herding as much as in antagonizing the animals, and he may never be a satisfactory herding prospect.

PROBLEM SOLVING:
Hard-hitting heelers

It is always better if dogs are trained on the type of stock they were intended for. Stumpy Tail Cattle Dogs, the Westerwälder Cowdog and other strong cowdogs are bred for strong heeling ability. They are doing what comes naturally. Trying to turn a cowdog into a sheepdog can be done, but it takes countless hours and patience. Dogs bred for cattle work may be too rough for sheep and maybe even goats, gripping so hard they can cause lameness. Ideally, they should be worked on cattle; however if none are available, then use a muzzle to prevent injury to the stock. (*See also* above: "Problem Solving: Biting or nipping (gripping).")

PROBLEM SOLVING:
Dog is paying attention to stock, but loses interest

Dogs lacking confidence may be attracted to stock, but can quickly shut off and quit if they feel pressure or are intimidated by an upsetting experience. The dog may start demonstrating anxiety or avoidance

Using a Muzzle on Your Dog

Using a muzzle is not recommended for the average dog. However, in extreme cases it can be used to enable a trainer to liberate the dog to move stock without worry of injury to the training animals. It is important, however, to be aware that your dog may become distracted or intimidated and focus all of his attention on the muzzle until he gets used to it. Ideally, the dog should be accustomed to wearing the muzzle prior to your working him on stock.

The appropriate muzzle is the wire-basket type used for racing Greyhounds, with a headstall and a padded leather nosepiece. It is designed to allow the dog to breathe and drink but not bite. It won't restrict the dog's ability to open his mouth to pant, which would put him in danger of overheating. When acquiring a muzzle, you'll need to take the dog's muzzle length into consideration so that it doesn't rub his nose.

Note: Do not use a muzzle on a dog working cattle, as cowdogs need to be able to defend themselves against recalcitrant animals. Also, the tip of the cow's horn or hoof can become caught in the muzzle and injure the dog.

behaviors by sniffing the ground, eating dung or grass, running to you, or going to the gate. This type of dog needs to be nurtured with gentle but cheerful handling and repeated exposure to livestock in short sessions. When the pup shows interest, praise him and end the session on a positive note.

PROBLEM SOLVING:
Dog lacks focus

Gather and move the stock yourself. Use a single animal to attract the dog's attention, and redirect it by separating it from the flock and taking it a short distance away from the other animals. Try using quick whistle signals, or you can hiss "tss, tss" to excite the dog and perk him up. Ask him to "watch 'em," then let the animal go to rejoin the others. Follow it back to the other animals yourself. This technique may trigger the dog's instincts and develop focus. Also, working another dog may help to increase your dog's awareness. If he takes an interest and tries to follow, let him go.

PROBLEM SOLVING:
Dog is reluctant to circle

If your dog is reluctant to circle, invite him to follow instead. Move the animals yourself. The strategy is to encourage the dog to move freely around the livestock in order to bring his instincts to the surface. The natural driving dog may be content to stay behind the animals, moving them forward. However, as his drive increases, he can be taught to block and turn stock by working half circles while the animals are contained along a fence line (as described above).

PROBLEM SOLVING:
Dog is reluctant to leave his handler or wants to play or retrieve objects (sticks or other things)

When the dog refuses to leave his handler's side, it may be the result of obedience training, where the dog's focus has been on the trainer—

Trainer is moving toward the sheep himself, which gives confidence to the pup.
PHOTO BY DEB CONROY.

especially in competitive obedience. The trainer should stay focused on the stock rather than the dog. If the dog has instinct, he will most likely settle and take notice with repeated exposure over several months.

If the dog is reserved because he is in an unfamiliar environment, you need to take the time to expose him to different places to help build his confidence. The dog may feel hesitant if he was injured or had a bad experience (such as getting kicked or butted) as a puppy. He may also feel inhibited if he was harshly corrected the first time he showed interest and lunged towards the stock. If the owner is nervous about the dog's reaction towards stock, the dog may sense that and be reluctant.

Ignore the dog. Focus your attention on the stock. Direct him to the stock by moving the animals yourself. You can whistle, use a hissing sound, clap your hands, or use a happy voice while pushing the stock to get the dog excited. Tell the dog "watch 'em" while you continue moving the stock. *Note: Don't use the command "watch 'em" if you have already used the command "watch me" for obedience training. It may confuse the dog.*

PROBLEM SOLVING:
Dog acts eager towards livestock, but shows no interest when allowed to go with them

There are several reasons why this may occur. If the dog was bred from proven working ancestry, be patient. He may be too young or may be a late bloomer and hasn't come into himself yet. You can give the dog repeated exposure to stock by letting him watch or follow along while other dogs work. When you take him in with stock, maintain your focus on the stock. Keep the sessions short, no more than five or so minutes, until he "sparks." It may take several weeks or even several months.

In the same way, some dogs seem really interested and lunge toward the stock while on a leash. Yet when unleashed they don't show any interest. When dogs see animals or other dogs working, they want to approach and investigate; naturally the handler changes his body posture and tightens the leash to better control the dog. The tension on the leash translates the handler's nervousness or other emotions and triggers the dog's guarding behavior. When the leash is removed, the dog no longer feels the threat. Sometimes the leash can be used to activate the herding instincts (providing they are buried in the dog's psyche) through defensive instincts. In this situation, if your dog tugs on the lead, don't correct him. The tension may bring out an assertive response, causing the stock to react—and in turn sparking the dog's interest. Be flexible.

Always give the dog the benefit of the doubt. However, if the dog is two years or older and doesn't seem to "turn on" after several months of repeated exposure, give him a break away from stock. Wait several months, and then test him again. If the dog doesn't show continued interest, there is always the possibility he isn't suited to the task of herding.

PROBLEM SOLVING:
Dog is troubled by the training stick

The dog may be very sensitive to pressure, including the training stick. Set the stick aside during the introduction, providing the dog doesn't pose a threat to the sheep. If the dog has been whacked with a stick, he may be frightened by it. To desensitize him to the stick, put the dog on leash so he cannot run away. Take it with you on walks, and softly tap the ground with it. When the dog isn't worried about it anymore, you can gently stroke him with it. Eventually, he will realize it is nothing to be feared.

PROBLEM SOLVING:
Dog is eager and biddable, but lacks appropriate herding instinct

This problem is commonly encountered in herding breeds that have been bred for purposes other than herding. A dog like this can be taught to herd, but will at the very best be mechanical. In other words, he will have to be continually instructed what to do. Mechanical dogs have earned herding degrees and even placed in trials, but are not reliable as practical working dogs in the real world.

Providing the dog isn't aggressive and doesn't demonstrate predatory behaviors, the owner should decide if she is willing to invest as much time as it will take to train a dog with limited potential.

A PROFILE OF

David Hartwig and Skidboot

 When you mention David Hartwig's name, it is hard not to think of Skidboot, a working ranch dog who gained national acclaim as one of the world's smartest dogs. In 2003 Skidboot won the $25,000 championship on Animal Planet's "Pet Star" competition. That recognition led to appearances on "The Tonight Show with Jay Leno," "The Oprah Winfrey Show," "The Late Show with David Letterman," "Crook & Chase," "Inside Edition," and many others.

The story began just outside the sleepy little town of Quinlan, Texas, on Christmas Eve in 1992. David was shoeing horses for a neighboring rancher, who gave him the pup, an Australian Cattle Dog mix, as a last-minute Christmas gift for David's wife, Barbara. He was halfway home when he decided that he should probably take a second look at the litter. When he did, he noticed one puppy standing apart from the rest. After a few minutes of watching him, David was won over, and he traded the first puppy back for the second one.

They named him Skidboot, which is a type of protective leather boot for reining, roping, and working cow horses. As the pup grew, he became unruly. He started tearing into things, and the neighbors complained that he was chasing their animals. After a couple of years of such behavior, David almost gave the dog away. He told his wife that if the dog was going to stay, he'd have to learn some manners.

Skidboot needed a job—that was certain—so his owner started teaching him tricks to keep his mind occupied. David soon realized that the dog was highly intuitive, so he taught him increasingly intricate tricks, including the "stuffed-ball trick," which became his signature act. David would tell Skidboot, "Now on the count of three, I want you to grab that ball." After his owner threw the ball, the dog waited in anticipation with his nose poised above the ball; David would count "one, two," then toss in a series of unrelated numbers, until casually adding "three"—Skidboot's signal that he could sink his teeth into the round stuffed toy, which he did instantly.

He served his master well and won the hearts of many Americans. While most people will remember his cleverness as a trick dog, he was so much more. In spite of all the national accolades, David Hartwig said his favorite memories are of seniors smiling or little children laughing or Skidboot snuggling up to a handicapped or old person. "The bond between me and Skidboot seemed more important than the tricks he did."

On March 25, 2007, at fourteen years of age, Skidboot passed over the Rainbow Bridge. His body was laid to rest, along with his favorite toy, beneath an oak tree on the property he had helped, through his fame, to purchase. In David's tribute to Skidboot, he said, "What a wonderful life of fourteen years he lived! Never has a last-minute, second-thought Christmas gift ever shone so brightly as Skidboot."

Chapter 7

Making the Most of Your Dog's Talent

TEACHING THE DOG TO FETCH THE STOCK

This is a continuation of the first lesson. The object is to teach your dog to move out and around the animals, then turn in and bring them to you while keeping them in a group. You don't need to worry about teaching your dog directional commands until he has learned this important function. These lessons may be practiced for several weeks or longer, until the fetch is well established, as you teach the dog how to control the flock while bringing them to you.

If the dog is eager to get to the head, he may cut in a little too sharply as he draws near the opposite side of the flock. As he gains confidence in his ability to turn and control the animals, he will learn to settle down and relax. Keep working on fetching as well as the half circle flanking exercises described in the previous chapter.

The most common mistake novice handlers make is that they
don't keep moving. They become an obstacle and cause the
stock to spill back over the dog. As one trainer aptly stated,
"Lead or follow, but get out of the way."

Move from one end of the training area to the other while the dog sweeps back and forth behind the stock, continually bringing them to you as you keep walking away from the sheep. When you get to the other side of the enclosure, swap ends with your dog. As you move counterclockwise, he should also move counterclockwise, picking up the opposite side to keep the flock between you and him. As you switch sides, the dog is also learning to move between the fence and stock with very little trouble.

Above: An eager, young dog cutting in as he nears the first head. Below: When the dog gets to the opposite side of the flock and turns them, the trainer should step back away so the dog can fetch the animals.

The trainer should continually walk backwards while the dog keeps the animals together and brings them to his handler. PHOTO BY DEB CONROY.

However, if instead of continuing to fetch, the dog tries to dash away to the head—turning them onto the fence—you will need to block him and send him back behind the flock.

Jo Thompson using her training stick to keep her dog Jewell in position along the fence, to bring stock away from it. Note: the trainer has left an opening so the sheep can escape the pressure. PHOTO BY DEB CONROY.

BALANCE IS THE FOUNDATION

Herding is a complex relationship between the handler, the dog, and the flock. In order for it to work properly, all three elements must be balanced. A dog in balance controls the stock by being in the right place at the right time to head off escapees—and by applying appropriate pressure (not too close, not too far) to move the flock at a relaxed pace.

Another understanding of balance is that the dog is opposite the handler in such a position as to maintain movement of the stock in a direct line to the trainer.

In other words, the dog's natural gathering instinct is to keep the stock between you and him continuously. When balance is understood in this way, the concept of balance can also be applied to driving. Once the trainer has indicated the desired direction he wants to take the stock, the dog is to maintain his "balance" to the stock in such a way that the speed and

Becky Parker's young dog Rein is maintaining the direction of the flock's movement by continually positioning herself at the other side of the animals from her owner.

As the trainer turns, her dog starts swinging around, picking up the opposite side to counterbalance her position. PHOTOS BY GARRETT PARKER OF DALLY UP PHOTOGRAPHY.

Trainer

direction of the stock remains on that established line of balance regardless of the trainer's position on the field. This concept of balance is extremely important to establish if the dog is to be left to work on his own while the trainer moves down the field possibly on horseback to meet the herd or flock at their final destination. There are multiple places in the world where dogs are expected to develop this ability and are left to move animals for miles.

Balance can be instinctive to various degrees in herding dogs. Developing and fostering balance and other herding instincts is the job of the trainer. The following exercises develop the dog's natural herding instincts so that they can be used in actual working conditions or in the trial arena. Repetition is essential to enable your dog to master his lessons. Keep the sessions short (about 5 to 10 minutes every few days) and enjoyable.

BUILDING ON YOUR DOG'S NATURAL ABILITY

Wherever possible, encourage the young dog to think on his own. A good example of this is when you are fetching stock and one head tries to break away from the others. The dog's instincts prompt him to stop the runaway and turn it back. Let him take action. Interfering with a dog's natural inclination discourages his inborn herding instincts, because it doesn't allow him to think for himself. The result is a mechanical worker who relies too much on the handler. You will have control of your dog once your dog has control of the livestock. You will also have a better dog.

When one head tries to break away from the flock, the dog's instinct prompts him to stop it and put it back with the others.

BAD HABITS

Bad habits can be inadvertently established if you keep drilling an exercise your dog just isn't getting. If your dog ever seems confused or frustrated, go back to the previous lessons to give him an opportunity to relax and be successful with something he understands clearly. Then take your time to set up the situation that was confusing him and work through it little by little, day by day. A good foundation laid at each stage of training will enhance the stability of your dog in the long run.

HANDLING TRAINING ANIMALS RESPONSIBLY

Every now and then, stop your dog with the *stand* command. Let your dog and the stock settle and relax before starting the exercise again. Panting with open mouths or beaks is a strong sign that the stock has been overworked. They must be given ample time to catch their breath and rest before continuing to train. During this time, they should be given access to shade and water. This also provides a window of opportunity to teach the dog how to relax around stock. Taking care of livestock is an important part of good stockmanship. Continually overworking stock will cause them to become sour and hard to handle.

PROBLEM SOLVING:
Ringing (circling the flock)

Sometimes, instead of going back behind the flock, a green dog with heading instincts keeps circling around and around the stock and trainer or cutting between them. Do not allow him to run excitedly around the stock, but correct his behavior so he understands that he is to keep the flock between him and you. If necessary, use your training stick to reinforce the correction.

For example, you are walking backward, positioned at 6:00, and the dog is moving counterclockwise around the stock (from 3:00, past 12:00 to 9:00). When he gets to 9:00 (on your left side as you are facing the animals), send him back clockwise. Walk opposite the direction in which the animals' heads are facing. This will compel your dog to move back behind the animals to tuck in the other side.

If he doesn't respond by going back behind, verbally correct him by saying "No!" to get his attention. Whack the ground with your stick to obstruct him from continuing in a full counterclockwise circle, and force him to turn back and go clockwise.

When he gets to 3:00 (on your right side as you face the flock), send him behind by stepping away from the flock and continuing to walk backward. If he doesn't automatically turn back and start moving counterclockwise, tell him "No," while at the same time you walk away from the direction the animals' heads are facing. If he ignores the verbal correction, reinforce it by swatting the ground with your stick.

Gwen Litz is using a crook to block her dog Babe from coming around to the head of the animals and send her back behind the flock. PHOTO BY DEB CONROY.

PROBLEM SOLVING:
Stock is crowding the perimeter fence and the dog has difficulty moving them away from it

Ideally, the flock should be standing in the middle of the training field away from any obstacles, but this is not always the case. If the flock is bunched together along the perimeter:

1. Move them off the fence together by stepping into the stock yourself, while keeping the dog at your side (between the fence and you). You can use a short but loose cord to keep the dog in place while you tell the dog "steady," "walk up"—until there is a sufficient gap or space so he can move forward.

2. When the flock moves away from the pressure of you and the dog, a gap or space will be created along the fence. As the space opens, let the dog move onward.

3. When he slips through the gap, the flock should veer away from him. He will be anxious to go to the head and turn them back to the handler, his pack leader.

4. As he turns the animals, quickly step away from the flock and start walking backward (away from the fence) so that he can bring them to you. The dog is learning to control the head and to contain the stock between himself and the trainer.

5. Sometimes he may get around to the head and instead of driving them towards you, he turns them back on the fence. If this happens, you need to be faster on your feet and block him with your training stick to send him back to push them off the fence. (*See also* Problem Solving: Ringing [circling the flock].)

Eventually, as the dog gains more experience, you won't need to go with him, but will be able to use your body and training stick to teach him to hold his position and talk him through with verbal instructions—"walk up," "steady."

Trainer moving stock away from a fence with the dog on a slack lead to keep him steady.

PROBLEM SOLVING:
Rating (working too close or too fast) while fetching

There is nothing wrong with a dog that moves quickly, providing he isn't putting unwanted pressure on the stock. If your dog is working too close to the animals and putting unwanted pressure on them, tell him to back out. To reinforce this, walk to the side around the outer edge of the flock and step into the dog to make him give ground and back out. When the dog is working at a comfortable distance, the stock won't feel so pressured—so in turn, he'll tend to relax.

If he continues to hurry and crowd the animals after you have told him to back out, you will need to teach him to move more slowly. To establish this *steady* approach, stop him with a "stand" command, and as soon as he pauses, tell him "easy" or "steady." Every time he rushes the animals, halt him and then tell him "steady." He will soon associate the command with changing pace.

When a dog works too closely and rushes the animals or slices off the edges, keeping the flock together can also be a problem. If some of the sheep split off from the flock and your dog automatically pursues them to head them off, let him go to the head and turn them back to the group. (*See* "Handling Breakaways.")

Dog is too close and must "back out," otherwise he will split the flock.

PROBLEM SOLVING:
The dog disregards the trainer—doesn't come when called, or stay when asked

In order to establish an effective team, the dog needs to recognize the handler as the pack leader. There may be times when the handler needs to be indulgent to encourage a dog in a certain phase of schooling. However, the trainer must always be in command of the dog when necessary. To do this, the trainer must follow through on his instructions, such as *stand, stay,* or *come.*

It is not uncommon for a dog with strong herding instincts to be distracted in the presence of livestock. A leash is very important to reinforce simple instructions such as coming when called. You need to practice the recall (described in Chapter 5: *Laying the Foundation*) with livestock both inside and outside the pen to develop a reliable "come."

PROBLEM SOLVING:
A dog that is difficult to stop

When a dog is working close, putting pressure on the stock, it is more difficult to reinforce the stop. Ask the dog to "back out." Then move in front of his shoulder towards his head to stop him. It is easier to get him to comply if you stop him when he is in the correct position to bring stock to a halt. Balance is necessary to reinforce it. In other words, when a young or an inexperienced dog is learning to fetch, his instincts tell him to keep the stock between you and him constantly. When the dog willingly circles around the stock and pauses (just before or after he turns in) to bring them to you, that is a good opportunity to reinforce the "stand." It may take a couple of weeks to get a reliable stop while herding.

Calm sheep are vital in teaching a young dog to stop when working livestock. If the sheep are flighty, the dog will be less inclined to stop and settle, he thinks they are going to escape. Remember, it is much easier to control a dog when he feels he is in control of the stock.

You can also move the animals to a corner where they can remain stationary. Get into a position between the dog and stock (closer to the animals), then ask the dog to stand. If he doesn't come to a standstill, step into him and make him yield to you by telling him "back out." When he does, praise him—"good dog." Then tell him to "stand." Practice this several times. Always speak calmly but with authority.

PROBLEM SOLVING:
Dog gets tense and bites when face to face with stock
When this occurs:

1. Step in next to the dog. Steadily ease forward, bringing your dog in with you. Do not force him, but urge him to move onward with the command, "steady, walk up," in a calm, reassuring tone. As he moves forward, tell him "good dog, steady, walk up."
2. If necessary, put a short slip lead on the dog (keep it slack) to steady him as needed and prevent him from darting away or diving in and taking a hold. Tell him "easy."
3. Turn the head(s) of the stock if need be to cause them to move away from the dog. This will reduce the dog's anxiety and build his self-confidence.
4. If one of the stock challenges the dog and tries to butt him, give the dog permission to grip the animal with the command "skit 'em up." If necessary, slap the animal on the nose to encourage the dog to nip the nose. Eventually, you will be able to simply talk the dog through face-to-face confrontations with stock. (*See also* "Problem Solving: Dog busts through the middle or grips when bringing stock off fence, out of a corner.")

As Phylliss Clark calmly steps in to lend support, it helps diffuse the pressure of the head-to-head between her Rottie and the cow with a calf by her side. PHOTOS BY DEB CONROY.

PROBLEM SOLVING:
Dog has strong eye, is tight in his movements, continually drops to the ground and is hesitant to walk up

A strong-eyed dog may work on his belly or in a low crouch and drops down (claps). He can become sticky if not handled well. Working small groups of stock will intensify the eye. Try to work larger flocks that move easily off a dog whenever possible. Practice exercises that encourage the dog to wear freely behind the stock while fetching to loosen him up. Change directions frequently, so he will have to keep moving to maintain balance. When you change direction, turn sharply (squarely, like military turns) and then walk in that direction. Every now and then, after turning, walk back in a tight circle, so the dog has to pursue the balance point (flanking off balance).

If the dog has the tendency to drop down (clap), ask him to "walk up." Keep him in motion as much as possible. Don't ask the dog to stop unless necessary—but when you need to stop him, it is important to keep him on his feet. Don't ask him to "lie down."

When an animal such as doe or ewe turns to face a strong-eyed dog, he can become so focused, staring at one animal, that he may not even hear your voice or notice when some of the flock strays off. This can be a huge problem in ranch situations where a dog is sent to gather stock at a distance and encounters an animal in a ravine. The dog freezes up. He's immobile, so the handler has to search for the dog.

When the dog gets stuck, try pushing stock towards him, but off to one side while telling him to "walk up," encouraging him to move. Whistle commands may be more effective breaking through the concentration. (*See also* "Problem Solving: Dog won't walk up to the stock.")

While loud, harsh sounds can startle the dog, thus breaking the intense concentration, they may also shock him enough to cause him to dive in and grab the animal with extreme force. The goal here is getting the dog moving without causing him to dart in and bite. In some situations, putting your hat or jacket in front of the dog's face has been known to distract him sufficiently enough to redirect him. (*See also* "Problem Solving: Dog gets tense and bites when face to face with stock.")

Commands such as "walk up," "come," and "that'll do" need to be well ingrained in extremely strong-eyed dogs. Play training is a very useful tool to instill these instructions. Lastly, do not keep this dog in situations (such as his kennel) where he can stare at livestock. It only makes him sticky.

PROBLEM SOLVING:
Dog won't walk up to the stock

There are several reasons a dog may be hesitant to walk up to the stock. Over correcting and over use of the training stick may cause uncertainty. A young or inexperienced dog may lack confidence when stock is hard to move or challenging and turns to face him. The same is true if the dog is sticky or lacks power.

Moving stock easily is essential to build the dog's self-confidence. Any time an animal turns to challenge the dog, the handler should step in as the pack leader and walk forward with the dog to move the stock together. If the dog tries to dart away, call him back in and continue moving forward. If necessary, use a short slip cord to steady the dog, while telling him "walk up, steady," in a calm but authoritative tone. When the stock submits and moves, the dog is encouraged to move as well.

Practice fetching stock short distances, with frequent turns to encourage the dog to swap sides, maintaining balance. Do not let the dog and stock get into a stalemate. Assist the dog in every way you can. When necessary, you should push the animal's face away from the dog and urge him to "walk up." If the stock tries to butt the dog, he should be encouraged to defend himself and allowed to grip. (*See also* "Problem Solving: Dog gets tense and bites when face to face with stock.")

PROBLEM SOLVING:
A dog that works so far off the flock it is difficult to get him to come in close

This is mainly a characteristic with strong-eyed dogs—primarily Border Collies—that are ultra-responsive to pressure. When working close they become uncomfortable and run off. This type of dog already runs wide and doesn't require being pushed out. If anything, they need to be encouraged to stay in contact with the stock. In order to settle this type of dog and build his confidence, you need to spend an appropriate amount of time working in smaller enclosures to keep him in touch with the stock.

If the dog is uptight or inclined to flee, work in a secure area or keep him on a light cord, but keep it slack. Spend time walking quietly around the stock to develop his comfort level and reliability.

PROBLEM SOLVING:
Dog dashes away, busts through the middle of the flock, or grips when bringing stock off a fence, out of a corner

Some dogs get uptight when working in confined spaces. It may be due to insecurity or a traumatic experience, such as being butted. The most practical thing you can do is teach the dog how to relax when working close in. Don't hesitate to step in and make the animals move away from the dog. Take your time to help him work through the problem. This will instill confidence in him.

If essential, use a loose leash or your training stick to prevent the dog from dashing in, while telling him "steady." As the stock gives way, tell him "walk up" in a quiet but commanding tone. This will encourage the dog to move forward as well. As his confidence grows, he will have the self-control to squeeze through a tight space and peel stock off a fence through vocal cues. (*See also* "Problem Solving: Dog won't walk up to the stock" and "Problem Solving: Dog gets tense and bites when face to face with stock.")

Brodie, a Bearded Collie owned by Mary Lott in Oregon, confidently moving sheep off a fence. PHOTO BY MARY PEASLEE.

PROBLEM SOLVING:
Barking while working

New Zealand Huntaways are noted for their big voices. Breeds such as the Huntaway and certain strains of Bearded Collies were developed to use bark. This is part of the dog's natural style to flush out lost or hiding stock, causing them to flock together. Equally, Kelpies and Mudis bark forcefully as needed to move large flocks without biting. On the other hand, young or inexperienced dogs may woof from excitement. Dogs lacking confidence or power may yap as a result.

If the dog starts barking when an animal turns to challenge him, you need to step in and cause the animals to turn away from the dog. This will help build the dog's confidence. As a dog develops confidence, the barking will become more purposeful and decrease in frequency. A dog may use his voice if he is confused and doesn't understand what his handler is trying to teach him. The dog can become frustrated if you are in the wrong position. A dog may also bark as an avoidance behavior caused by anxiety from harsh or untimely corrections.

PROBLEM SOLVING:
Dog loses interest, quits working or wanders off
When a keen dog quits working, physical problems causing pain or weakness—such as from injury, hip dysplasia, heartworms or even feet—should be examined. Stamina is affected by physical condition and a dog's requirement for adequate water. Always be on guard for heat-related issues such as heat stress.

A dog may eagerly run around the stock, but lose interest when asked to change direction or stop, or when he is pushed away from stock to get him to widen out. A frightening encounter with a stubborn or aggressive animal can intimidate a sensitive dog. This type of dog requires lots of encouragement, gentle handling, and mild correction.

Dogs lacking concentration and desire may lose interest due to boredom. Some signs of losing interest are wandering off, not paying attention, or sniffing the ground and eating grass or animal dung. Don't correct him, but redirect him. Keep the training sessions short and enjoyable. You may need to re-evaluate the dog's suitability to the task. You cannot take for granted that just because a dog comes from a herding breed or bloodlines that he has inherited the traits or desire necessary for herding.

Some dogs are easily distracted and stray off to explore things in the training area. Males can also be distracted by the scent of females in estrus. If your dog's attention wanders, call his name in a cheerful voice or whistle to attract his attention, then redirect him back to the flock with the words "watch 'em" in an excited voice. Lure him back to the flock by moving the animals. You may need to give this type of dog a freer rein to encourage him and to build confidence. Instead of using the stick, give a verbal correction to send the dog back behind. (*See also* "Developing focus.")

PROBLEM SOLVING:
Dog leaves stock behind

Dogs that lack balance may not adequately cover their stock, thereby allowing the animals to spread out and fall by the wayside. Fetch short distances and spend time zigzagging around the pen, changing direction often. Practice figure eight patterns where the dog has to continually tuck in the corners to heighten his awareness. Consider working different animals in a variety of situations as well.

Likewise, when a dog is paying attention to the trainer rather than the stock, he can leave animals behind. A highly sensitive dog or one lacking confidence can become distracted and also lose track of the animals. The trainer needs to be very careful not to over-command this type of dog, and to give him plenty of opportunities to think for himself.

Mechanical dogs lacking the appropriate herding instincts—balance and a certain degree of eye—lack awareness also and may not notice when some animals go astray. This type of dog needs a lot of work on focus. You might want to reconsider the dog's suitability to the task of herding.

PROBLEM SOLVING:
A dog that has been started incorrectly

Sometimes a dog is started incorrectly, but you can work through it. Good training and humane treatment can go a long way toward rehabilitating a damaged dog. He may require much positive handling to correct undesirable habits and create a new attitude toward training. As you work with him, walk to him many, many times just to say "good dog." Do this when he is performing well. This will create a very desirable relationship between you and your dog.

You may need to start with the basic exercises and retrain. It may take a lot of repetition, but you must not assume the dog knows anything. Work calmly with the dog so he doesn't become anxious and confused or frustrated.

PROBLEM SOLVING:
A male dog who continually lifts his leg on the fence posts as he works

This generally occurs with dominant, loose-eyed males trying to mark territory. Having a male neutered can reduce territorial marking with urine. It may also occur from the scent of a female in estrus or when a dog loses interest. (*See* "Problem Solving: losing interest.")

Chapter 8

Developing a Useful Dog

PUTTING ON THE MILES (WALKABOUT)

Once the dog has been bringing sheep wherever you walk, you can help him gain experience by taking many walks around a pasture or field while your dog brings the flock (keeping them in a group). It is always a good idea to work first in a larger fenced area, in the event things get out of control. Stop every so often and allow the flock to rest and even graze while your dog settles. It's important for him to learn that the flock does not need to be moving every moment.

Walkabout—Deb Conroy and her dog Mick are taking a walk about the pasture.
PHOTO BY LORI HERBEL OF XP RANCH PHOTOGRAPHY.

Louanne Brooks and her ACD, CH Hillhaven's Chompin's Sparkplug, PT, HASs, TDI taking a break to allow the stock to rest. PHOTO BY DEB CONROY.

Handling Breakaways

When an animal bolts away from the bunch, the dog should automatically turn back to pick it up. If he is unsuccessful, tell him "that'll do" to let him know that he should leave the stray and come back to you; so you can take the group to the single. Use the flocking instinct to help draw the individual back to the main bunch. The closer the bunch comes, the stronger the attraction and the easier it will be to reunite the group. If your dog naturally understands balance, distance, and rating, breakaways are much less likely. As your dog's skills get better and your handling skills improve, the likelihood of breakaways should diminish. If this problem recurs too often you may need to re-evaluate your situation and take measures to minimize breakaways. Gentler stock, better rating and balance, or more attentiveness on the trainer's part should be considered. You and your dog are never so far along that you might not go back and revisit earlier lessons. Breakaways may be an indication that this might be needed.

FURTHERING BALANCE

Balance is the underpinning for all stock training and handling. To increase your dog's balance, have him bring the sheep and hold them to you by containing them against a fence or gate. If the stock is very light (that is, flighty) you can use a corner of the field. Stop your dog and tell him to "watch 'em."

Watch the animals' heads and ears to determine the appropriate distance the dog needs to be to hold the stock in place. Your job will be to help him recognize where he needs to stop. If your dog gets too close or puts too much pressure on the bunch, one or more may try to break away and flee from the others. Let your dog head off the escapees and put them back with the bunch. Encourage the dog to think on his own. Give him a chance to respond to his natural inclination to put the animal in its place.

After the dog has held the sheep to you on the fence or in the corner of a field and apprehended any escapees, you can then walk along one side of the sheep and let the dog bring them off the fence while you lead them away.

Vary this exercise working gradually off of the fence to give the dog more control of the situation. Don't overdo it. This exercise is intended to help you and your dog, not to become your regular practice.

Dog holding stock to his trainer on horseback along a fence line.

In 1991 I was invited to work my dogs at the Livestock Expo in Tepatitlan, Guadalajara, Mexico. The exhibition was held in a bullfighting lienzo while a mariachi band played lively music with trumpets blaring away.

The stock was wild. They had come out of the hills and had never been worked by dogs before. The wind was blowing and the music was loud. My dogs, Fleetwood and Reanna, couldn't hear any of the commands I gave, so I simply turned them loose and let them balance and work purely on instinct. The crowd—watching the dogs work like cutting horses to keep the stock from bolting away—cheered. Had it not been for their well-developed balance I wouldn't have been able to do that.

The author's dog Reanna stopping an escaping ewe.

BUILDING CONFIDENCE

Stubborn stock that challenges a dog or tries to fight with him can easily destroy the confidence of a young dog. If your dog lacks the self-assurance to defend himself against attacks from an animal testing his authority, step in to give him confidence by turning the aggressor's head away from your dog. If the stock chooses not to move away from your dog and keeps facing or challenging him, encourage him to use force. This is a controlled situation in which you give your dog permission to grip by telling him to "skit 'em" or "skit a hold." As soon as he has done so, tell him "good dog, that'll do." Don't overdo it; you want to teach him to use his authority appropriately. You must also keep the welfare of the stock in mind and be sure that your dog is not abusing the stock—just gaining their respect.

If the stock continually challenges your dog, you might need to acquire stock that is better suited to him, gradually developing his ability until he has acquired the skills and confidence to meet with success or at least give his best attempt in every situation.

MOVING TO THE NEXT PHASE OF TRAINING

Once your dog has been taught to reliably control stock and bring them to you, you will want to move to a larger area to further his skills on

Teaching Bark and Bite

A forceful, purposeful bark in brushy country—or when pushing stock crowded in sorting races or through footbaths—can be useful and necessary, but yapping can be detrimental when working certain types of stock, such as cows with calves. You can easily teach the dog to bark in a game format when you know what triggers the dog to bark. Some dogs are easily excited when you "woof" at them, and they reciprocate. Ask the dog to speak or "woof." Praise him when he does and reward him with a treat. Do this several times. If he continues to bark, tell him "that'll do." In that way you are modifying natural behavior in a beneficial way.

There are times when bark must be backed by bite. If an animal challenges the dog's authority, however, by all means encourage the dog to put it back in its place.

When feeding, use the dog to keep stock from trampling over you until you are finished putting out the hay and grain. If the animals rush towards the feed, give the dog permission to "skit 'em up." Working stock through sorting chutes is another time to teach bite. Grip can also be taught in the game format, as described in "Herding Games and Commands, Skit a Hold."

 Note: At no time is teaching a dog to bite compliant training animals ever part of good stockmanship. It is also detrimental to coaching a dog to read and rate stock correctly.

Dog getting ready to nip the cow's poll. The correct areas for a dog to nip are the nose, the poll, or the lower legs (fetlock or hocks). A mild pinch (quick nip and release) to the neck, rib area, or the ear may be considered reasonable in sheep or goats when necessary, providing it doesn't cause bruising or an incision, since sheep's skin is so thin. A bite on the body can bruise and tear the flesh, making the animal susceptible to fly strikes, infection, etc.

different terrains. You can tell that he is ready to move to the next level of training by assessing the following factors:

- The dog realizes that his place is on the opposite side of the flock from his trainer.
- He knows how to keep the stock together in a group.
- He knows how to yield when you apply pressure.
- He responds to your instructions to stop, walk up, and come.
- He is rating (moving the animals at a relaxed pace) and knows how to counter attempts to escape.

Author and his dog Poco swapping sides to continue fetching.

FLANKING

When the dog has been programmed always to bring the sheep to the trainer and stop attempts to escape, he is ready for the next level of training. The trainer is able to reliably stop the dog on command and call him off the stock. The dog is ready to hone his ability to group livestock in a larger area and fetch them to the trainer wherever he walks. This is the stage at which the flanking commands are introduced and the distance the dog works away from the handler is gradually increased.

Teaching Flanking (Directional) Commands
Flanking is the circling movement that the dog uses to go around livestock. Although he has not been taught the flanking commands formally, he has already been executing the behavior around the flock. The flanking com-

mands are "away to me" for counterclockwise movement around the stock (think of it as "going back in time") and "come bye" or "go by" for clockwise movements around the stock (think of it as "time goes by"). Your dog may not understand at first what the directional commands mean, but he'll soon learn to associate the command with the action by your marking or naming the behavior as it is being performed.

It is easier to teach the flanking commands beginning with quarter turns. You will also introduce the command "there" to indicate to the dog when he is in the desired position to turn in and walk directly towards the animals. Calm, docile sheep are highly helpful for teaching this exercise.

1. Have your dog fetch the flock to the center of the training area. Let them settle so he is not concerned that they will get away.
2. Instruct your dog to "stand–stay." When you stop the dog, he should not move closer to the sheep until asked to.
3. Move to a position fairly close to the flock. It is usually the dog's natural inclination to go to the animals' heads. Keep this in mind as you get into position around the flock to send the dog.
4. To send him in the clockwise direction, call the dog's name and ask him to "come up." Pat your leg to draw him around your body clockwise, and as he starts to circle, tell him "come bye."
5. If he begins to go the wrong way, say "no!—stand" and cross over in front of him to block him from continuing in the wrong direction.
6. While the dog is moving around the flock, you should also be walking around the flock in the same direction, but nearer to the animals and slightly behind the dog (walking just behind his shoulder). Your position is extremely important. When you step in front of the dog's shoulder, you will cause him to switch directions. Your position keeps the dog from coming in too tightly and causing the flock to move away.
7. If the dog cuts in or moves in too closely, step toward his shoulder and force him to yield. When he gives to the pressure, relieve the pressure (step back next to the flock), staying in position to correct when necessary. This will also increase the dog's awareness of the invisible perimeter around the sheep and show him the right distance while you are teaching the side commands.
8. Flank the dog a quarter of the way around the flock, and then stop him with the "stand" command.
9. Send him clockwise again by telling him "come bye."
10. After you've done this two or three times, reward him by letting him fetch the sheep. As he is circling the sheep, tell him "there, walk up," instructing him to turn in and move toward the flock as you back away from them, so he can bring them to you.

11. Practice flanking several times going clockwise, and then try it going counterclockwise.

Gwen Litz is positioned near the sheep, but just ahead of her dog Babe on a "stand, stay" in the imaginary circle. To flank her dog counterclockwise, she will step to the side (behind the dog's shoulder) to open the door.
PHOTO BY DEB CONROY.

Training Tips

Always be in a position to make certain that your dog goes in the desired direction—as well as maintains appropriate distance to the sheep—while flanking. Make sure your dog stays far enough from the stock so that he does not put too much pressure on them, but not so far that he loses contact with them. Note that the emphasis of "there, walk up" is placed on the "there."

If your dog is excitable and charges into the stock prior to fetching them to you, back him out, stop him momentarily, and then calmly ask him to pick up the stock with the "steady" command. The stock should move quietly away from your dog. When you practice this, you are helping your dog understand how to lift the stock in a controlled manner. Dogs with a calm approach do not need to be stopped prior to lifting the stock.

Trainer's position is too far behind the dog to prevent him from cutting the corners as he flanks the sheep.

As you cast your dog from your side to the other side of the livestock, you are laying the foundation for the outrun, in which your dog moves from your side to the opposite side of the stock without disrupting the animals or sending them bolting in the wrong direction.

Square Flanks

When your dog maintains the appropriate distance on sheep while flanking, it allows him to move to the point of balance (by skirting the stock's fight/flight zone) without causing the flock to bolt or panic and split. If the dog is cutting the corners, he may be putting unwanted pressure on the animals before the handler is ready to move them. To "square" a dog up, you should stand the dog, and then step to the side and flank the dog around your body—as the dog passes you, put gentle pressure on him by walking toward his shoulder and telling him "back out." The dog should yield to your position and give ground, but he should continue moving in the desired direction while keeping his focus on the stock. If the dog "turns tail" or turns away from the sheep, you have pushed him out too far. Some dogs are very responsive to pressure. As soon as he responds, step back to reduce the pressure.

If a dog is pushed out too far, he is no longer in contact with the animals and has lost control. This situation indicates weakness to the livestock and allows them to gain the upper hand over your dog. It may also cause a soft dog to quit working.

Note: When teaching flanking with extremely light or flighty stock, set up the exercise so that the animals can be contained in the corner of a field or against a fence. You will still assume the position between the flock and dog, while the dog is flanked back and forth in front of the animals.

Square flank illustrated by Deb Conroy and Mick. PHOTO BY LORI HERBEL OF XP RANCH PHOTOGRAPHY.

▼

The term "square flank" is relatively new terminology, introduced in the late 1980s.

▲

TAKING TIME OFF FROM STRUCTURED TRAINING SESSIONS

Dogs can benefit from being allowed to perform everyday jobs without constant handler direction, giving them an opportunity to think things through and make decisions. Sometimes either you or the dog has an "off" day. In that event, it is better to put the stock away until another day. Any time your dog seems confused, tired, or reluctant, give him a break for several days or even a few weeks. This should be a time of moderate exercise and play but no structured training sessions.

It is not unusual for a dog to become physically and mentally worn out and need time off. When your dog has finished his break from training, he will be fresh, with renewed interest and excitement. A short vacation can be a good idea for the trainer, who might also be feeling tired, confused, or frustrated. And finally, the training livestock will often benefit greatly from a rest as well. This practice is a necessary part of structured training, not an easy out from a difficult situation.

PROBLEM SOLVING:
Dog seems to be one sided
A dog may circle easily in one direction, but become difficult to flank on the opposite side. He may have a preferred side. His discomfort may be made evident by cutting in, shutting down, and gripping. Handle the dog calmly to reduce the dog's anxiety. When working on the dog's weaker side, do not pressure the dog with force. You can increase the dog's skills little by little with quarter flanks, as described above. Make sure to practice both sides equally so the dog learns to circle well in either direction.

Secondly, make sure you are using your training stick properly. (*Refer to:* The Training Stick and How to Use It Correctly.)

PROBLEM SOLVING:
Dog flanks fast and tight
Try instructing the dog with calm, quiet commands. Keep everything relaxed. Flank the dog, then stop him; let him settle before sending him again. As you gently back the dog out, be careful not to push him out of contact with the animals.

A PROFILE OF

John Payne — The One-Armed Bandit

Loading livestock *in* a trailer can sometimes be a difficult task, but loading them on the *top* of a trailer is not something most people will ever attempt. John Payne, an expert horseman and dog trainer who makes his living in the saddle, created a rodeo act doing just that with the help of his Cur heading dogs. Payne uses his expert horsemanship skills and herding dogs to round up steers and load them on top of a stock trailer to entertain rodeo audiences across the country.

He acquired his moniker, the One-Armed Bandit, because of an electrical accident that happened when he grabbed what he thought was a dead power line. He sustained 7,200 volts of electricity and lost his right arm and nearly his life. In true cowboy fashion, he recovered—and two months later returned to ranching and riding.

John grew up in Oklahoma, where he has spent his entire life on horseback. For over forty-five years he was in partnership with his father and four brothers, running the family livestock operation and a cattle-gathering business. Their expeditions have taken them across the country, from southern Florida to the western plains.

The men discovered that the heelers they were working in the early years didn't have the type of nose necessary to track and locate cows in brush and vines so thick it is almost impossible to walk through them, much less ride a horse. They needed dogs that could handle feral cattle in heavily wooded areas with dense undergrowth. John had seen Florida Curs (bay-and-catch dogs) on a cattle-gathering expedition in Florida and was impressed with their ability to trail and control maverick cattle, so he started breeding and training Curs. He has worked his dogs on many wild cattle-gathering jobs, where they handled 800- to 1,000-pound horned steers and 1,000- to 1,500-pound bulls in bad terrain with lots of undergrowth, and sometimes in swamps, where alligators lay waiting for thirsty animals.

Although John has since retired from the dangerous job of gathering untamed cattle for other outfits, he continues to perform his signature act at fairs and rodeos across the country. John has earned the Pro Rodeo Cowboys Association (PRCA) Specialty Act of the Year award eight years in a row, an honor that would have been impossible without the help of herding dogs.

Chapter 9

THE OUTRUN

TEACHING OUTRUN AND LIFT

The outrun enables you to send your dog sizable distances to gather and bring stock. In some trials a dog could easily be working a quarter of a mile (.4 km) away from his handler. In certain ranch situations dogs are required to gather and bring stock to corrals or holding areas from a half mile (.8 km)—if not much farther—away, like a speck on the horizon or out of sight, depending on the terrain and the type of stock.

The ideal trial outrun is described as a pear shape—starts out tighter and widens out as the dog approaches the sheep. In the real world, the dog needs to maintain whatever distance is sufficient to gather all the stock and keep from pushing the stock in the wrong direction before he can lift them to his handler.

Outrun, lift, and fetch.

The way you set up the outrun will determine the path the dog takes. When the handler is between the stock and the dog and the dog is set off to one side (or the trainer steps off to one side) the dog is pulled around the trainer, and that will widen the dog's path. When the dog is started off closer to the handler he may choose a narrower path, but your goal is to be able to eventually send the dog from your side.

Reanna is maintaining a path around the sheep at a distance suitable for the flock's comfort zone.

The ground work for the outrun was laid when you taught the dog how to flank. When sending your dog from one side to the other, do not allow him to come between you and the stock. Otherwise, when working at greater distances, he may be tempted to cut back and "cross over," or take the direction he prefers rather than following through on the flanking command you gave. Crossing over in front of the animals may cause them to run off in the wrong direction before the dog is in position to bring them to you.

1. Let the dog bring the stock to you, as you've been practicing.
2. Stop in a place where the flock is positioned in the open, away from fences.
3. Call your dog to you and walk a short distance away (50 yards, or 15 to 46 m) from the flock.
4. Stand the dog facing the direction you intend to cast him.
5. Leave him there with a "stay" command.
6. Walk back toward the flock, staying closer to the flock, so that you can discourage him from cutting in or running straight at the flock.
7. Give your dog a directional command to send him to one or the other

side around the stock such as "come bye" to flank or cast him clockwise. As he passes by you he should bend out around you and proceed to the far side of the sheep. If he tries to run straight at the animals, walk toward the dog's shoulder—not in front of it—as he passes by and instruct him to "back out." Follow him around to the back of the sheep. Dogs, similar to livestock, respond to pressure. If you get in front of the dog's shoulder or head, you can cause him to cut back or go in the wrong direction.

Reanna turning in at the far side positioned at the top of the flock—not too deep or shallow—for the "lift."

In this position, the trainer is able to prevent the dog from cutting in.

Ty is positioned to cast his dog Poco to the opposite side of the flock. If necessary, he'll bend the horse around and ride towards the dog to encourage an appropriate path around the sheep.

Training Tips

If the dog goes in a different direction from the one you commanded, stop him with the "stand" command and redirect him. If he is still determined to go the wrong way, cross over in front of the dog and block him from taking the incorrect side.

When the dog gets to the other side of the flock, tell him "there" to instruct him where to turn in, and "walk up" to bring the animals toward you. If the dog bolts towards the animals, stop him and tell him "easy" or "steady." Once he's settled, let the dog bring the flock to you. Walk to the other side of the pasture, as you've been practicing with the walkabout. Repeat the process.

Training cannot be hurried. You need to take the necessary time to fix whatever problems may occur. Otherwise, they will soon become bad habits. Build the length of the outrun a few feet at a time. It is important not to send the dog too far or too wide too soon. If at any time your dog cuts in, stop and redirect him.

Training Tips (continued)

Steadily, increase your dog's distance from the flock, so that you are starting the outrun from farther away. Gradually, move closer to the dog, until you are able to send the dog from your side. Stay near the flock as long as necessary to get the top of the outrun as it should be.

Once you send the dog—even if he starts poorly—stop him, but don't call him back. Re-direct him from there. Next time, send him a shorter distance to the flock.

As training progresses, the author casts his dog situated by his side. He is letting stock drift farther away and settle before sending Poco.

Years ago, I was working a young Border Collie named Fleetwood who had been started on cattle and was now being trained on sheep. When I sent him on an outrun to gather the flock, he would lunge in as the sheep were moving away and heel, gripping one. I would scold him, and it became a bad habit encouraged partly and unknowingly by me. He bit out of frustration because he didn't clearly understand what I was expecting of him—and was anticipating being reprimanded. He was redirecting his frustration onto the sheep. (continued on next page)

One night, while everything was very calm and quiet, I sent him out to the pasture to gather a small group of 20 or 30 head. Naturally, when he got to the top side, he lunged in and gripped a ewe, but this time I didn't say a word to him. He was surprised. He looked at me, expecting to be corrected. Instead, I quietly let him bring the sheep to me.

I sent him twice more. The second time he dove in, and again I didn't say anything to him, just let him bring the sheep. The third time, and ever after, he didn't jump in and bite the sheep when he got to the end of the outrun. The lesson I learned was that some of the problems exhibited by a dog are created by the trainer. Whenever there is a problem, you need to take time to analyze your strategy. A video camera can be a useful tool to help you examine your training methods. Working with a friend can also give you that second set of eyes. Some of the best trainers work with others and both trainers benefit from the collaboration. There are many times when both the trainer and the dog can get locked into reacting and not thinking about what they are doing. Working with someone else helps keep the process thoughtful.

PROBLEM SOLVING:
A dog that runs better to one side

Shorten the distance of his outrun on his weaker side. Flanking exercises can help the dog build confidence when working on his off side. When the dog seems at ease flanking on his weak side you can go back to building the length of his outrun little by little. Work close until the dog is more relaxed. In the meantime, you can continue sending the dog on his strong side.

PROBLEM SOLVING:
A dog that takes a narrow path (runs tight) on its outrun

Developing an efficient outrun in upright, close working breeds can take time. When you position the dog to send him, step off to one side of the sheep (or set the dog off to one side) and pull him around them, causing him to take a wider path.

Practice flanking exercises to widen the dog as he passes the sheep and nears at the top of the outrun. Stay near the flock as long as necessary to get the dog to widen out as he approaches the sheep to pass them and nears the top of his outrun. It is important to increase the distance a few feet at a time. This is an ongoing process.

PROBLEM SOLVING:
Dog overruns the top of the outrun

In order for the dog to bring the animals straight to the trainer, the dog will need to stop at the back of the sheep in a position approximately opposite yours at about twelve o'clock. However, if after you send the dog clockwise, the sheep start heading towards four o'clock for example, the dog may have to compensate by stopping at maybe one or two o'clock to head them to six o'clock. In this situation, the dog is reading the sheep and balancing correctly. This is true when fetching also.

As the dog is fetching to his handler, he is positioned on the flock's heavy side (direction the lead sheep is inclined to go towards). PHOTO BY LORI HERBEL OF XP RANCH PHOTOGRAPHY.

After you send the dog, move to approximately four or five o'clock. This will encourage the dog to counterbalance your position when he gets to the top of the outrun.

Always hold the training stick vertical (not to one side or the other). Otherwise, the dog may be reading it as a cue to under or over flank.

If the dog over runs and then starts ringing, it may be an indication that you aren't cueing the dog with "there" or asking him to stop at the top of the outrun. Shorten the distance you send the dog and work up little by little.

PROBLEM SOLVING:
Dog doesn't complete the outrun or stops short

Fences or other outer structures creates external pressure on a sensitive dog and can cause him to pull up short. When you place the sheep for the outrun, it is important to position them far enough away from fences so the dog can get around the sheep freely.

Send the dog clockwise, for example, and when you see he is starting to slow down or stop short at ten or eleven o'clock, repeat the flanking command "come-by" ("go-by") while you move toward him. If the dog is highly responsive, you might get a better result by stepping away from him. It depends entirely on the dog. Be mindful of how your training stick is positioned so you don't cause the dog to stop short. Use flanking exercises to circle the dog past the balance point before asking him to stop.

Finally, never send a dog to gather stock if there's none to be found. Otherwise, he may become confused and give up. When you send a dog on a blind outrun—over a hill, for example, where he may not be able to see the animals—make sure there is always stock to be gathered. If you ever need to send him to search for real lost stock, he will work hard because he knows there is an actual task to be performed, not a game.

PROBLEM SOLVING:
Cutting in on the outrun

A dog with strong heading instincts can be tempted to cut in to head stock that is facing him. Also, tame, dog-broke stock can get in the habit of going to the trainer when they see a dog. It is not uncommon for a dog to cut in if the sheep start moving toward the trainer before he gets to the top of the outrun.

Sending the dog on an outrun in narrow pastures enclosed by a fence or natural hedge, creating pressure, can cause sheep to shift out of position before the dog reaches the other side of the flock. It may be necessary to use a drop-pen or put feed out to hold the stock in place until the dog is in position to make his lift.

When a dog is pushed out too far too soon it can cause him to cut in to re-establish contact. The dog should be widened out gradually as described in the flanking exercises.

If there are obstacles in the field, a close-running dog has an inclination to cut to the inside of them rather than go around them. Try to keep this in mind when setting up the outrun.

PROBLEM SOLVING:
Dog is hesitant on lift
A dog that lacks power or is sticky may have difficulty lifting heavy sheep or one that faces him, stomping her foot. In order to avoid a stand-off at the end of the outrun it is better to let the dog pick up the flock with out stopping him at the end of the outrun. When he gets to the top of the outrun and begins to slow down or hesitate, tell him to "walk up." Encourage the dog to keep moving forward to pick up the flock.

PROBLEM SOLVING:
Dog starts out wide, but flattens or slices off the top of his outrun
Instead of maintaining the circular path around the sheep, the dog comes in tight. There are several reasons this can happen, one of which is the trainer has started the dog too wide and he loses contact with the sheep.

If you push the dog too wide, he may feel he's not in contact with the sheep and comes in tight. Practice the outrun as described in the steps numbered above, and when the dog nears the top follow him around to the back of the sheep. Stay near the flock as long as necessary to get the depth at the top of the outrun as it should be. When setting the dog up, face him straight toward the sheep at twelve o'clock (not left or right).

PROBLEM SOLVING:
Dog takes a wide path on his outrun and stops far away at the top of the outrun
When sent to gather a pasture, a dog that runs wide is much more likely to see animals that may be scattered farther away and widen out to gather them as well. Therefore, he is less likely to leave some behind. While running wide has its benefits, it can be problematic in some ranch situations, such as when working willful stock in large, unfenced pastures that require the dog to block the stock from escaping. If, instead, the dog casts out too wide, going around natural obstacles such as trees and rocks, he will lose control of the animals.

The dog usually keeps distance to avoid pressure from the handler or horse and rider and the stock. Practice short outruns. When you set this dog up for an outrun; start him close to your side rather than from a distance or by pulling him around you. If the dog continues to widen, step back farther away from the flock to draw him in closer to the animals. Stepping away from the dog may release enough pressure to correct him. If the dog starts running wider at the backside of the sheep, correct him in the same way by stepping away from the flock. If that doesn't draw the dog closer toward the stock, use a simple "here" or some quick, short whistles to pull him in tighter.

PROBLEM SOLVING:
Trainer only has small areas to practice in

Not everyone has the perfect training situation. Ideally, you will be able to work in a variety of situations. However, if the dog is taught the fundamental exercises correctly, the dog will very likely perform correctly in a larger area. Take advantage of fun and training trials to broaden your dog's horizon.

PROBLEM SOLVING:
Dog lacks excitement

If you have over corrected the dog he may be hesitant. Instead of using a flanking command to send him to the other side of the stock, try a hissing sound or "shoo" to encourage the dog and help speed up his outrun. Try to give the dog a freer rein. As long as the dog isn't making any big mistakes don't nitpick him. The dog may lack luster and need some time away from training.

Chapter 10

DRIVING SKILLS

DRIVING

A dog is driving whenever he is behind the stock and they are moving away from him. He has been learning to stay behind stock while fetching or bringing the stock to you. The only thing that is going to change is your position. Now you will teach him to work on the same side of the stock, pushing them away—and to drive them from your right (or left) to the other side at varying lengths and distances (cross driving). A good time to teach your dog to drive stock away from you is when he is responding well to his flanking commands. During the first lessons in driving, it is helpful for you to walk beside your dog. This will give him confidence, and he won't be looking back constantly for direction.

Driving may frustrate a natural heading dog by making him feel he is about to lose control—so he will try to head the flock off at the first opportunity. The heading dog may be reluctant to take the driving position, whereas a natural driving dog will readily fall in behind the stock and move them.

To teach the drive:

1. Send your dog to gather and bring the stock to you.
2. As the stock come closer, walk toward your dog but off to one side. He will probably start to swing away to go to the head of the flock. If this happens, stop him—on his feet—by instructing him to "stand," and bring him back behind the sheep by using the appropriate flanking or side command: "come bye" for clockwise or "away to me" for counterclockwise.
3. When he has come behind the flock, tell him "there," to indicate you want him to turn in. This further instills in him the need to pick up and lift the stock in a controlled manner.

The only thing that changes in driving is the handler's position, which is now behind the dog. PHOTO BY LORI HERBEL OF XP RANCH PHOTOGRAPHY.

4. Ask him to "walk up." At this point, you are on the same side of the stock and walking forward with the dog.
5. After your dog has driven the stock a short distance—a few yards, perhaps—flank him around you; bring him from behind the animals and around your body in a semicircle to change his direction and turn the stock 180 degrees.
6. Tell him "that'll do," then praise him and walk away from the stock.
7. Reward him by sending him to lift and fetch the stock back to you.

Training Tips

Only ask your dog to drive the flock several feet at first, then several yards. Increase the distance gradually. If your dog pushes the stock too fast, slow his pace with the "steady" command. Keep the sessions short and enjoyable; little by little he will master what you are trying to teach him.

Author walking on the same side as the dog, driving steers along the fence so he can keep her in his eyesight.

To change direction, the dog is called away from the stock and brought around the trainer's body so he can head the stock and turn them.

Increase the distance little by little as the dog becomes more comfortable moving the animals away from you.

PROBLEM SOLVING:
Can't get dog to settle into driving—but continually breaks away to circle and fetch

This may be the result of letting the dog fetch sheep from the drive position. There needs to be a clear distinction between fetching and driving. Always bring the dog away from the sheep before sending him to gather and bring them back to you.

PROBLEM SOLVING:
Dog constantly looks back when driving

The dog is not accustomed to having you positioned behind him. Do not rush training. Progressively, drop back as you gradually build the distance between you and the dog, increasing the length of the drive. Refer to beginning of chapter.

USING A LONG LINE TO TEACH THE DRIVE

Some dogs have such strong heading instincts that a novice trainer may experience a lot of difficulty teaching the dog to drive. In this case the use of a 25- to 50-foot (7.5–15 m) light cord may help the trainer settle the dog into driving.

1. Attach a lightweight cord or line to your dog's collar.
2. When he tries to race to head the stock, stop him with "stand."
3. If he does not automatically respond, give a quick tug on the cord and give the appropriate side or flanking command: "come bye" or "away to me."
4. When the dog is in driving position behind the flock, tell him "there, walk up."
5. After he has been driving for several yards, reward the dog by letting him fetch the flock to you.

USING AN ALLEY OR FENCE TO TEACH THE DRIVE

A fenceline or return alley can also be used to teach the drive to a dog that is inclined to head the stock. Begin with the flock moving forward, with the fence on one side and you and the dog on the other, covering the open flank. This will help the strong heading dog to relax. Position yourself toward the front but off to the side (as with fetching). This allows your dog

Moving the Stock

When you want to guide stock in a particular direction, bring the dog on the opposite side from where you want them to go. The stock will move away from the dog. In other words, if you want the animal or herd to move left, place the dog on the right side. Stock is also influenced by other sources of pressure such as a fence, which can cause them to turn back.

1. To urge the animal forward, place the dog toward the rear.
2. To turn the animal or herd or to stop sideways drift, bring the dog toward the shoulder.
3. If the dog moves too far forward, the animals will stop or turn back.

The author is in position slightly in front of the dog, but off to one side to start driving the steers around the pen.

▼

If your dog becomes frustrated at any point
in his training, go back to the basics!

▲

Steve Shope and Gus, his very talented Australian Shepherd and working buddy, cross driving in a trial arena. PHOTO BY GARY R. ANDERSON.

to keep you in sight without turning his head or losing contact with the livestock, which can be frustrating to him.

TEACHING A DOG TO CROSS DRIVE

Cross driving is a continuation of driving. Instead of being positioned next to you, your dog moves the stock parallel to your position. The dog is not bringing the stock to you or moving them away from you, but is moving them in front of you. For example, you are facing the dog, who is moving the stock along a fence in front of you horizontally from either the right or left side. Picture the letter "T"—you are standing at the bottom while the dog is crossing the top with the sheep.

A round pen is helpful for teaching this concept, just as horsemen use the round pen to longe a horse: The horse moves around the trainer either clockwise or counterclockwise. Your dog holds the animals on the fence while he moves the stock continuously in a circle first one way, then the other. This way he can keep his eye on you without having to turn and look around.

If he tries to move between the stock and the fence to lift them off the fence and bring them to you, give him the appropriate flanking command to keep him behind the animals. When you draw him towards you, he'll be flanking on the inside.

Above and below: Mac, a Border Collie handled by Kent Herbel, in a cross drive, moving the sheep parallel from his handler's right to left side.
PHOTOS BY LORI HERBEL OF XP RANCH PHOTOGRAPHY.

Cross driving in a
round pen.

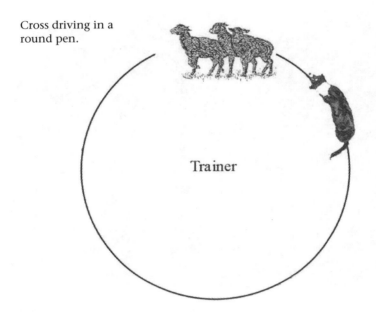

Trainer

To have the dog change direction, use the correct flanking command to bring him to your position and then send him around you the other way.

Out in the open, your dog can practice moving the stock in a circle around you. In time you can increase the distance by enlarging the circle, ultimately varying the length of the cross drive in both directions to expand your dog's adaptability. You can also take advantage of a fenced field or arena to teach your dog to move the stock from the left to the right or right to the left in straight parallel lines from your position. Your goal is to cross drive without the aid of a fence.

Chapter 11

BALANCE AND PENNING

By this stage of training, your dog should have developed the skills necessary to handle livestock in various situations on all sorts of terrain. Now it is time to sharpen the previously learned skills and further your dog's experience. By the time a dog makes the transition from the intermediate to the advanced level, he and his handler have become a team. He is well versed in the flanking commands and clearly understands what the trainer is asking; he can be sent to gather, fetch, and drive. At this stage of training the dog should be furthering his ability to perform different tasks in a larger area while handling more challenging stock in a variety of situations.

Lastly, as your ability as a handler increases, you will learn to watch the livestock—instead of watching the dog—to indicate where your dog needs to be positioned and how to instruct him.

MAXIMIZING BALANCE

Good balance is the underpinning for the ultimate stock dog. You can hone your dog's balance by having him put three light sheep into a corner of the field and hold them to you against the fence. If he goes in too close or too tight, the stock will be inclined to split in different directions. It is your goal to help the dog realize when he is getting in too close. If any of the animals try to break away, then your dog must block (head) them and put them back together. This exercise can be repeated by moving to different corners of the field. You can do this once or twice during a training session. It is *also* important for the dog to quietly contain stock without moving them for five or ten minutes at a time.

Clinician Jim Hartnagle using the corner of a field to maximize balance in Robby, an Australian Shepherd owned by Janna Cowen. PHOTO BY DEB CONROY.

Jim watches the lead ewe's reaction to determine the appropriate distance. PHOTO BY DEB CONROY.

When your dog exhibits good balance in the corner, you can practice the same exercise by standing with your back against a straight fence—while your dog brings the stock to you and calmly holds them there. Balance can also be utilized while the dog holds stock away from an open gate or the feed bins while you feed. Balance is important not only when holding animals in one position, but also when moving them. These exercises prepare the dog to pen stock out in the open in freestanding pens.

PRACTICE PENNING

Teaching a dog to pen stock has many practical uses, such as moving animals into holding pens, moving stock through a confined area such as a chute or narrow bridge, and moving animals into a stock trailer. Penning is a team effort. Stock animals do not like to move through narrow openings, so penning requires you to be able to read their reactions so you can instruct your dog. Your position is every bit as important as the dog's; you must be in charge of your side of the pen at the gate, while the dog is responsible for the rest. You need to stay out of the way so you don't block the entrance, yet be in position to apply pressure when necessary and limit the flock's options by presenting the path of least resistance into the pen.

When you practice penning stock in freestanding pens, start with generous openings so that your dog can put livestock in without a lot of difficult maneuvers. It can put unnecessary pressure on a dog when he must make many tight movements to get the stock into a small pen. Your job is to work the gate while your dog contains the stock and eases them into the enclosure. When the stock is penned, close the gate and tell your dog "that'll do" and walk away. This gives him a sense of accomplishment.

Forcing livestock into a pen will just cause trouble. They must be eased in, but if one tries to break away, your dog must turn it back. Once your dog has foiled any attempts to escape, he should continue to exert enough pressure to keep the animals contained as he is easing them into the opening. Once they start moving in, follow them with the gate, closing it so they can't bolt out. You will not have much success if the livestock is panicky, the pen is too small, you are in the wrong position, or your dog is out of balance.

Training Tips

When asking the dog to flank very short distances—as occurs in penning—it may be helpful to shorten the commands. For example, instead of using "away to me" try "away."

Above and below: Merlin, an Australian Shepherd owned by Andrea Mellor, holding the herd while working from side to side to pen them. PHOTOS BY BECKY PARKER OF DALLY UP PHOTOGRAPHY.

▼

The stock must be looking toward the opening in order to go there. When you are working difficult stock, a single animal can be haltered and tied inside the enclosure to help lure the others in.

▲

This Aussie is working like a cutting horse to block the heifer and turn her back to the rest of the herd. PHOTO BY GARY R. ANDERSON.

Kent Herbel—with the aid of his Australian Cattle Dogs, Cotton and Bow—loading a 1,600-pound cow that had not been caught in eight years. PHOTO BY LORI HERBEL OF XP RANCH PHOTOGRAPHY.

PROBLEM SOLVING:
Dog over-flanks

Penning light, fresh stock can require short flanking movements. Try giving shortened flanking commands—such as "way" or "by"—to encourage the dog to respond more quickly. Also, try using a softer tone of voice. Commands given in loud, harsh tones may cause the dog to overreact.

PROBLEM SOLVING:
Stock goes readily into pen

Training animals get trained, too. Working the same, familiar, tame training animals is relaxing for a dog, but it can contribute to sloppy re-actions. To enliven stock—if you don't have fresh training animals—and increase their resistance to entering the pen, you can place a second dog at the back of the pen or behind it.

PROBLEM SOLVING:
Dog nips and bolts away during penning

When a dog nips and dashes away in a penning situation, he does so because he is anxious and lacks confidence. Tight flanking work with lots of commands—one after the other—can really put a lot of pressure on a dog. If the dog is insecure or tense when working in close proximity to the flock, practice flanking gentle stock in a smaller enclosure. Calm handling and quiet but deliberate instructions are required to help a high-strung dog relax and settle down.

Chapter 12

Working With the Advanced Dog

FOCUS ON SHEDDING AND HOLDING

There are times when you want to separate a small group of livestock for veterinary attention, a trip to market, or for sorting your stock from a neighbor's. At these times, a dog that can separate stock into smaller groups or isolate an individual animal can be invaluable in the corrals or on the open range.

In ISDS-style trials, part of the competition involves *shedding*. Shedding is a method for sorting stock without using chutes. In essence you are letting the stock pass through an imaginary sorting gate between the dog and yourself. In other types of trials there is a sorting exercise, testing the dog's ability to work as a team to separate one or more animals and hold them to his handler.

Until this time the dog has been taught to keep the stock contained in one group by working on the edge of the flight zone. Now you are going to ask him to penetrate the flight zone and move through the middle of the animals. Shedding should be attempted only after your dog knows how to read and control livestock. If shedding is attempted too soon, an inexperienced dog can get into the bad habit of splitting stock. The first goal is to teach him to move calmly between two groups of animals.

1. Use a fence to help line the stock out. Take whatever time is necessary to set up the correct situation, with the stock settled and calmly standing along the fence, so they will be more likely to divide into two groups. You should be standing against the fence with your dog positioned at the other side, with the flock strung out to the right and left between you and your dog.

2. Since you've practiced the dog's ability to balance sheep against a fence, instruct the dog to remain stationary until the animals create a large enough space.

3. When there is a sufficient gap or opening after the stock is strung out, call your dog to you with "come here." As your dog comes to you, step inward to help split the stock into two groups.
4. When the dog comes through, praise him. The animals may stay separated or may regroup on their own. In any case, send the dog to gather them and bring them back.

Pamela Frost setting up a shed with her Rottweiler, HTCH Pepperhaus Luna von der Mond. When there is sufficient space the dog is called through.
PHOTO BY ELSIE RHODES.

When your dog readily comes to you between groups of stock, the next phase of the exercise is to call him through and have him drive one group with you and away from the others a distance of a few yards. At this point you should be walking with your dog, using "walk up" and whatever flanking commands are necessary to keep the dog in a driving position.

Training Tips

It is helpful to use a larger group of animals—perhaps 100 head. Different groups or types of stock that naturally and easily gravitate to their own breed—such as a group of Indian Runner ducks and a group of Muscovy ducks or a group of sheep and a group of goats—can help your dog understand this concept more clearly.

This exercise should be done only once or twice in a training session, and it is important to praise your dog when he does it correctly.

Kent Herbel and his dog, Sadie, in the shedding ring driving one group away from the others during the BSCA Nationals. Photo by Lori Herbel, XP Ranch Photography.

SHEDDING WITHOUT A FENCE

When setting up a shed without the aid of a fence, you should have the dog hold one side while you move back and forth on the other side of the sheep to line them out. Once they are sufficiently strung out, call your dog through and let him take charge, either driving or fetching one group away from the others and bringing them to you while blocking their attempt to regroup.

Splitting a single or a pair of sheep from the rest of the flock is a more difficult task, because they prefer to stay in a group. To increase the dog's ability to hold a single or a pair of sheep, you can practice having him hold them to you first in the corner of a field, then on a straight fence line.

WORKING SINGLES

In practicing singling off one head, the dog needs practice to allow the stock to pass between you and him, similar to working in a sorting race or

Conroy's Cato, a Border Collie, working hard to hold and prevent the sheep sorted off from regrouping with the rest of the flock. PHOTOS BY LORI HERBEL, XP RANCH PHOTOGRAPHY.

Steve Waltenberg of California with his Border Collie XP Deuce, getting ready to sort off a single ewe. PHOTO BY LORI HERBEL OF XP RANCH PHOTOGRAPHY.

chute. Allow them to pass through freely, until the animal you need to cut out presents itself.

TEACHING YOUR DOG TO LOOK BACK

When your dog can reliably shed several sheep from the main flock and drive the smaller group away, introduce the "look back" command. This teaches your dog to leave one group of stock and turn back to look for the second bunch.

1.   Shed a few head from the flock and have your dog drive them a short distance away from the others.

Training Tips

Give him the "look back" command, followed by the appropriate flanking command, to help him understand. Eventually, he will need only the "look back" command.

The trainer flanks the dog to pick up the remaining group.

2. Instruct your dog to "stand."
3. Walk up to him, say his name, and instruct him to "look back;" then encourage him to walk with you toward the remaining stock.
4. Send him in an outrun to the second group. If your dog is overly worried about leaving his original charges, take him by the collar and turn him in the direction of the other group.

LIFTING A SECOND GROUP

A dog's ability to gather more than one group in real working situations greatly increases his usefulness. When the dog is comfortable turning back to pick up sheep that have been sorted off, this is a good time to teach him to look for the second bunch of stock in a different part of the field or that are hidden out of the dog's sight.

This skill can be practiced by placing a second group farther away or on a different side of a field. As before, send the dog for the first group, and when they get near, stop him and re-direct him as described above to "look back" for the second group. Adding variety to your training routine will help keep your dog keen and ready to learn.

PROBLEM SOLVING
Dog hesitates to pick up the second bunch.

From the dog's eye level it may be difficult to see the stock in hilly terrain. Practice blind outruns. Use the dog to drive the training animals to a location behind a hill, clump of trees or in a ravine, for example. Walk some distance away. Face the dog toward the stock and tell him *"look back."* Even though the stock is out of sight, he knows where to find the animals.

WORKING IN CLOSE QUARTERS

In earlier lessons the dog has learned how to bring stock out of a corner when necessary. This skill is helpful when bringing stock down an alleyway or out of a small enclosure, such as a holding pen, shearing shed or stock trailer.

To increase the dog's ability, practice flanking him around sheep and goats in a small enclosure such as a holding pen. Give him guidance, but don't rush him. Let him think things through. Flank him one way and

As Jo Thompson practices calmly bringing stock out of a confined enclosure, her dog Jewell develops a relaxed approach, which in turn keeps the stock quiet and easy to handle. PHOTO BY DEB CONROY.

Powder River Strawboss—deliberate in his approach—is confident working in close quarters as he brings sheep out of the corner. COURTESY JIM AND SUE FOSTER.

then the other. Do this on different occasions until the dog is comfortable with stock in close quarters.

When bringing stock out of a holding pen, teach the dog to take his time to ease the stock out, giving them an opportunity to respond. Don't forget—the smaller the enclosure, the bigger the flight zone, unless the stock is already conditioned to dogs working in close quarters. Sometimes an alleyway gets crowded or stock becomes jam-packed and hard to move in close quarters. With experience the dog will learn how to push between the animals and the panels or shed walls. Bark and grip may be necessary, but should always be used appropriately. (*See also* "Teaching a Dog to Back" in Chapter 15.)

PROBLEMS YOU MIGHT ENCOUNTER IN ADVANCED TRAINING

Most of the problems that can occur at this stage of training can be avoided if each lesson is built on a solid foundation—moving ahead from one level to the next only as the dog is ready.

HTCh Peaslee's Honey, HRD III-s, HTD III-d, HTAD III-d,s, RLF III-s, an English Shepherd, bringing a draw of sheep from holding pens. COURTESY MARY PEASLEE.

Sometimes the dog doesn't have enough drive for the type of fine tuning that comes with trial training. However, he may still be a useful farm or ranch dog. In trial competition a dog must exhibit a keen response to his handler while performing different tasks. After several years of intensive training and trialing, a dog can get burned out. It doesn't have to be that way, but more often than not dogs get dreary—they lack luster. Avoid over-training and burning out your dog. Always watch your dog for signs of fatigue, and always allow for a day of rest and leisure. Giving the dog tasks with a purpose, where he can successfully accomplish the work without a lot of extra instruction, will go a long way to keep a dog keen and motivated.

A PROFILE OF

Joe Taylor — Instinct Pure and Mysterious

Joe Taylor is the fourth generation raised in the family tradition of ranching. At one time, the Taylor ranch (both deeded land and BLM leases) encompassed 200,000 acres. For over a hundred years, the Taylors have grazed their sheep and cattle on the lush grass on the meadows of the east face of the La Sal Mountains in Utah. In the spring they drive their animals from the desert to the high country, and they winter them in the Moab Valley, where water comes in the form of snow.

Without the help of dogs such as Taylor's Whiskey, an Australian Shepherd, it would have been much more difficult to manage the cattle and sheep. Once, when Joe Taylor's brother D. L. was in the hospital from a horseback riding accident, Joe and his father, Lester, needed to move over 300 head of cattle. Seventy head of these were bulls and the rest cows with calves. It was very late fall—almost Thanksgiving—with the threat of a heavy snowfall.

They contemplated going to town to see if they could get an extra hand to help them, because normally they wouldn't try to handle that many head of cattle in such rough country with just two riders. Experienced help was usually hard to come by, and inexperienced help can often be more trouble than help. Joe and Lester decided to go ahead and move the herd by themselves. "We were headed north across a big open draw," said Joe. "Whiskey's natural instinct was to go ahead of me. He worked the sides. He would go up the right side of the herd and then come back around behind me and then head up the left side." Joe noticed that Whiskey went back up the left side a second time. He was half a mile away. "He would disappear for 10 to 15 minutes at a time. Then I could see him leave the herd and go straight west and run with his nose to the ground. I really needed some help in the rear. The calves were trying to cut back on me, but he was so far away from me he couldn't hear me yell at him. I was pretty mad. A little while later, I saw Whiskey bringing a 2,000-pound horned Hereford bull back to the herd at a dead run. Not long after that, he brought back a huge polled Hereford bull."

Only when Taylor came upon a rise could he see what was happening. "It's the bulls' nature to go off by themselves," he reflected, "and how Whiskey knew to keep those bulls from escaping is not something you can train them to do. It is instinct pure and mysterious." It is a perfect example of how farm and ranch dogs bred for the real world need to be able to think for themselves and take action accordingly.

Chapter 13

BOUNDARY TRAINING FOR TENDING DOGS

TEACHING BOUNDARIES

Boundary skills can be a useful tool for dogs that will be used for brush control and other types of contract grazing in unfenced areas. It is also the type of training required for dogs preparing for continental-style trials such as Course C in AKC Herding Events and the CKC tending trials.

Boundary work is used to keep livestock off adjacent pastures when livestock are grazing in unfenced areas next to gardens, berry bushes, flower beds or crops of bloat-causing legumes such as alfalfa and clover (red and white). It is also beneficial to keep stock concentrated in a certain area for more intensive grazing management. Trotting up and down the edge of a meadow to keep the sheep in their designated grazing area comes quite naturally to German Shepherd Dogs from true herding lines. Other loose-eyed breeds with good territorial instincts—Belgian Sheepdogs, Beaucerons, Briards, Dutch Shepherds, Laekenois, Malinois, Tervuren, and Picardy Shepherds—also do well in boundary work, although they may be much more relaxed and less methodical in their approach to patrolling boundaries than GSDs.

When the flock first enters the field they fan out and begin to forage, drifting as they eat and fertilize. The dog will move along the boundary to establish the perimeter while the animals settle. When the flock is content to graze in a specified area, the dog may stand quietly (or even sit or lie down) and watch the animals graze. If any of the animals try to go across the perimeter, the dog springs into action and patrols the edge as necessary to keep them from leaving. If by chance some of the animals slip by the dog, he herds them back to the designated grazing area.

Dogs can be taught to observe boundaries at any stage of training. However, they need to have good basic herding skills in order to gather and move livestock to and from grazing areas. In real working situations,

Alf von Fafnerhaus, otherwise known as Nicky—a true working GSD from a bloodline of top herding champions—establishing a boundary on an open grassy meadow. COURTESY ELLEN NICKELSBERG.

shepherds school young dogs by introducing them to a boundary while a more experienced dog is used to move and contain livestock during grazing.

Your dog is ready to start boundary work if he is focused on the sheep and responds to vocal correction. Unless you are working with a GSD with appropriate instincts, it is easier to start teaching boundaries with a well-marked natural or man-made border. If you don't have the benefit of a trained dog to contain the animals while you begin training the inexperienced dog, start in an area that is enclosed by two or three fenced sides so the dog only has to cover one or two sides.

Four basic instructions are used to direct a dog working on a boundary: to come toward you "come in;" go away from you "go on;" to stop moving "stand;" and when the dog trespasses the perimeter, "keep out." Dogs can be trained to observe the boundary either by positive vocal reinforcement and correction or physical restraint (a long line) and vocal correction.

Champion Las Rocosa Jessica Jazz CDX, ATDd, OTDsc, an Australian Shepherd, patrolling a designated perimeter.

Trainers may stand at the inside edge of the boundary with their dog on or dragging a check line or light cord. The trainer instructs the dog to "go on" and moves along the edge of the perimeter with him as necessary. The dog is restricted only if he crosses the boundary to disturb or bother the grazing animals. If that happens, the trainer steps into the dog and tells him to "keep out." Otherwise, he is allowed to move freely along the perimeter. That way the sheep are free to graze without restraint within the boundary. If the sheep attempt to cross the limit, the dog is allowed to turn the animals back into the grazing area. The check cord can be removed when the dog demonstrates respect for the perimeter.

Some trainers will introduce the dog to a boundary where sheep are grazing by walking him along a path clearly marked by different terrain; by a natural barrier, such as an irrigation ditch or furrow; or by some type of indicator, such as boundary posts or flags. The concept is similar to teaching a dog to respect a wireless or underground fence system, where he receives a reminder (a warning tone from his collar) when he comes too close to the edge. If the dog ignores the warning he is corrected.

If you take the time to do this kind of work whenever possible, the dog will soon become interested in the job, learning to watch the sheep and patrol the boundary. Working with bigger flocks is helpful because it is easier to get them to string out; this encourages the dog to work the entire length of the perimeter. Once the stock is settled, the dog can relax and move only as necessary.

A Method of Handling Aggression

Some trainers use the concept of boundary training as a method to handle aggression in an overeager dog—and to keep an inexperienced dog from causing mayhem with the stock. For this purpose the dog is put on a long line and given free rein to run along the boundary while you stand inside the area with the sheep. This allows the trainer to channel the energy of a strong, aggressive dog without letting him make contact with the animals. However, boundary training is not a long-term solution for gripping or an out-of-control dog lacking herding instincts. Aggression and biting must be dealt with as described previously in Chapter 6.

Chapter 14

BASIC STOCKMANSHIP

UNDERSTANDING LIVESTOCK

There is an abundance of training information, herding clinics, and books on the market on this topic. There are as many different training methods and philosophies as there are trainers. Still, even when fortified with step-by-step instructions, people are often frustrated by a lack of progress in training. Why?

Your dog's progress ultimately lies in his natural ability to benefit from his exposure to stock and constructive handling by you, his trainer. It is part of the trainer's job to understand the minds of the animals—both dog and stock—and be able to manipulate their behavior to produce the desired results.

If you as the trainer view the sheep as simply a tool for teaching the dog to herd, not only is the well-being of the sheep neglected, but the quality of herding is greatly hindered. Handlers whose living depends upon their stock's welfare—and who are more considerate of their sheep's handling when training their dogs—will see better results, because they will be training with "stock savvy."

Stock savvy is vital for both dog and handler. Trainers who can read livestock—who can recognize the point of balance and the flight zone—will be more successful in bringing out the dog's innate herding instincts and in teaching the dog to handle livestock efficiently. Without it, herding becomes a game of chance. It is far easier to help your dog reach his full potential if you have a clear understanding of the behavior of livestock; it is also safer for you, your dog, and your livestock.

DEVELOPING STOCK SAVVY

In order to be an effective trainer, you must be able to understand, "read," and out think the livestock just as skillfully as you do your dog. Stock savvy comes from understanding the nature and habits of different kinds of stock, being able to predict how the animals will react to the dog in a given situation, and knowing how to exploit the stock's behavior to accomplish the task at hand.

The stock animals' disposition and level of conditioning will determine the way you have to handle them. Brahman cattle and Barbados and Cheviot sheep, for example, are more nervous and more easily upset if they have not been adequately acclimated to dogs and people. On the other hand, stock like black baldies (Hereford-Angus crosses) and Dorset sheep are not as high strung and are easier to work with.

UNDERSTANDING FLOCK INSTINCTS AND HERD BEHAVIOR

Grazing animals prefer to be in a group for protection. Unlike sheep, cows stash their newborn calves for the first few days to keep them safe from predation. When faced with an apparent threat, the entire herd will turn as a group to keep track of the predator. Sometimes when an unfamiliar dog enters a pasture with a herd of cows, they will group together and move in unison to investigate the perceived intruder or chase him off.

In order for the dog to bring the ducks to his handler's right side and continue clockwise around the handler's post, Lachlan, owned by Debbie Willoughby, has to head off the lead duck so the others will follow. PHOTO BY LORI HERBEL OF XP RANCH PHOTOGRAPHY.

When sheep are threatened, they either band together or flee. Sheep are followers by nature and will readily follow the leader. This hierarchy is ingrained from birth as newborn lambs are taught to follow their mothers. By applying their instinct to bunch and follow, you can handle and move them more easily. If you control the leaders, the rest of the flock will follow.

Some breeds are more gregarious than others, meaning that they have stronger flocking instincts and will readily band together. This is especially noticeable with white-faced wool breeds like the Rambouillet sheep, a Merino derivative. They graze fairly close together, and at night they sleep close together. Indian Runner ducks are another example of gregarious stock. They act almost like a school of fish when in a group. Gregarious livestock are ideal for teaching young or inexperienced dogs to work because they are not as likely to split into multiple directions unless they are scattered by the dog. Muscovy ducks, on the other hand, tend to string out and gravitate in various directions, requiring more work by the dog to keep them bunched in a group. And goats—although very social animals—do not flock as well as sheep.

UNDERSTANDING THE SENSES

Herd animals, having evolved as prey animals in the wild, are always on alert for predators. They have highly developed senses, particularly hearing and vision. They tend to react quickly to noises or objects that seem threatening, so it is important to be aware at all times of what is going on around the stock animals and what might affect their behavior. For example, they will look and incline their ears toward whatever attracts their attention. Excessive noise, especially high-pitched noise, is stressful to livestock; a rattle paddle (a device often used in sales yards and feedlots) or the bark from a dog will get sheep on their feet and moving away from the noise. In contrast, calm, low-pitched tones tend to quiet stock.

Herd animals have wide peripheral vision. Their eyes are set on the sides of the head rather than in the front, like predators such as wolves and coyotes; this increases their ability to spot predators. Because the eyes are not set in a single plane but are on the lateral surfaces of the nasal bone, a grazing animal has a narrow field of binocular vision in front of its head and a broad peripheral field of monocular vision—unlike humans, who are able to focus both eyes simultaneously to achieve good depth perception.

In a herd animal, each eye sees individually, and the two visual paths do not converge until they reach 10 feet (3 m) in front of the animal;

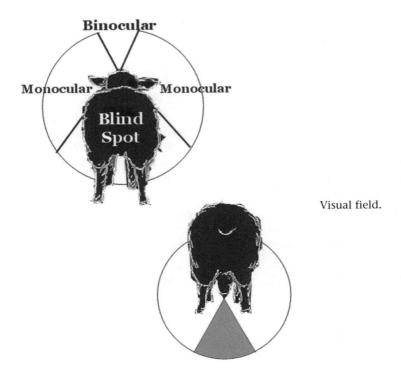

Visual field.

this creates a blind spot, as binocular vision requires full convergence. This is one of the reasons livestock sometimes run into fences or other obstacles when frightened. Furthermore, in order to focus on the ground, herd animals must lower their heads. Their depth perception at ground level is restricted and can cause them to balk at shadows and dark areas, which explains why they are often reluctant to walk into a dark pen or alley.

Livestock see better to the side and to the rear than to the front, though there is a small blind spot directly behind the animal when the head is raised. When an animal turns its head, it can see what's behind and to that side, depending on the amount of wool on the face or the bulkiness of the animal's body. When a dog is directly behind a ewe or a steer, the animal may not actually be able to see it—but may run even faster to try to escape the perceived threat. In order to stop or turn the animals, the trainer needs to bring the dog out from behind the animal into the range of its peripheral vision.

Canine Vision

A dog's typical field of vision is about 240 degrees, compared to approximately 100 degrees for humans. Their night vision is keener than ours because reflective tissue behind the retina focuses the light. They have binocular convergence (visual overlap) that enhances depth perception in the middle of their visual field, somewhere between 30 and 60 degrees. While they have much less depth perception than humans do, it's more than adequate for jumping a fence or catching a ball.

Dog breeds with brachycephalic head shapes and frontally placed eyes, such as the Rottweiler, have more binocular vision but less peripheral vision (about 200 degrees) than breeds with normal, mesocephalic head shapes, such as the German Shepherd.

UNDERSTANDING THE FLIGHT ZONE

Livestock are prey species, or "flight animals." Fight or flight is an automatic response of grazing animals to predators. Their survival generally depends on running away rather than fighting, but when cornered or threatened most herd animals will try to defend themselves. The flight zone is an invisible perimeter or bubble around the stock, a minimum distance of comfort or security—the animal's safe zone.

If they have a choice, cattle and sheep will generally turn and move away when the dog or trainer enters the edge of the flight zone. Some animals become defensive or sullen and will fight; mothers with babies in particular are less likely to turn their backs on a predator for fear of attack.

The distance that animals keep between themselves and a perceived threat—depending on how tame or wild the stock—is their comfort or safe zone. Range animals kept in large open pastures usually have a larger flight zone than those contained in small fenced enclosures or those that receive frequent gentle handling. The distance of the flight zone will decrease with repeated conditioning. The more often livestock are worked with dogs, the smaller their flight zone will be.

To keep the stock calm and moving easily, the dog should work on the edge of the flight zone. If the dog is perhaps 40 to 60 feet (12–18 m) out to one side, the animals can still see him, and he will be able to turn or stop them without entering their flight zone. If more pressure is needed to get the animals moving, the dog or trainer should step into the flight zone. But if too much pressure is placed upon the animals (i.e., the dog comes too close), the stock might panic, turn back, and run past or over the handler and dog.

Greer, an Aussie owned by Grete Krause, entering the duck's flight zone.
PHOTO BY DEB CONROY.

Excited animals bunch together and are more difficult to work with. A herd animal that becomes separated from the others will attempt to get back to the safety of the group, though if really frightened it may run away in a panic. Livestock at a run are out of control and in danger of being injured or killed; livestock that are calm are easier to handle and move. When herd animals sense that you don't intend to harm them, they will usually continue to drink, forage, and feed their young.

THE CONCEPT OF BALANCE

Once you understand the animal's flight distance, the next requirement is knowing where to position yourself or your dog to get the animal to move in a desired direction. Because animals inherently react to pressure by moving away from it, the animal's shoulder is the point of balance you must work from. When a dog is positioned behind the animal's shoulder, or point of balance, the animal will move forward. When the dog is parallel but still behind the shoulder, the animal will turn away or move to the side. When the dog steps in front of the shoulder, the animal will stop, back up, or turn and change direction.

When the dog is positioned behind an animal, he will push the animal forward.

Dog positioned at side between the shoulder and rear will keep animal moving forward, stop sideways drift, or turn them.

Dog positioned between shoulder and front will stop or turn animal.

Above: Pressure points on livestock.
Below: The dog positioned behind the shoulder is driving the steer back to the rest of the herd.

Little Wolf, an Australian Shepherd, is positioned behind the animal's shoulder to ease the cow into the sorting alley.

Position of handler in front of heifer's head and shoulder is causing the animal to balk. PHOTO BY DEB CONROY.

Defensive Behavior in Livestock Animals

Although livestock usually move away from danger and toward safety, they will turn and fight if they feel they have no other way out. Herding dogs may be perceived as a threat. If livestock are pushed too hard by an overly enthusiastic or inexperienced dog, they may balk or become sullen, hold their ground, and fight the dog.

Sheep are typically passive animals. Ewes are gentle and generally don't exhibit aggression to humans or to other sheep, except for pushiness at feeding time. However, they may become defensive after lambing to protect their offspring. They will stomp their feet and perhaps snort as a warning that they may charge. Lambs and young kids may freeze at the sign of danger and refuse to move.

Ewe with aggressive posture—stomping her foot—is challenging the dog. PHOTO BY DEB CONROY.

A ram, on the other hand, can be aggressive with humans or dogs, particularly during the breeding season. He won't bite—grazing animals don't have upper front teeth—but he will back up and charge forward with his head down to smash into a target.

(continued on next page)

Just before charging, a ram usually tilts his head to the side. Though goats are similar, when a buck exhibits aggression he rears up on his hind legs and lunges downward. Rams or bucks can badly injure a dog or a human; they should never be trusted and should be avoided for general training purposes. If you do have one on your property, use only experienced dogs to handle him.

Cattle are better equipped to defend themselves by kicking and butting. When cattle react defensively to an intruder invading their flight zone, they lower their heads. Reactions such as pawing the ground, backing up, tail swishing, and snorting also indicate that the animal feels threatened and may charge.

Due to their size and unpredictable nature, all bulls should be regarded as unsafe. They can severely injure or kill a person or dog. To signal aggression from a distance, they turn sideways, posing broadside and arching their backs to look bigger when a human or dog has invaded the flight zone.

LEARNING HOW TO READ LIVESTOCK

The quickest way to learn how to handle livestock and where to place the dog is to work them yourself on foot. Turn a single animal into the arena or practice pen. Practice driving, turning, and stopping the animal without your dog. Work quietly. Take your time to think about the cause and effect of your actions. Then work with a group of animals.

Notice what happens when you step in front of an animal's shoulder—it will back away. Placing a dog in front of the shoulder will cause the animal to stop, turn, or back away. Notice what happens when you step behind the animal's shoulder—it will move forward.

While you are moving the animals, always watch them for signs of agitation or stress. When livestock are at ease, especially when they are chewing their cud, their ears will be carried in a normal (for the breed) relaxed position. When something attracts their attention, they shift their ears toward the cause. When they are moving away from a dog, for example, they rotate the ears towards the side to stay focused on the dog. One indication that livestock are nervous or flighty is that they carry their heads up high and look around. When they become excited or aggressive, the ears are drawn back and held close to the head.

The sheep are paying attention to the Border Collie behind them, as indicated by their head and ears. PHOTO BY LORI HERBEL, XP RANCH PHOTOGRAPHY.

The manner in which an animal carries its tail is also an indicator of its frame of mind. When goats are in a non-threatening environment, they carry their tails up, while sheep carry theirs down. When cattle are comfortably grazing or walking, their tails hang in repose. When they are nervous or agitated, they either swish their tails or tuck them between their legs, but when they are threatened or running, they lift their tails away from their body.

Even though this heifer is moving away, she is keeping an eye on the dog behind her. PHOTO BY DEB CONROY.

Pressure on stock by a dog that is moving too close or pushing too fast causes them to explode into quick flight to escape. Working in small, confined enclosures where the stock is unable to freely move away could place the dog and you deep inside the flight zone; this may cause the animals to run right over both of you or even through the fence in an attempt to escape the pressure. You should obviously try to avoid this situation.

Give the stock plenty of breathing room to keep them from panicking. Always give them the opportunity to ease away from the pressure. If the dog does come so close that they bolt, send him around them wide enough to turn them. Keep adequate distance between the dog and the livestock to allow the dog enough opportunity to outmaneuver the livestock or counter their moves—otherwise, the dog is playing catch-up.

While some animals may flee at the mere presence of a dog, others may be put on the defensive and want to fight. If an overeager or pushy dog pressures the stock to turn and fight, give the stock a little ground by moving the dog "back out" a few feet; then stop him momentarily with a "stand" or "lie down" (making sure he is not in danger of getting butted or charged).

When you drop the dog with a "lie down" or back the dog away with a "back out" it changes the dynamics, reducing the threat felt by the stock and allowing the animals to relax. When you relieve the pressure, the animals may watch the dog momentarily but will usually turn and move away when they no longer feel in danger. Resume by walking the dog up steadily, and make sure to stop him before he intrudes beyond the comfort zone. On the other hand, when the dog and trainer are at a critical stage in penning, for example, where each step forward needs to be highly controlled, downing a dog and then bringing him to his feet again can break the necessary contact and diminish the control the dog has established over the animals.

MAINTAINING CONTACT

This is a good time to talk about contact and loss of contact. In order to control the stock, your dog needs to have the correct amount of contact or communication with the animals. This is partly established through his presence and approach; the stock must be aware of him in order to respond to his movements. In other words, he needs to learn to maintain the appropriate, effective distance for the animals being worked.

If the dog is too far off the stock, he has no influence over them and the animals are not paying attention to him. He has lost contact. If he is too close, they will be alarmed and may feel panicked, possibly causing him to lose control. Some stock that have been handled a lot are "heavy" and do not readily move without direct pressure applied at a working distance of two to three body lengths. This is in contrast to "lighter" stock like the Barbado sheep and Brahman cows, which tend to be more responsive to the dog's movements from farther away (perhaps 50 yards, 46 m, for instance).

METHODS OF MOVING STOCK

When the stock—cattle, sheep, poultry, or goats—have been gathered by you or by the dog, there are several methods for moving them from one point to another. One method is for you and the dog to push from behind to guide the flock to its destination. A second method is for you to lead the way, on foot or on horseback, with the stock in the middle and the dog bringing up the rear. A third method is especially effective when gathering wild cattle that are likely to break away from the herd: you push the herd from behind, generally on horseback, while the dogs—usually a team—work at the head of the herd to keep the cattle contained.

When moving a herd along a fence line or through a chute, having the dog wear back and forth behind the stock (or along the side and behind) to the point of balance and then back in the opposite direction, keeps the animals moving along and can speed up the movement of the flock or herd. The same principle applies when livestock start milling around in a circle. The most effective way to get them lined out and moving is to move from the front to back (opposite the direction they are traveling) to encourage forward movement.

When moving stock from behind or along a fence line, the dog needs to stay to the side and rear where they can see him. Keep in mind the range of the animals' vision. When the dog is directly behind the animals, in their blind zone, they will move forward because they sense the dog's presence, but they will often turn their heads to the side as they move along to see where the dog is.

When the dog is driving animals along a fence, the pressure of the fence may cause them to turn away from it. The dog needs to be in a position behind but to the side to be able to apply enough counter-pressure to keep them moving forward without doubling back—containing the animals but pushing them forward at the same time. The dog needs to be where he can counter any attempts to escape.

A PROFILE OF

Clyde Hall — Just Having Fun

Every spring competitors from all across the United States gather on the green pastures of Clyde Hall's 46-acre Twin Oaks Farm outside Murfreesboro, Tennessee. Hall is a member of the Middle Tennessee Stock Dog Association, sponsors of the annual Sheep Dog Trial.

Clyde discovered trialing later in life. Although he was born shortly after World War II and lived on a farm as a child, when he got out of school he joined the military, then went to college to become a Certified Registered Nurse Anesthetist. It wasn't until 1991, when he saw the movie *City Slickers*—in which a man and his friends who were having midlife crises find renewal and purpose while cattle driving in the West—that Hall was drawn back to his own country roots with renewed interest.

Shortly thereafter, he acquired some acreage and bought a small herd. One day at the hospital where he worked, he was talking to a coworker, who convinced him that he needed to get a Border Collie. It just so happened that a woman who worked in the X-ray department had one she needed to place. Now equipped with a dog, steers, and a farm, he was well on his way to step into his new role as a *former* city slicker.

He took his new dog, Jessie, to monthly stockdog training sessions with the Middle Tennessee Stock Dog Association. He found that he enjoyed working with the dog and the sheep so much that he sold his steers for less than they were worth and bought some sheep for the dog.

When Clyde took Jessie to their first sheep trial, he won the Novice Class with her. He hadn't had so much fun in ages. As it turned out, however, his Border Collie was loose-eyed. She worked cattle just fine, but she wasn't a great sheepdog. Hall decided to find another dog, one that was good enough to compete in Open Sheep Dog trials. The result of his search was Tip.

The little black and white pup grew into a first-class sheepdog. She was only 18 months old in 1996, when they finished eleventh in the Open Class in 2000 at the National Finals in El Reno, Oklahoma. Clyde also received the Nation's Rookie of the Year Award from the United States Border Collie Handler's Association, which he claims was the most satisfying of all the prizes he ever won with Tip. The prize goes to the highest rookie handler and dog at the National Finals and is sponsored by Rural Route Videos.

When Clyde started working the dogs, he found his niche in a sport that was the most fun he had ever known. His concern is that a lot of people go to a trial and see the dogs work or they see the movie *Babe*, and they decide to get a Border Collie. "They don't take the time to research the breed's history to understand what they are getting into," he claims. "And they are not willing to put the time into training. They want instant gratification, but when the dog gets underfoot, wanting to do something, and is driving them crazy, the dog ends up being destroyed or placed in rescue."

Chapter 15

WORKING LARGE FLOCKS AND HERDS

HANDLING LARGE FLOCKS AND HERDS

While moving as few as 50 or as many as 3,000 head of animals to and from the grazing areas, the handler can either lead the group or work from behind. The dog will naturally move along one side toward the head and then move back behind, cross over, and move up and down the other side. This is a form of "wearing" (*See* Chapter 5, *Herding Terms*) but instead of staying behind the group, the dog covers all sides of the flock (front, side, and rear positions).

Taylor's Oscar working along the side of a herd during roundup.

As the dog works from the side, he strings the sheep out and urges the animals to move forward. Dogs sometimes work towards the head of the flock to keep the leaders pointed in the correct direction. If the leaders are moving too fast and get far ahead of the rest of the animals, the dog goes to the front to contain them and keep them on track.

When moving along a trail or road, the dog works up and down the length of one side of the column to move the animals over far enough to open a lane for oncoming traffic.

The bottom line is that the dog is positioned wherever necessary to control the stock, whether it's at the head, along the side, or behind. When working pens and corrals, the dog can be sent inside to bring the stock out or positioned outside to prevent them from getting away.

Champion Las Rocosa Just Jake ATDd, OTDs, STDc wearing behind 1,500 head of range sheep on the Taylor Ranch.

DEALING WITH MILLING

When stock is pushed too hard from behind and they aren't adequately strung out, they get bunched up. The lead animals start milling around (moving in a circle) and refusing to move forward, obstructing the animals behind. When this happens, send your dog along the side of the animals toward the front of the flock. He should break up the milling by moving in the opposite direction the animals are traveling and then redirect them in the desired direction. Once the animals are moving, the dog then moves back to the rear of the flock or herd to keep them strung out so that they continue to travel freely.

Just Jake and Doggie, an upright, close-working Border Collie, on the Taylor Ranch keeping range sheep strung out so they don't get bunched up and start milling while being trailed to winter range.

CHANGING DIRECTION

When changing the flock's direction, a dog is sent to the appropriate side to push the leaders to the desired route. If you want to turn the flock to the left, you send the dog to the right side to drive the leaders left.

MOVING THROUGH NARROW OPENINGS AND BRIDGE CROSSINGS

If the flock or herd is being moved into a narrow area—such as through a gate, onto a bridge or overpass—your dog can be sent ahead to hold a stationary post at the front to thin them out. Alternately, he can work from front to rear (on the side) to keep the animals moving along in a narrow row and prevent them from turning back, balling up, fanning out, spilling around (or over the edges), or straying into nearby fields. A single dog may have to cover a lot of territory in this situation.

Bridge crossing can be hazardous. If too many animals are crossing the bridge at the same time, some of the animals near the edge can be forced off the bridge. They need to be thinned out. This is where a dog posted with a *stand stay* at the side of the entry is ideal.

Preventing Stock from Turning in the Wrong Direction

When moving stock past an opening, gate, or a fork in the road, the dog can be sent to block the open space and keep the stock from turning in. When working a pair of dogs, one dog can be sent to hold a stationary post, while the second dog will continue to keep the flock moving along.

D. L. Taylor thinning the herd out to lighten the load across Dewey Bridge on Highway 128 in Moab, Utah.

TEACHING A DOG TO BACK

When sheep get jammed in chutes or a sorting alley or otherwise bunched up, breeds like the Kelpie and the Patagonian Sheepdog are well known to "back," or jump on the backs of the tightly grouped sheep and run to the front of the flock to start the animals moving again.

Kelpie moving across the backs of sheep in New South Wales, Australia. Courtesy of the Australian National Travel Association.

Teaching a dog to back livestock can be very useful if you have to move sheep out of a crowded stock trailer, up congested ramps, and into sheds and trailers. *Backing* describes the action of the dog in jumping on top of the sheep's backs and moving from the front of the flock to the back, causing the lead animals to move forward.

A dozen or so sheep work best for training purposes, but you can teach this skill with as few as four animals. The dog must be small to medium size, as well as quick, agile, and self-confident. To introduce this technique, you can crowd the animals into a narrow or small pen (you can use a panel to contain them in the corner of a pen), making sure there are no spaces between them where the dog could slip through and be injured.

Start by setting the dog on the animals' backs. Do this several times, so the dog becomes acquainted with the idea of standing on them. Once he is comfortable, you can use a lead to invite him to jump on the top of the sheep. Praise him lavishly when he jumps up, even if it is only for a few seconds. For some dogs this will be a natural behavior, but not all dogs will like it. Making it fun and turning it into a game can change the dog's attitude and build confidence.

▼

Pulis have been depicted as leaping onto the back of a runaway sheep and guiding it back to the flock; this is not very likely. However, Tibetan sheepdogs, from which they may originate, have been described assisting shepherds journeying down steep mountains in the treacherous terrain of the Himalayas and leaping onto the backs of sheep tightly banded in the narrow mountain passages to move them along, very much like Kelpies "backing" tightly packed sheep in races.

▲

Chapter 16

THE RANCH DOG

There is very little difference between training the sheepdog for trial competition and teaching the working cowdog to be a useful hand on the farm or ranch. The basics are the same—except that in the real world, the job is not always accomplished with finesse. Dogs often learn best when they can apply their skills in practical working situations in all kinds of terrain.

WORKING IN THE REAL WORLD

Both you and your dog must be flexible, because the stock is not always predictable or cooperative. Often in ranch work there are uncontrolled situations, and precise techniques are not always as important as getting the job done effectively. Your dog must be able to think for himself. There are many times you may need to send a dog out to hunt for and gather stock and then bring them to corrals or a holding area.

As with all training, your dog gains confidence by being successful. If he is not successful, go back to the basic exercises. Then you can present him with new challenges. Never place unreasonable or unfair demands on the dog during training. Remember that your dog will be unable to think clearly and function properly when he is hot or tired. When he is tired, he is more prone to getting injured.

THE WORKING COWDOG

Working with cattle requires a dog that is more forceful than the average sheepdog. Study the other training chapters, because the same teaching principles used on sheep and ducks can be applied to cattle; all teaching transfers from one class of stock to another, but there are some particular

Little Wolf was an outstanding cowdog. We used him to work cattle on the average of three or four times a week. There wasn't much he couldn't handle. I wanted to work him in some trials, but I needed to widen him out for sheep.

One day I decided to work on his outrun. We had just gotten some new ewes. I had worked them with dogs only a couple of times, but I thought they'd do fine in the open. I sorted three head off and asked Little Wolf to bring them to a pasture on a hillside. It was about 25 acres of unfenced land. We took the sheep in the middle of the field and left them standing. I placed him about 150 yards away and sent him to gather them. When he took off, I walked in a straight line toward the sheep. He was a little tight, but gave some ground as I stepped into him and asked him to "back out." When he reached the far side of the sheep I told him, "there." About that time, one of the ewes bolted off. He raced around to head her off and grabbed her nose to turn her around and put her back with the others, now heading in my general direction. When the sheep got near I asked Little Wolf to circle around to contain them. After they came to rest, we took them back to the middle of the field and left them about the same place as the first time.

When they were settled—about as much as they were going to get—I sent him on an outrun and started walking toward the sheep. Only this time, the renegade ewe took off before he could get on the backside. He started to cut in to head her off, but I stopped him and asked him to continue his outrun to the back side of the remaining sheep. They took off stampeding towards the renegade, who by now was in a dead run going in the wrong direction. He was able to stop the two, but the renegade ewe was heading down the lane towards the railroad tracks.

I decided to get Reanna, one of my Border Collies very good at handling singles. We found the ewe traveling along the tracks. The tracks were fenced along one side with a creek and a steep embankment on the other side. It was such a narrow strip of land that every time I tried to send the dog around the ewe, it only pushed her to go faster. I had to wait until we could get to a clearing. It took several miles to get around her. Finally, we were able to catch her.

The lesson I learned was there are times when you need to let a dog get control of the stock regardless of how the job gets done or how it would score in trial competition. A good ranch dog can take the place of several men if you let them do their job in the most effective way.

This moment in time captured by photographer Gary R. Anderson merely suggests a dog working cattle must be quick and athletic to avoid injury.

techniques for working with cattle. Don't even think about turning an inexperienced dog loose on cows unless you have taught him the basic obedience commands, such as to come when called and to stay put when instructed. A dog's trained response to basic obedience is fundamental to success.

As with sheep, you should begin with at least four head of docile cows: 300- to 900-pound (136–408 kg) steers or heifers work well as long as they are calm and have been exposed to dogs before you start training. When you introduce an inexperienced dog to cattle, it is preferable to work in a space where the cows can move freely away from your dog. In a small, confined area, there is a greater risk of injury or challenges from the cattle to your dog. On the other hand, you don't want such a large area that the dog can't control them.

As with any other type of stock, dogs working cattle need to work at an appropriate distance—not too far and not too close—to keep the animals moving calmly at a relaxed pace. A dog should be efficient and deliberate in all of his moves to conserve valuable energy. If a dog expends all of his energy in the first hour of a 12-hour day, he may be of little or no value later that day. Often at the end of a long, hard day, when stock are tired and have become difficult (sticky), the dog may have to exert more force.

Never stop your dog or ask him to "lie down" in a vulnerable position where he can get kicked or butted.
PHOTO BY JEFF JAQUISH AT ZINGPIX.COM.

Risk of Injury to the Cowdog

Working with cattle is riskier for dogs than working with sheep. Cattle are large animals and more likely to kick or to step on a dog. Your dog should not wear a collar, because it can get entangled on a horn or hoof. If your dog is kicked, do not say anything to him right away, because you do not want him to associate the kick with you. If your dog is kicked or trampled, check for limping.

Blinking or rubbing the eye with a paw could indicate that he was kicked in the head. Seek veterinary care immediately if you notice any of the following signs of head injury:

- Pupils of eyes are different sizes
- Cornea looking hazy or gray
- Blood or clear fluid draining from the ears or nose
- Poor coordination (unsteady walking)
- Convulsions
- Fatigue or excessive sleepiness
- Intolerance to noise
- Slow thinking
- Vomiting more than twice

▼

Cattle have a broad visual field to the side and to the rear.
They are in a good position to kick with accuracy
while they are standing still.

▲

USING BARK AND GRIP

An old cattleman once said, "One bite will move one cow, but one bark *at the right time* will move 25 cows." When working a large herd of cattle or while working with "blind" stock (i.e., cattle afflicted by pinkeye), a dog that does not bark or growl at a critical point (and if necessary back it up with grip) may be totally ineffective.

An Aussie using appropriate force to block his charges from escape, stopping them in their tracks.
PHOTO BY GARY R. ANDERSON.

Barking can alert and move the lead cows, while gripping places pressure upon the animals in the rear, which will then push the group ahead. A cowdog with good stock savvy will learn when and how to use bark effectively. For example, a barking dog working around cow/calf herds can put the mothers on the fight (due to their mothering instincts). Cowdogs should bark or grip when necessary to convince the cows to move, stop, or turn. (*Refer to* "Teaching Bark and Bite.")

DEALING WITH BULLS AND RAMS

Although bulls and rams are not recommended for training dogs, in the real world, stockmen have to handle them. Bulls and rams can be irritable and often prefer to go off by themselves, unless of course it is during the breeding season. At that time they can be extremely dangerous, especially if you are working inexperienced dogs.

When this bull tried to break away, Oscar, one of the Taylor Ranch dogs, turned him back to the rest of the bulls.

To keep them together, Poco must continually work back and forth between the flock and the ram that is lagging behind.

PROBLEM SOLVING:
Body biting and swinging on tails

Body biting on the cow's belly, flank, hamstring, or shoulders is undesirable. The inclination may start when a dog—not yet physically mature enough to out-maneuver cattle—gets kicked and then resorts to gripping wherever he can, but most likely it is genetic.

Swinging on tails tends to occur in dogs that heel naturally high (midway or higher) on the hocks and may start out accidentally (as the dog is going in to grip). For some dogs, it may be considered fun. People have wondered if training through play—triggered by prey drive when dragging a lure on a pole—increases a dog's tendency to grab the switch on tails. It is a fair question. However, dogs have been known to do this long before the concept of play training. There seems to be a genetic predisposition for the trait. In any case, it is undesirable and can become a very bad habit—causing potential injury to the cow's tail and leaving a dog more vulnerable to getting kicked. Through the years, we've heard many different ideas for discouraging the habit, but cannot recommend any consistently successful methods.

FETCHING CATTLE

Ideally, you can start by using the first lesson described in Chapter 7: *Making the Most of Your Dog's Talent / Teaching the Dog to Fetch the Stock*. Be sure the cows are in motion before you let an inexperienced dog make contact with them. When they are standing still, cows are in a better position to calculate a kick with deadly aim. Cattle can kick forward and out to the side. They can also kick directly backward. It may take a couple of sessions to condition cattle to the concept of fetching. In this case, it is highly effective to begin teaching a dog to first contain cows along a fence, which also serves to condition the animals, and then to bring them off the fence.

You will not be working directly in front of the cattle but should maintain a position toward the front and off to the side, depending on how tame they are. For example, you might be walking at somewhere around 12:00 and 2:00, while the dog is moving between 4:00 and 5:00. The cattle should be moving forward along the fence.

Let the dog move the cows along the fence line for a distance of 50 to 200 feet (15–61 m). Don't hinder the dog from wearing along the side to move the cows along together and keep stragglers grouped with the herd. If a cow starts to break away, let the dog put the animal back into the herd.

In this position the author—toward the front of the animals, but off to the side—is preparing these steers to the idea of moving into pressure with someone in front of them.

If he tries to circle around the stock to the head, step in front of him to block him and send him back behind the animals. If he ignores your instructions, tell him "no," and use your training stick to block him, tell him to "get back."

The next step is to flank him around to the head, bringing him from behind the animals and around your body in a semicircle, to stop and turn them. Natural heading dogs welcome this opportunity.

When he gets to the head to turn them, tell him "there," to further reinforce the use of the command for turning into livestock when flanking. If an animal breaks away, let the dog head it off and bring it back to the herd. If things get too hectic or out of control, stop your dog with the instruction to "stand" and "stay." This will give you the opportunity to regain control.

Repeat the above, going the other way. As the cows move along the fence line, you can work as a head gate, meaning that you use your position toward the front of the cows (but off to the side) to regulate and control their speed or keep them from running off. When you want to stop them, you instruct the dog to "stand," and then you step inward toward the head of the lead animal to shut down the flow of motion, but not so much as to turn them back.

BRINGING COWS OFF A FENCE OR OUT OF A CORNER

Your dog has practiced moving stock along a fence from one end of the enclosure to the other and then back again. The next step teaches him to bring them away from the fence. Teaching your dog to bring the cows off the fence is not difficult; it just takes time to set up the situation for the dog to succeed.

When your dog is sent through a space or gap to move the cows off the fence, it is important for him to have sufficient room to get through and avoid injury. Ideally, the fence or panels should be designed with an escape route, so that your dog can duck under if necessary.

1. Lead the animals toward the inside of the pen while your dog brings up the rear.
2. As the herd moves away from the fence, send the dog in behind the cows. If necessary, use your training stick to block him from swinging out to the head. Send him in behind the cows.
3. If you aren't successful after several attempts, try sending your dog to the head. More than likely, the stock will veer away from him and give him an opportunity to move them off the fence. Otherwise, take your dog with you (between you and the fence) and move the cows out together.
4. When you get to the opposite end of the pen, turn around and go back to the other side. Vary the distance that you have him bring or fetch before you change direction.
5. Allow your dog to bring the stock behind you as you walk from one end of the arena to the other. If your dog starts moving them too fast, stop him by standing him.

Training Tips

A lot of your success in teaching this task will depend on your position. If necessary, walk between the cattle and the fence and call your dog in with you. This same type of move applies to getting stock out of a corner.

If your dog has difficulty in getting the stock to move in one direction, try the other. If that doesn't work, stop and take a moment to reevaluate the situation. Make sure you are not blocking the cattle by your position or by putting undue pressure on them.

(continued on next page)

Training Tips (continued)

It is not uncommon for a strong heading dog to swing out, forcing the animals back against the fence or into a corner even after you have brought them away from the fence or out of the corner. If this is the case, you need to stop him *before* he swings out from behind.

Some dogs lack the confidence to move stock away from the fence or out of a corner. If your dog is reluctant to move in, don't be in a hurry or put a lot of pressure on him. Walk in with him and bring the animals out together.

WORKING A COW/CALF HERD

When working cows with calves at their sides, you need a calm, quiet dog with a deliberate approach. Mother cows with calves will immediately be prepared to fight, especially if they have been subjected to wild predators. A dog that begins to yap or harass the cows will alert the whole herd to come to the rescue.

Above and on next page: Trinity Gamegards Lasting Image, a Rottweiler female, is using a deliberate but calm approach to ease this cow and her calf along. PHOTOS BY DEB CONROY.

With experience, some of the grittiest working dogs will learn that when a mother cow turns on them, she will usually turn back into the herd without incident if they back off and give her a little space. If she does not, then the dog must use necessary force to gain the upper hand, or he will continue to be challenged.

WORKING STOCK FROM HORSEBACK

If you plan on working your dog from horseback, you first need to accustom him to being around horses. Working a dog next to a horse can be difficult if the horse and dog are not familiar with one another. Some dogs want to work anything that moves, including horses. The first rule for handling dogs from horseback is this: don't allow the dog to harass, work, or bark at horses.

We've always had a seasoned horse that we could introduce our pups to. Even if you do not, you can take your pup along when you feed your horses and do other chores. The young dog gets used to seeing horses, and the horses become familiar with the dog. Make it a habit to handle the dog around horses and vice versa until they get used to each other. For example, pull up a chair in the barn and spend some quiet time brushing the dog while the horses eat. When you keep everything quiet and calm, both species will learn to relax.

The best way to get acquainted. Tyler Taylor and his buddies, Gabe and Dancer.

Introducing a horse to flock animals during feeding time in a pasture.

It is also important for the horse to be accustomed to livestock. One of the ways our horses become accustomed to sheep or goats is by grazing them in the same pastures. Even with plenty of room for them to maintain a comfortable distance, they soon will be grazing side by side. When hay is put out in smaller paddocks, the horses become accustomed to the smaller animals moving around them and sometimes touching their legs.

Unless your horse is familiar to dogs and stock, don't start working from horseback until your dog is well trained with stock. Once the dog has a good foundation on stock, then you can introduce the concept of working while you are on horseback; since he already knows what is expected, it will be easier to keep him focused on the job rather than the horse.

Training a Dog on Cattle and Sheep

When a dog is punished for gripping sheep, it can also discourage him from using grip on cattle. You don't want to take all the bite out of the cowdog. Teaching the dog to respect the flock's flight zone will minimize the incentive to grip, as he learns to rate the sheep. If you plan to use a dog on both sheep and cattle, work him on the two as much as possible. Your dog will learn that he does not need to grip unnecessarily to move the sheep. You must teach your dog to grip discriminately to gain the upper hand. Once sheep are compliant, your dog should back off. This is where your discretion as the handler is very important.

In the meantime, use a muzzle on the dog when training with sheep. In this way, you can liberate him without risk of injury to the animals. If the dog has good stock savvy, he may figure out he doesn't need to grip as much on sheep.

TEACHING TEAMWORK

In real working situations there are times when a team of dogs is more effective than one dog alone. It is always helpful to use more than one dog when you are working rough country or when large herds or flocks need to be managed. Two dogs might be necessary when working difficult stock such as rams and bulls. Working together gives both dogs more courage and power, and they can support one another when difficult obstacles need

A team of dogs, Poco and Little Wolf, work together to put this testy ram in his place.

to be negotiated. In goose patrolling, an effective dog can herd geese off the tarmac or grass into the water. Without doubt, geese may double back on a single dog, but a team of dogs are fairly effective to prevent that from happening.

A good team consists of two or more dogs that get along and that are willing to support one another, not compete with each other. It is helpful to have individuals that complement each other's working style. For example, a heading dog that can control the direction of the herd can work well with a driving dog that keeps the herd contained and moving along. A closer working dog can be used for immediate pressure, while a wider runner can counter the escape attempts by creating a second pressure point from farther away.

A young dog that has mastered the basic commands of "come here," "stand," and "stay," and is taking the flanking commands is at the ideal stage to start working with an older, more experienced, dependable dog. An individual that is willing but unable to handle the pressure created by the demands of high-level training might make an excellent backup dog in farm and ranch work.

Before you start working your dogs as a team, each one should be solid in controlling stock alone. Each dog must understand how to listen for his

Reanna and Little Wolf demonstrate how a team of dogs—each with a different working style—can work together while easing a flock to a new grazing area.

own commands. It is beneficial to use each dog's name with the command. Soon each dog learns to respond only when he hears his name. Ideally, each dog should have his own set of commands—for example, one dog can be worked with whistle signals while the other dog is given the verbal commands.

Start by practicing the basic commands with the team away from the distraction of stock. Using their names, instruct one dog to "stand" or "lie down" and "stay," while you walk a short distance away with the other dog. Now ask the second dog to "stand" and "stay" while you call the first dog to you. If necessary, you can put one or both of the dogs on a long line to reinforce instructions until they get used to obeying a stationary instruction while the other dog is in motion.

Practice working with the dogs in a number of different locations. Vary the type of exercises you use to practice teamwork. For example, you can have both dogs come to you from a distance and tell one to "stand" halfway while the other one continues to come.

Games and play training can be valuable tools to prepare dogs for teamwork. For example, tell one dog to "stay" while you toss a ball or toy to the second dog. When he brings it back, instruct him to "stay" while you release the first dog to fetch the ball. Take turns with each dog. Or you can

Just Jake and Doggie, moving sheep down John Brown Canyon from Moab, Utah into Gateway, Colorado.

have both dogs come to you and tell one to "stand" while you ask the other to retrieve an object.

When both dogs respond favorably to the basic commands away from stock, they can be worked with stock in a controlled situation using the same types of exercises. If necessary, you can start working them as a team by having one dog on lead next to you while the other one works independently. Then instruct the first dog to "stand" while you release the second one to perform a segment of work. On stock with a small flight zone or with large groups, you can let both dogs work freely together, especially if you are covering a fair distance or difficult terrain.

During each phase of training—whether working an individual or a team of dogs—it is important to continue to improve and perfect the previous lessons. By working a variety of stock in many different situations, you will keep your dog keen and versatile. Not every individual will make a top trial dog, but with plenty of practice you can develop your dog to his fullest potential and gain an enjoyable, useful stock dog.

On Special Assignment

In 1987, we got a special assignment working wild bison in Yellow-stone National Park. Bison management problems had developed during the late 1970s and '80s in various National Parks through-out the western United States. I was contracted to assist the Department of Interior in a bison control and management project. We went on location for actual fieldwork with stockdogs and wild bison.

Part of the challenge lies with tourist liability. Tourists don't think of this huge, nonchalant creature as a wild animal. Lone bison bulls wander into campsites and along roadsides, drop their heads, and graze. They aren't easily spooked, which makes them appear docile and easy going. Despite numerous warning signs along roadsides and in camp areas, people still walk right up to pet and photograph them. Each year, multiple incidents are reported where individuals are charged and injured and sometimes killed.

Park rangers had been trying to find an effective method of dis-couraging bison bulls from "setting up camp" near tourists. Con-ventional fences won't deter them; they can jump as high as six feet. Rangers have resorted to using thumper guns loaded with vials of water; this inflicts a harmless sting to encourage the bison to move along. The effectiveness is minimal, though. The bulls might run only fifty feet to fifty yards before dropping their heads to continue grazing at their leisure.

Many other options have been considered for the program, includ-ing using horses to haze the bison. The shaggy monarch of the plains is deceptively fast and agile, and because his windpipe is four times larger than that of similar-sized animals, he can pump in large quantities of air. Horses can't compare when it comes to overall en-durance. Bison also don't react to pressure the way cattle do; in-stead of moving away, they'll charge at a horse and throw him.

These drawbacks triggered the next phase of the program: using stock dogs. It sounded like an interesting project, but one that warranted some research. After all, these bison weren't raised in somebody's back yard, and they weren't accustomed to being handled, let alone herded, by domestic dogs that resembled

(continued on next page)

On Special Assignment (continued)

predators. These were not bison trained to follow "cake wagons" (vehicles dispensing cubes or pellets of processed food with molasses). As a whole, a herd of bison is mellow. When the calves are born, bison cows become extremely protective, not unlike domestic cattle. While the cow will be the first to get you, it is the lone bull, especially if he's been whipped out of the herd, that is the most cantankerous.

After deliberating the pros and cons with my family, we concluded this would be the supreme test for our dogs. I carefully chose each individual dog. Only the most experienced cattle dogs in the fittest condition would survive. Along with miles on rough stock, each individual had to have "heart" if the going got tough.

Our first working location was out in an open meadow. A lone bull stood grazing peacefully and hardly took notice of the crew of rangers, cameraman, and other officials, including an armed marksman.

I chose Leo as my anchor dog to begin with, because of his deliberate approach. He was powerful, but wouldn't take any foolish chances. As Leo approached the fight/flight zone, the bull lifted his head and charged. Leo dodged him and slipped around to heel him from behind, but bison bulls don't turn in the same manner as a domestic bull. When a bison spins, he pivots on his forelegs, which frees his hindquarters to kick out while he meets his challenger with his substantial head and horns.

Leo and Rogue on assignment during the 1987 wild bison experiment at Yellowstone National Park in Wyoming.

(continued on next page)

On Special Assignment (continued)

Leo avoided the attacks of the bull, and turned and repositioned himself to counter his moves. He pressured the bull and then gave him an opportunity for retreat. The bull would back up a step or two and then stand, waiting like a concrete statue.

I sent Rogue, a gutsy driving dog, to back Leo, also a strong driving dog, but naturally, the bison was not going to allow the dogs to get behind him. At one point, after backing a few steps, the bull dropped his head, waiting for an opportunity to start grazing. I asked them to "get 'em up." Rogue moved in and grabbed the hair between the bison's eyes, and jerked it. Silver strings of saliva blew across the air; the bull dropped his head and bulldozed his way out of the meadow and through the woods past us, shaking the earth, with the dogs in relentless pursuit.

It could easily take forty to fifty minutes to move a single bull 500 yards in one direction. I felt extremely confident after seeing the dogs in action. Even though it took that much time to move the bull a short distance, it was the acid test for the dogs' ability to maneuver around the bulls.

One of the locations where we worked the dogs was an actual campsite with tents and trailers, which required careful reading of the situation to prevent things from getting out of hand. A couple of the areas were open, some with natural obstacles. At times it appeared as though the bison were trying to work the dogs towards a fallen log to catch them at a disadvantage "against the wall," so to speak.

My entourage of dogs would not have been complete without Just Jake, a courageous little fetching dog. His style proved extremely effective. He never penetrated beyond a certain fine line, but kept constant pressure driving towards the bull. Every now and then he'd growl and let out a throaty bark.

Before long, several more bulls had wandered into the area we were working, which was a clearing in the wooded area. I teamed Jake up with Hondo, a friend's gritty blue Australian Shepherd. Together, they rounded up those bulls and put them on the move across the open space, with the ground thundering beneath their feet.

(continued on next page)

On Special Assignment (continued)

Rogue working a lone, wild bison bull.

The inevitable did happen. The afternoon was warm. The dogs had already worked several bulls when Rogue was caught beneath the piston strokes of an enraged bull's hoofs. He was able to pull himself free, but his left hind leg was limp, dragging behind. With true Aussie character, he spun around ready to stand his ground. He wasn't going to give up until I called him. His teammate Leo kept the bull's attention, allowing Rogue to get out of the line of fire. He had been stomped and gored. The horns tore deep into the flesh of his muscles, but luckily no vital organs were hit. With some major stitches, he survived to herd again.

Herding wild, lone bison bulls is extremely difficult, like trying to stop a freight train. While stockdogs proved not to be a long-term solution to the bison problem, I feel that my dogs met the supreme test with success. Handling wild bison bulls is something to approach with a healthy respect. After all, they are the king of the plains—the ultimate challenge.

Chapter 17

TRAINING ANIMALS

TYPES OF LIVESTOCK

For many people the whole point of having a herding dog is to have a partner to help handle livestock. These are the people who own livestock as a way of life or a serious hobby and use their animals for brush mitigation or else to produce milk, wool, meat, or eggs. Other people start with the dog, become fascinated by the herding life, and eventually find that it makes sense to keep a few animals and work them regularly. They may keep poultry or sheep just for the enjoyment of working with their dogs, or they may decide to go into small-scale farming as a result.

There are many choices of species and breeds of livestock available for teaching stockdogs. While meat, milk, fiber, and eggs take precedence in the selection of stock for a particular region or commercial purpose, choosing livestock for herding training is different. Stamina and athletic ability are factors to consider when choosing a species and breed of livestock for

Peaslee's Honey—an English Shepherd, the classic farm collie—working a flock of production geese. PHOTO BY ELSIE RHODES.

training. Not surprisingly, docile animals are easier to work with. The stock best suited for getting started in herding will have a good disposition and be gentle, not wild or combative. Additionally, using calm, tame animals is very important to prevent bad habits from starting. Stock must also be easy to care for, sound, and healthy.

Your personal budget and property considerations will naturally dictate your choices of livestock. Ducks, geese, and turkeys are the least costly type of stock to purchase and keep. They are omnivorous and can be kept in a small yard. Sheep and goats can be kept on limited acreage as long as you have appropriate fencing. You may even be able to have cattle if you have a few acres and suitable zoning.

▼

For effective brush control you need at least four mature regular-sized goats of any breed (6 to 8 miniature goats) per acre, but that is subjective to the density and type of brush to be controlled and the amount of time required to clear the area.

▲

While cattle are generally easier to maintain—because they don't need as much daily attention or require dog-proof fencing and can be maintained with a strand-wire electric fence—sheep and goats are initially less expensive than cows and easier for beginners to manage while they learn about livestock. Dog owners with breeds from cattle-working lines might choose goats as an alternative.

Available forage is a factor, too. Poultry will eat grass, roots, seeds, stems, berries, fruits, and insects if allowed to free range. Cows prefer grass to other types of forage and are less likely to eat weeds than are sheep or goats. In general, sheep utilize uneven, steep hill pastures better than goats or cows do. They are grazers, preferring broadleaf plants and short tender grass and clover, while goats favor leaves, twigs, vines, shrubs, and brush. They will eat as high as they can reach by standing on their hind legs. Consequently, goats are not considered the most effective "lawnmowers." Sheep are better suited to that task. Goats on the other hand will very often forage a wide variety of vegetation (and noxious weeds) that other grazing animals won't. Goats shouldn't be allowed access to certain plants that are toxic to them, but they are highly effective in clearing an area of poison ivy and poison oak with no ill effects.

If fodder becomes limited because of overgrazing or drought, supplemental feeding of hay may be necessary. You also need to think about the climate where you live and choose a breed that was developed to do well

An Azores Cattledog pushing a herd of purebred Hereford cattle out to pasture at Vattukorven Farms in Finland. COURTESY SATU HUUSKO.

in, say, an arid climate with scarce vegetation rather than one more suited to a damp, cold region with high rainfall.

OTHER CONSIDERATIONS

A major consideration is that livestock used for training purposes must be physically able to move freely and without restriction. An example of restricted movement is the Large Dewlap Toulouse (Exhibition) Goose, one of the biggest breeds, and shaped a little like a tub of lard. It often weighs up to 30 pounds (13.6 kg) and has short legs, a large dewlap, and a deep keel (breastbone). It is quiet, calm, and gentle, but it is too bulky and too restricted by its big body and short legs to use for training stock. Similarly, a Southdown sheep is short-legged and has a tendency to be fatter, slower, and not as agile as other breeds.

The following chapters outline some of the most common breeds encountered in the North American herding world. After you determine what type and breed of stock best suits you, do some research on that breed and class of stock so you will know how to properly care for it *before* purchasing any animals.

Training Animals to Avoid

Intact male stock animals (bucks, bulls, and rams) are not an option for training, especially if they have been bottle raised. They can be territorial and dangerous to handle. They also tend to become more difficult as they age. While dogs can be very useful for handling hogs in real farm situations, hogs aren't a good choice for training and practice; they don't handle stress well, and they can easily overheat and even die. It should also be pointed out that they are as intelligent as a dog and can bite to defend themselves.

WHERE TO ACQUIRE TRAINING ANIMALS

Ducks and geese can be purchased from a hatchery, a feed store, newspaper ads and from other herding enthusiasts. Trials, training clinics, and online e-mail lists are other sources to locate training animals. Sheep, goats, or cows may be obtained similarly and from livestock auctions and breeders. A good starter flock or herd may be developed by purchasing older animals culled from other flocks or herds. Although seven-to-eight year old animals may be considered beyond their prime and replaced in a breeding

Green's Boots, a courageous Australian Shepherd, handling hogs on his owner's farm in Kansas. PHOTO BY DOUG MACSPADDEN.

program, they may still be productive until 10 or 12 years of age. These animals can be purchased at a lower cost than prime young breeding stock.

For training you want healthy animals. Avoid skinny animals and any animals that are lame or have eye problems, including any condition resembling pinkeye. Soft dung may be due to lush seasonal pastures; however loose droppings may also indicate illness and internal parasites. Lumps or swelling around the jaw and under the chin may also indicate certain parasites. Find out from the seller when the animal(s) were de-wormed and what agents were used.

Stockmen will offer large discounts for sick animals, but the cost of doctoring them can well exceed the initial savings. Secondly, when purchasing sick animals, there is an elevated risk of death loss that must be considered. Reduced prices for thin animals are larger in the fall than spring due to concerns about animal health during cold weather.

Signs of Healthy Animals

The feathers in poultry will be smooth, not ruffled; goats and cows will have smooth coats with lick marks. Their eyes will be bright and clear (no discharge) and their ears will be in a normal erect position. Their noses and muzzles should be clean with no discharge and saliva shouldn't be drooling from the mouth. Healthy animals lick their noses. They will exhibit patterns of usual behavior and chew their cuds. Their breathing should be smooth and regular at rest. They will have normal firm feces and their urine should be clear. When it is time to eat they are ready. They will not be off by themselves (abnormal behavior). They'll remain in the group.

A Bearded Collie owned by Mary Jo Tilford in Indiana working a healthy flock of Barbados. PHOTO BY LORI HERBEL OF XP RANCH PHOTOGRAPHY

Older animals can usually be purchased for a lower price and can be satisfactory for training, providing they are healthy. Avoid animals with over or undershot jaws unless you are willing to consider special feeding requirements.

Avoid sheep with wool that covers the face because of wool blindness, unless you are willing to keep the face trimmed. Shearing is fairly labor intensive, so unless you're prepared to shear or hire a sheep shearer, you'd be better off considering hair sheep for training purposes.

ESTIMATING AGE BY THE TEETH

Cows, sheep, and goats are cud chewers. For example, sheep have incisor teeth on the lower jaw, not on the top. The thick hard dental pad on the upper jaw gives them a surface to tear off grass. There is a large gap between the dental pad and the back teeth. They have molars on the upper and lower jaws in the back of the mouth.

A lamb has eight deciduous or temporary incisors called milk teeth. These teeth are small, narrow, and have some spaces between them. Lambs have four pair of incisors. When sheep mature they have 32 permanent teeth. At one year of age, yearlings have one pair of permanent middle incisors. The mouth of a two-year-old sheep has two pairs of permanent incisors. The temporary centrals have been replaced with two large, white, sharp permanent incisors.

With each year sheep gain another set of permanent incisors. By three years of age they have their third pair of permanent incisors and respectively get their fourth set at four years of age and have a full mouth with four pairs of permanent teeth. By five years all their permanent incisors close together. When they are older than five, their incisors begin spreading apart, and they are called "spreaders." When a sheep reaches eight or nine—and sometimes as early as five or six years of age—they start losing teeth and are referred to as "broken mouth." Between 10 and 12 years of age all incisors are missing. Once a sheep has lost all its incisors, it is called a "gummer."

Cattle develop in a similar fashion to sheep and goats, except that cattle don't usually have a full mouth until five years of age instead of four. When they are four years of age they have six permanent incisors, and by five years of age they have a full mouth (32 teeth). By ten years of age every tooth, especially the central and first intermediate incisors, shows considerable wear. Some teeth may be worn away entirely. They are referred to as "gummers" when all their teeth are gone and only the root stubs are left.

Animals grazing in certain conditions, such as sandy soil, may show more wear than those in better conditions. Old animals with worn teeth will not eat as well as younger animals, no matter what the grazing condition.

Chapter 18

POULTRY

TRAINING WITH POULTRY

Ducks and geese are a popular choice for training and are easy to keep, though they can be quite messy and they need to have a source of water available, such as a pond or wading pool. Their natural tendency to flock together makes them a good choice for training herding dogs. These birds are hardy and resistant to many common poultry diseases. They can feed on free-range pasture, grazing on grass, plants, and seeds. They are wonderful around the barnyard for keeping down insects. They consume all sorts of bugs, including slugs and snails, and they help eradicate mosquito larva from waterways.

For herding purposes select robust, strong-legged birds. You will need to have at least one group of no less than four. At trials, ducks are usually worked in groups of five. Maintaining a flock of 10 or 15 allows the trainer to work one group while the others rest. Ducks should be fully feathered and no less than three months old before being worked.

Chickens can be worked with dogs. They can be a fun diversion for seasoned dogs, but are not recommended for training inexperienced dogs. They are excitable and fast. They don't flock well and are often broody (nesting and hatching eggs).

WORKING WITH DUCKS

Ducks are a diverse species of waterfowl. Wild mallards are the ancestors of all domestic ducks except Muscovies. With the exception of some of the bantam breeds, domestic ducks are unable to take flight, as their wings are

Aussie working flock of Indian Runners. PHOTO BY DOUGLAS MACSPADDEN.

A variety of different medium-body ducks. PHOTO BY DEB CONROY.

too small to support their bodies. The average lifespan for ducks is between six and eight years. Duck breeds are generally divided into egg layers and meat birds, with many different varieties, ranging from bantam (miniature) ducks to light-framed to large (heavy) breeds.

Egg-Laying Breeds

All breeds of ducks lay eggs, but some are more prolific than others, including the Indian Runner, the Khaki Campbell, the Magpie, and the Bali (or Crested Runner). The Runner is active and somewhat nervous but rarely broody. It is a quick bird with an upright stance (they don't waddle) and a strong flocking instinct. Runners are sensitive to a dog's presence and move like a school of fish, which makes them well suited for herding. Crossbred Runners are generally sturdier.

The Khaki Campbell (derived from Runners, though calmer and not as fast) and the Magpie are good all-around breeds that work well for herding. They are fairly sturdy and upright. Campbell ducks are excellent foragers and do very well in cool climates. Duck breeds such as the Welsh Harlequin are quieter than the Campbell breed, from which they originated. They are docile and inquisitive and work well.

Bantam Ducks

Bantams are miniature breeds, bred for smallness and weighing 4.5 pounds (2 kg) or less. People choose to own them for the novelty, because they require a smaller space, and because they are not usually as noisy as the large duck breeds. Some of the miniature breeds, such as Call ducks, are good fliers; this can be offset by clipping a couple of inches (5 cm) off the outer flight feathers of one wing to prevent the duck from taking to the air. The Call duck has short legs and an upright body. It is noisier, too. The Call duck has been used in some trials successfully and works nicely, but it is more fragile than larger ducks.

Honey, a nice working English Shepherd owned by Mary Peaslee, working a flock of Call ducks. PHOTO BY ELSIE RHODES.

Meat Breeds

The larger and heavier meat breeds include the Aylesbury; the remarkably attractive Cayuga; the Pekin, Muscovy, Rouen, and Saxony (a dual-purpose egg and meat bird); the Swedish and Silver Appleyard. These breeds tend to be very tame, with large, deep bodies and full breasts. They gain weight quickly, so they are slower, unlikely to fly, and don't have a lot of stamina, which makes it more difficult for them to sustain an adequate pace for herding. Leg injuries may also be a problem due to the heaviness of their bodies.

Despite the drawbacks, some trainers prefer to use meat ducks for gentle, slow-working dogs because these ducks are calm and generally flock well. In this case, you might want to consider the Swedish. Though somewhat larger, they are considered medium-weight birds. Ducks crossed from these breeds, such as the Rouen Clair, a farmyard utility duck, are smaller and more upright than the Rouen and therefore better suited for working.

While it can be interesting for experienced dogs and useful for teaching certain skills such as shedding, the Muscovy is not the perfect bird to use for training. They tend to string out instead of flocking nicely. They can be aggressive, and some of the lighter hens can fly well enough to clear most training pens.

WORKING WITH GEESE

Geese have long been kept in small farm flocks, primarily for meat and eggs. They are one of the most economical farmyard birds to keep, and they make excellent "watchdogs," being quick to sound the alarm by honking when intruders are spotted. They are hardy, active foragers that graze grass and some broad leaves, consume insects, slugs, and snails. They can adapt equally well to cold climates as to hot climates, providing they have shade. They can be kept on a fenced-in range with good grass, but they require a source of fresh, clean water to bathe in.

The average lifespan of geese is between 8 and 15 years. A flock of at least four to six makes a good bunch for training purposes. When working in larger flocks, geese tend to string out, making them a good choice for boundary training.

A good choice for training dogs is the Pilgrim goose. They are medium sized, hardy, docile, and quiet. This gentle, friendly goose has a strong flocking instinct. While it is protective of newly hatched goslings, it is gentle and less aggressive than other breeds. Pilgrims are unique compared to other geese, in that the male and female come in different colors: The male is white, and the female is olive gray.

By contrast, the delightful and elegant Chinese goose, a dual-purpose breed, is talkative or "chatty," and sounds off if confronted by intruders.

The Chinese goose is the smallest and lightest breed, making it ideal for crossing with other breeds. It is an active forager and is the most prolific egg layer of all the breeds. It is agile, has strong legs, and is quite suitable for working, but is spirited and considered one of the more aggressive breeds. The knob, or protuberance on its head, is susceptible to frostbite. Chinese geese can be defensive when watching over broody females and may intimidate inexperienced dogs, as can the ordinary gray Toulouse.

The general purpose production or "utility" Toulouse strain is quieter than the Chinese. It is hardy and does well in cold winters. The Toulouse is the most common and popular farmyard breed, being smaller and less bulky than most meat breeds, with longer legs and no keel. It is easygoing and trusting and works quite well for training and herding.

Meat production breeds can also be calm, but their size may present problems. Large breeds, such as the stately African goose (a close cousin to the Chinese goose), the Embden, and the Large Dewlap (Exhibition) Toulouse, are raised for meat production. A pond of fresh clean water for swimming and to bathe in is a must. They have mild, pleasant dispositions and do fairly well in confinement, but their bulky size limits their effectiveness for stock training.

Moderation sometimes presents the best compromise. Medium-size geese such as the tall Pomeranian, the Brecon Buff, and the Roman (also known as Roman Tufted) are very calm, quieter, and slower than the light-framed breeds and are less likely to flap their wings when aggravated. They require grazing and a water source for swimming and bathing.

Minka, a Shetland Sheepdog owned by Linda Rorem, working Shetland geese, a long-established barnyard goose from the Shetland Islands with coloration similar to Pilgrim geese. Shetlands are distinguished for their foraging ability. PHOTO BY JUDY CUMMINGS.

What About Turkeys?

Turkeys are native to North America, are fairly hardy, and do well as free-range birds, eating crickets, grasshoppers, and other insects. In previous centuries, herding dogs were used to drive turkeys to market. They can be fun to work, although in small groups they don't generally flock as well as ducks or geese. Turkeys are flighty and like to roost. It takes a talented dog to be a career turkey dog. If turkeys are pressured, their natural inclination is to take to the air. If they are too heavy to fly, they just leap up.

In small groups, turkeys don't flock well. Certik—a multiple titled herding dog—working a small group of the many thousands of turkeys raised at Turkey Run Farms in Indiana.
PHOTO BY ADRIANA PLUM.

Early maturing breeds, such as the Broad-Breasted Bronze and Broad-Breasted White, are commercially developed breeds that are raised for the table. They have potential leg problems and are not feasible for training because of their fast growth and overdeveloped keels.

Heritage breeds (domesticated varieties descended from wild turkeys) have a slow to moderate growth rate, so their legs are generally much stronger. Narragansett turkeys are thought to be calm and easy to work. Like the Narragansett, the Buff turkey is a good choice, but hard to find. Similarly, Midget White Turkeys are considered quite friendly and less excitable than most breeds, but rare.

Chapter 19

SHEEP

TRAINING WITH SHEEP

Sheep are the most popular type of stock used for training purposes. There are over 200 breeds that have been bred for wool quality, meat production, and flocking instincts, among other uses. Breed characteristics have also been influenced by climate, environment, and forage quality. In North America, sheep breeds are divided into six types: hair and double-coated, dual purpose, fine wool, meat, long wool, and the minor breeds.

While you can raise sheep in almost all environments, some breeds are better suited to certain climates. For example, hair sheep such as the St. Croix were developed in tropical conditions for heat tolerance and parasite resistance, while breeds like the Navajo Churro do well in hot, dry climates where forage is in short supply. In areas where the climate is cold and wet and feed is more plentiful, certain double-coated and long wool breeds and meat breeds may be preferable—and less likely to suffer foot rot or die of pneumonia.

HAIR AND DOUBLE-COATED BREEDS

Common breeds include the Barbados, the St. Croix, the Katahdin, and the Dorper. Hair sheep such as the Barbados and the St. Croix are becoming quite popular because they are easy to care for and do not require shearing. They are more parasite resistant and tolerate heat and humidity better than wool breeds; they manage well on low-grade forage and demonstrate good fitness. The meat has a milder flavor than the fine wool breeds. The double-coated or "shedding" breeds, such as the Katahdin and the Dorper, have a mixture of hair and wool that grows over the winter. As with the hair breeds, this type of coat usually sheds completely off in the spring and doesn't require shearing.

Cato, a blue-eyed Border Collie, owned by Conroy Farms, working Dorper cross sheep. PHOTO BY LORI HERBEL, XP RANCH PHOTOGRAPHY.

The Barbados is like an antelope—fast, wild, and a good fence jumper—but it possesses a strong flocking instinct and is easy to herd. It is one of the most common sheep used in herding activities and is rarely combative with dogs. Commercial sheep producers don't usually raise the Barbados, because it doesn't produce wool and has a small carcass. However, it is low maintenance and adapts well to a broad range of environments; it tolerates low-grade forage, and possesses an unusual tolerance to heat and humidity as well as to cold. Naturally, it becomes tamer with handling and exposure to dogs. It tends not to sour as easily in training, as many of the other types of sheep do.

Meg, a Border Collie owned by Mary Swindell, working Barbados hair sheep. PHOTO BY LORI HERBEL, XP RANCH PHOTOGRAPHY.

Barbados crosses, such as the California Red (Barbados x Tunis), look like deer, but they have a gentle, easygoing disposition and respond well to quiet handling. Other Barbados crosses, such as with the Dorset breed, tend to be docile and less nervous and work well for stock training.

The St. Croix is a docile, calm, but free moving and responsive breed with good flocking ability; it is not as excitable as the Barbados. In colder climates it produces a heavy winter coat of mixed wool and hair that sheds in the spring. The St. Croix is a healthy, hardy breed used for both meat and dairy production.

Katahdins and Dorpers flock fairly well and are docile, even tempered, and easily handled. Both are free moving but not flighty, with average flocking instinct; the Dorper is heavier, more docile and pushy. Both breeds are hardy and adaptable to any climate; they are nonselective grazers and perform well under a variety of production systems.

DUAL-PURPOSE BREEDS

The useful dual-purpose breeds produce both meat and wool; they include the Columbia, the Panama, the Corriedale, the Finnsheep, the Polypay, and the Targhee.

The Columbia is a hardy, long-lived, gregarious breed with good flocking instincts, well suited to the western range though larger and somewhat less compliant than its Merino forebears. It was developed in the United States by crossing Rambouillet rams with Lincoln ewes. The Panama is another American breed, resulting from the reverse of the cross used for the Columbia—but it tends to have better flocking instincts and is not as large.

The gregarious Corriedale is a docile, medium-size, white-faced sheep whose numbers are declining in range country as demand increases for larger-bodied sheep. They are well adapted to farm life, where they are maintained in fenced pastures rather than on the open range.

The smaller Finnsheep or Finnish Landrace is hardy and adaptable to a variety of management conditions, eating leaves and bracken as well as grass pastures. It is well-known for its friendly nature and does well on small farms. A prolific breed, the ewes usually have triplets or quadruplets with short tails that don't need to be docked.

The Targhee is an American breed that was developed from crosses between the Rambouillet, Columbia, and Corriedale. It is a medium to large breed, fairly complacent in character with reasonable flocking instincts. The Polypay, also a composite breed (developed from the Targhee, Rambouillet, Finnsheep, and Dorset), is medium sized, has good flocking instincts, and is easily managed. This hardy breed adapts well to the varied climates and forage conditions of ranches throughout the American West and the northern states.

WTCH Las Rocosa Bonny Kyle RDX working Dorset sheep on the Hartnagle's Lazy 3 Mill Iron Y Ranch.

FINE-WOOL BREEDS

Prized for their luxurious fleece, fine-wool breeds are developed from the basic Merino; specific breeds include the Debouillet, the Delaine-Merino, and the Rambouillet.

The Merino originated in Spain. It tends to be small in body and have many long, loose folds of skin. It is strictly a wool producer, as its carcass is narrow and leggy. Merino sheep are gregarious and well known for staying together unless they become panic stricken. They are easy to handle and will readily follow a leader, even if it is a billy goat with a bell. When handled by a person and dog, the flock will readily accept the trainer as the bellwether. Merinos off the range, however, can be unpredictable when they are separated from the flock and handled in small numbers. They become restless and may stand and fight or panic and bolt headlong into a fence. They tend to get dogged fairly easily.

Merino derivatives such as the Debouillet and Delaine-Merinos are hardy and have well-developed flocking instincts. They can be counted on to stay in a flock in unfenced regions, but are somewhat temperamental and stress easily when singled out from the flock. Both are hardy breeds, foraging well in less productive regions and suited to hill country locations.

The Rambouillet was developed in France and Germany from Spanish Merino stock. This breed has a well-developed flocking instinct. It is the foundation of most range flocks and is kept on the open range by the thousands in the western United States. The Rambouillet is rugged and adapts to a wide variety of arid range conditions. In a strange environment such as a trial situation, it may panic and run over anything standing in its way. In a training situation, Rambouillets are easily conditioned to follow the trainer, and in fact tend to cling to the trainer for safety. Over time, they become less responsive to a dog and more difficult to drive away from the trainer.

LONG-WOOL BREEDS

The so-called long-wool breeds have large bodies and coarse wool that grows much longer than that of other breeds. The long-stapled fleece is well-liked by hand-spinners for making yarn. In certain areas—such as the northern United States and Canada, with cool, wet climates and good pastures—these breeds may have an advantage, such as a reduced propensity for foot rot. Some of the long-wool breeds, with their coarse but utilitarian fleeces, include the Border Leicester, the Lincoln, the Perendale, and the Romney.

The Border Leicester is medium size and well known for its quiet nature. This breed can be fast and free moving, but not flighty. They are smart and easy to work with.

The medium sized Perendale, a Cheviot/Romney derivative, was developed to be an easy-care breed. It is hardy and highly adapted to marginal forage-producing areas, but is nervous and flighty and requires gentle handling.

The Lincoln is the largest of all the sheep breeds. It is docile and easily handled, but not well suited to cold, wet weather because a part runs down the middle of its back fleece, exposing its sensitive backbone to cold rain. The Romney, on the other hand, was developed to withstand cold and wet conditions. It is also less susceptible to foot rot than many breeds, but it doesn't do well in hot climates. It is considered quiet and easy to work with, but the breed doesn't have a strong herding instinct, so needs to be managed as a farm flock kept within fenced pastures.

MEAT BREEDS

Breeds commonly raised for meat include the Cheviot (Border and North Country), the Dorset (polled and horned), the Hampshire, the Montadale, the Suffolk, and the Southdown.

Cheviot cross sheep with clean faces (free from wool). PHOTO BY LORI HERBEL, XP RANCH PHOTOGRAPHY.

The Cheviot is very alert and active, resourceful, and highly adaptable to a variety of climates. It was developed specifically to live in rugged terrain, and it thrives on poor forage conditions. This breed is fast, high strung, and lacks strong flocking instincts, but is not inclined to challenge a dog unless pushed. The Montadale, a Cheviot/Columbia derivation, can be restless like the Cheviot, only slower and more inclined to run than to challenge a dog. Cheviots do well in farm flocks, but they lack the strong flocking instinct for open-range grazing.

The medium-sized Dorset was developed in England and at one time was kept as a dairy sheep. It is mild mannered, flocks well, and works nicely off a dog. It is a stable and excellent breed for starting dogs. Smaller, traditional production Dorset sheep are the most desirable for herding.

The Hampshire and the Suffolk also originated in England. Both breeds have brown or black heads, noses, feet, and legs. The Suffolk is the most popular breed in the world and the preferred meat sheep in America, although because it is not a particularly gregarious breed and somewhat temperamental, it does best in farm flocks. The Suffolk is quiet and quick to settle down once disturbed, but is less responsive to a dog and more likely to challenge its authority (especially a weak dog); it may need to be convinced to comply. The Hampshire is a little more agreeable.

The Southdown is extremely docile, nonaggressive, and slow working. This breed is easily maintained and is sometimes preferred for starting a dog in the round pen or for working slow dogs, even though it doesn't have exceptional flocking instincts and does not tolerate heat well. Baby-doll sheep are a dwarf form of the Southdown.

MINOR BREEDS

Many herding dog owners are attracted to the minor breeds, such as the Icelandic, Scottish Blackface, and Shetland sheep, because of the sheep's significance to their herding breed's heritage. Others are interested in preserving a rare breed, such as the Navajo-Churro.

The Scottish Blackface is a beautiful and hardy breed that is the backbone of the Scottish sheep industry. The Blackface is smart and can take care of itself, but does not have good flocking instincts and can be tough to handle. They have horns and can be aggressive. It can take a very determined dog to convince them to move.

Minka, a Shetland Sheepdog owned by Linda Rorem, working a couple of Shetland sheep with a white Dorset cross ewe. Photo by Judy Cummings.

Icelandic and Shetland sheep are primitive short-tailed breeds noted for their ability to survive under harsh conditions, in marginal pasture and changeable climate. The Icelandic sheep is a medium-sized breed, short legged and stocky. This intelligent, high strung, and reactive breed is not docile and doesn't flock well. The flock can be combative with a dog and is not a good choice for beginning dogs or trainers. The Shetland is a somewhat smaller breed but similarly independent; it doesn't flock well and is easily scattered. The Navajo-Churro sheep, by contrast, is a delightful breed. It is a smallish sheep tracing back to the Churra sheep the Spanish Conquistadors brought to the Americas for mutton. The breed was developed in the Southwest by the Navajo tribe and thus is well adapted to the harsh desert environment. It is gregarious, friendly, and even-tempered; intelligent and alert, yet docile. The wool is extremely coarse and is used almost exclusively by the Navajo Indians in the production of traditional blankets and rugs.

Chapter 20

GOATS

TRAINING WITH GOATS

Goats, sometimes referred to as the poor man's cow, were an integral part of American colonization. A few head can generally be kept on less than an acre of land with sturdy fences; the space required to keep one cow will support six goats. Their size and ability to eat a wider assortment of less desirable vegetation than other livestock made them highly valuable to early settlers, as did the fact that goats produce milk, meat, and cashmere. They do well both in arid and moderately wet climates.

For training purposes goats are calmer and less quick to respond than the flighty breeds of sheep. They are inquisitive and curious creatures and are often compared in workability to the slower working black-faced Hampshire or Suffolk sheep. Goats tend to be more independent than sheep and don't flock well. They are conditioned to being led to pasture by the billy or lead nanny, so they will respond well to being led by the trainer.

You can choose from among the dairy, fiber, and meat breeds, depending on what qualities you desire, as long as you choose a healthy and approachable breed and work with the flock regularly. Left unattended, goats will return to a wild state as easily as the domestic cat does. In order to have friendly goats that you can handle, you must buy already tame adults or raise kids from an early age.

▼

Myotonic, or fainting, goats should be avoided for herding. They have a neurological disorder that causes their muscles to freeze when they're startled or nervous, triggering a "fainting spell" that is characterized by a stiff-legged walk or shuffle and often accompanied by an actual collapse and temporary paralysis.

▲

Champion Las Rocosa Leslie CSD flanking counterclockwise around goats in one of the first ever ASCA Stockdog Trials held in May 1974.

Lastly, goats are curious and escape artists. Sturdy goat-resistant fences with goat-proof gates are necessary to keep goats contained where desired. Surprisingly, miniature goats such as the Pygmy generally require a higher fence than a calmer breed such as the Angora.

DAIRY BREEDS

Goat milk is becoming increasingly popular, both to drink and to produce cheese. It is more digestible than cow's milk and is often given to young children or to people with digestive disorders. The one drawback to working with goats that are fresh (bagged up for milking) is that their bags can become bruised and injured, making them more susceptible to mastitis. They also need to be milked every 12 hours. The main dairy breeds are the Nubian, LaMancha, Alpine, Oberhasli, Saanen, and the Toggenburg.

The medium- to large-size Nubian is considered the Jersey cow of dairy goats because of the high butterfat content in its milk. It was developed in England and is more heat tolerant and less cold tolerant than Swiss breeds and also more vocal. Some herding trainers find this breed to be mulish. A fairly congenial and fun breed, it can be stubborn and may lie down when it no longer wants to participate. The Nubian is easily identified by its Roman nose and long lop ears, which are always in jeopardy with dogs that naturally grip.

Gabe, owned by
Tyler Taylor,
bringing in Elly
May, a Nubian-type
doe.

The medium-sized LaMancha, an American breed, on the other hand, is distinctive for its very short, nearly nonexistent ears. It is highly unlikely dogs will rip or tear ears with this breed. The LaMancha is popular because it is naturally friendly and easy to handle. It is laid back and cooperative, making it suitable for training purposes. It is well suited to the Northwest, but does fine in warm climates.

The Alpine, Oberhasli, Saanen, and Toggenburg breeds originated in the French and Swiss Alps. These breeds are best suited to temperate climates; they perform poorly in hot regions with high humidity. The highly popular, multicolored Alpine has alert, upright ears and a straight or slightly dished face. The breed is inquisitive and friendly; it is easy to keep and work with and herds well. Individuals can be good jumpers and escape artists. It is medium to large in size, generally hardy.

The Oberhasli is a smaller, medium-sized goat with an alert appearance. It is nonaggressive, tolerant, and works well with people and dogs.

The gentle Saanen, the largest of the dairy breeds, is considered the Holstein of the goat world. It does best in cooler climates and can be susceptible to sunburn. It is fairly laid back.

The robust Toggenburg breed is a small to medium-sized breed noted for its hardiness and adaptability to different climates. It typically does better in cool conditions, but is more heat tolerant than the Saanen.

FIBER BREEDS

Fiber goats are small-framed goats not suitable for meat production, instead being valued for the fine fleece they produce. Common breeds include the Angora, the Cashmere, the Pygora, and the Nigora.

The medium-size Angora breed is docile, flocks moderately well, and is fairly laid back. It is the source of mohair, which is similar to wool but much finer in composition and lacks the felting properties of wool. The Angora is small compared to the average dairy breed; the does weigh between 70 and 110 pounds (31.2–49.9 kg). The much larger bucks weigh between 180 and 225 pounds (81.7–102.1 kg).

The Angora isn't as hardy as other breeds and must be shorn twice a year. Care must be taken to keep newly shorn Angoras out of adverse weather, as they are susceptible to pneumonia. Colored Angoras are slightly hardier than white ones but still are considered more delicate than other livestock animals. Although the breed is not as tough as some other breeds—doesn't take the heat well, and tires easily—it has been used successfully for training and trialing.

Fiber goat breeds other than Angoras produce cashmere, the fine downy undercoat that is harvested annually by combing. So-called cashmere goats are not a specific breed but a type of fiber goat, mainly the Spanish meat or cashmere goat.

The Pygora, as its name suggests, is a cross between the Angora and the Pygmy breeds. It is small and usually hardy and calm. The Nigora, a stocky little goat with a gentle disposition, is a cross between the Angora and the Nigerian Dwarf. It is nonaggressive and pleasant to work.

▼

Unlike other goats, Angoras graze more than browse.

▲

MEAT GOATS

Many producers raise goats for meat, a market that is ever increasing. Boer and Spanish are the primary meat breeds.

The Boer goat, a horned breed with a beefy frame, has a Roman nose and pendulous ears similar to those of the Nubian, but its body is primarily white with dark coloration around the head. The Boer is gentle and flocks fairly well, but it is less hardy, less parasite resistant, and higher maintenance than most breeds. It doesn't seem to do well in areas with hot temperatures and high humidity, and tends to be picky about its diet, preferring grain and hay to brush. Crossbred Boer goats are healthier and work well with dogs.

Spanish goats, also known as brush goats, are raised primarily for meat. This is not a standardized breed and exhibits quite a bit of diversity in size due to infusions of Angora and dairy breeding. From the smaller framed to the somewhat larger, rangy type, Spanish goats generally have large pendulous ears similar to the Nubian. They are agile, hardy animals, able to thrive in hot climates on whatever forage is readily available. They are generally preferred over Angoras for herding in difficult mountainous terrain or controlling woody briars. Docility is variable, but when they are tame they can be congenial and friendly. Their athletic build makes them good for herding work.

Miniature Goats

Miniature goats are popular because they are adaptable, small, and sociable. Their calm, gentle temperaments are attractive to herding hobbyists and make them good for starting dogs. The friendly Nigerian Dwarf is a dairy animal and is more disease resistant and heat tolerant and requires less feed and space than the larger dairy breeds. This is a social breed that mixes well with other animals and is easy to handle with dogs.

The Pygmy goat is a sweet-natured, cobby meat breed, but its short legs and other dwarf features may hinder its ability for training walkabouts. Because of their small size, Pygmy goats are popular pets, playful and easy to handle. They have horns and can be feisty with a dog. Some trainers use Pygmies for starting a dog in the round pen, although Nigerians are generally preferred.

A PROFILE OF

Matt Mason DVM — From a Vet's Point of View

While in Veterinary School at The Ohio State University, Matt Mason wanted a dog of his own, and was attracted to "the little blue dogs" he frequently saw and learned were Australian Shepherds. He acquired his first Aussie in 1991 from Leslie Frank of Propwash Kennels.

Although "Polo" didn't show instinct and never worked livestock, he was a trusted companion that led Matt into the world of working dogs. While completing a veterinary externship in Snohomish, Washington, Matt met Marti Parrish, an Aussie breeder and stockdog competitor. She invited him to "try herding."

Dr. Mason had always been fascinated by the partnership between dogs and handlers that worked well together. The encounter peaked his interest in competition and led him to acquire his second Australian Shepherd when he finished school in 1995. Dr. Mason never imagined that he would be able to earn an ASCA Working Trial Championship, but in May 1999, he and his dog, Mason's Rugby, successfully earned a WTCh. He says, "With a lot of diligent practice and guidance from herding dog clinicians, Rugby became the basis for many stockdog titles." Since then, Matt has successfully completed Working Trial Championships on two other Aussies and a couple of Border Collies as well as titled other Aussies.

Matt has enjoyed working with his dogs and has learned a lot about dogs, livestock and human nature through them. They have taught him a great deal about communication between humans and animals. He became aware that the herding dogs are so tuned into their chosen humans that it is difficult for their master to deceive them. He said, "When the handler's mind is settled and task oriented, the dogs are too. When the handler is stressed, confused and unsure about the task at hand, the dogs are too. Although your words may be one way of stating your intentions, your thoughts and body language all need to agree to have a successful transfer of information between the dog and handler." He pointed out that confusion, frustration and misunderstanding occur when communication is not clear, and this seems to be a constant state in today's pet owning community.

From his viewpoint as a veterinarian and experienced stockdog handler he believes herding breeds require a lot of understanding and competent handling for them to be successful in life. They tend to be very perceptive and can be easily overwhelmed in our "pet life styles" when they are primarily asked to just "look good" and not use their minds. "These dogs have been bred for generations to be a working partner with a human being, and when they are underguided and overstimulated, they can become obsessive/compulsive, and develop other negative habits such as biting, car chasing, barking and digging."

Chapter 21

CATTLE

WORKING WITH CATTLE

For centuries cattle have provided milk and meat; oxen or castrated bulls were used for draft purposes. Cattle aren't usually as excitable as sheep and will generally tolerate an eager dog moving freely around them better than sheep. A general rule of thumb is that an acre of land that will support six head of sheep or goats will support one cow, depending on the location and available forage. On lush ground with good quality forage, you may be able to stock two head of cows per acre without overgrazing or overcrowding. In the West, it may take 25 acres to support one cow, depending on the region and available forage.

In North America there are many different breeds divided into two species: British and European breeds such as Angus, Hereford, Charolais, and Simmental are examples of the *Bos tarus*, while the *Bos indicus* species includes humped cattle such as the Brahman (Zebu), which were developed in India.

A gutsy Corgi blocking and turning a commercial steer at a trial. PHOTO BY LORI HERBEL OF XP RANCH PHOTOGRAPHY.

MEAT OR BEEF BREEDS

The majority of cattle used for training or trialing in North America are grade or commercial, meaning they are not registered with a breed association. They can be any type or color. The Hereford, Angus, Shorthorn, Swiss Simmental, French Charolais, Brahman, Corriente, and Longhorn are among the specific beef breeds commonly found in North America.

The Hereford is one of the most popular breeds of beef cattle in the United States. It can be either polled or horned and is a medium-frame cow with distinctive red and white coloring. It is generally a docile, quiet cow and remarkably easy to handle. It is extremely hardy and does well in a variety of climates, including cold harsh weather.

An Azores Cattle Dog working Hereford bulls on the Vattukorven Farm in Finland. COURTESY SATU HUUSKO.

The Angus is highly popular for beef production. It is rugged and adaptable and can survive harsh weather. A good-natured breed, it is much more excitable than the Hereford and will fight a dog when agitated. Both breeds are used widely in crossbreeding and are a mainstay in commercial herds. When crossed together, the Hereford-Angus produces what is known as the Black Baldy, which is an excellent cow to handle with dogs.

The Shorthorn originated in the British Isles and can be either a beef or dairy cow. It is quite hardy, vigorous, and long lived. The Shorthorn is known for its quiet, docile nature, which makes it easy to work with dogs. Shorthorns are red roan to white in color.

A pair of Milking Shorthorn cattle moving away from Bella, a Malinois owned by Donna Haworth. PHOTO BY ELSIE RHODES.

The calm Simmental is considered one of the easiest breeds to manage with dogs. Its quiet, gentle nature can be related to the breed's use as a draft animal; it is a medium to large cow with sound, strong feet and legs.

The Charolais is a medium- to large-frame cow commonly used for crossbreeding because it is docile and easily handled, thanks to its development as a draft animal. It is fairly adaptable and can stand moderate cold. This breed is more likely to challenge a dog and doesn't usually group as easily as the Hereford.

Brahman cattle, often referred as "Brahmas" (even "Brahmers"), are easily identified by their long, floppy ears and the hump on their back. Purebred Brahman are intelligent, inquisitive, and reserved, but can also be a little nervous, flighty, and temperamental. With calm, gentle handling, they can be docile and easily fetched with a dog if given enough distance. If you don't crowd them or overwork them, Brahmans can be fine to handle, but if they get hot and agitated, they can become difficult and even aggressive, and may challenge a dog. They are very quick and athletic and have been known to jump fences if they become angry.

WTCH Twin Oaks Bull working a herd of Brahman-type cattle.
PHOTO BY CEE HAMBO.

Windsong's Troyabby STDcsd racing to the head of a Brahma.
COURTESY JOEL FINCH.

The Santa Gertrudis (developed from the Brahman and Shorthorn) and Brahman cross cows are popular in southern states because they do well in hot climates; they are frequently encountered at stockdog events. Four of the main crosses are Braford (Brahman/Hereford), Brangus (Brahman/Angus), Charbray (Charolais/Brahman) and Simbrah (Simmental/Brahman). They have more ear than the British and European breeds and are therefore known as "ear cows." Brahman-type cattle are hardy, with proven resistance to parasites and disease and excellent foraging ability. As far as workability, they are compatible, usually mellower and less excitable than purebred Brahman.

▼

As a rule of thumb, cows with a broad head and kind, large eyes tend to be calmer, less flighty, and easier to handle than narrow-headed cattle with small, close-set eyes.

▲

The Corriente is a lean, narrow-bodied cow with curved horns that is commonly used for roping and bulldogging because it is quick and agile. The breed traces back to the original cattle brought to the New World by the Spanish in the fifteenth century. This is an extremely hardy, adaptable breed, chosen especially to withstand the ocean crossing and adapt to the new land. The Corriente has been known to go from one pasture to another by dropping down on its knees and going under a fence—as easily as it can jump over. It is a tough, fast, agile breed and has good endurance, which makes it ideal for training cowdogs. It is quite capable of using its hooves and horns, however, which can be dangerous.

Champion Las Rocosa Leo 4A ATDc in a showdown with a Corriente roping steer.

The Longhorn, the cornerstone of the cowboy culture, is an intelligent breed frequently used in crossbreeding. The Longhorn behaves similarly to the Corriente but is faster. With its massive horns, it can protect itself against predators and can be relatively aggressive with dogs.

DAIRY BREEDS

As a rule, dairy cows are not as excitable as many range or beef breeds, because they are handled on a daily basis. The main dairy breeds (all *Bos taurus*) found in the United States are the Holstein, the Ayrshire, the Brown Swiss, the Guernsey, the Jersey, and the Shorthorn. The dairy cows you will encounter at trials are most likely to be the Holstein, sometimes known as the Fresian—the prototypical dairy cow found on nine out of ten dairy farms in the country and easily recognized by its distinctive black and white markings. This breed doesn't herd as well as beef cattle; they have few herd instincts. When they get hot or tired they can be difficult to drive, especially if they've been raised as bucket calves.

Winterbound's Fortune Teller HSAs, STDs, better known as "Tell," a Rough Collie owned by Haydee Kuner, herding Holstein calves. PHOTO BY HILDY MORGAN.

Miniature Cattle and Small Breeds

Cows of any breed developed for smallness may be ideally suited
for small acreages. The Dexter, which is about half the size of an
average Hereford, the miniature Hereford, and the Lowline Angus,
among other miniature breeds, don't require as much feed. Their
smaller size allows you to run more animals per acre. They tend to
be intelligent, sweet natured, and docile, making them ideal stock
for first time cattle owners, 4-H projects, and for introducing young
or inexperienced dogs to cattle—as well as for teaching larger cattle-working dog breeds that may be too forceful for sheep or goats.

A PROFILE OF

Mike Ryan — Staying Connected to Rural Heritage

Growing up the son of a horse and cattle dealer, Mike Ryan had many occasions to become acquainted with stockdogs. As a boy, he'd spend endless time getting to know the stockyard dogs at the local auction barn in Belle Plaine, Minnesota, petting or watching dogs move or load stock. Some of them mostly just guarded trucks and trailers. He could tell from their attentiveness to any action in the pens of the stockyards that they knew more than they were showing when they were laying around scratching fleas.

"I'm not sure if simply being a member of a herding breed truly qualifies a dog as a stockdog," he mused. "It seems to me that stockdog is a title that ought to be earned." At that time, the Australian Shepherd and Border Collie were the two breeds he saw most often that were consistently out there doing the real work.

After the death of his mother in the mid-seventies, Mike, who was in his late teens, sold all his livestock, gave notice at the local farm store where he worked and left for the West Coast. He ended up moving to Oregon and was living in a rental property.

He wanted to work his dogs, but he didn't have any stock to work. As it was, there were quite a few people who had moved outside Portland and kept small acreages that were fenced in woven wire. They'd buy a few Barbados, which had become popular in the Northwest to keep the weeds from getting out of control, but not everybody's fences or dogs could handle them. The sheep would jump over the fences and away they would go. Mike started gathering stray flocks. He had a little pickup that got 30 miles to the gallon in which he could easily haul his dogs.

Mike quickly saw the opportunity for free grazing, so he bought some nice wool sheep. Land owners agreed to let him keep his sheep on their property. For a period of ten years he sold lambs and wool. He learned to shear his own sheep, so the biggest investment at that time was his labor. In the winter he'd decrease the size of his flock so he didn't have the extra expense of providing hay.

During the decade of the 1990s, he was able to supplement his income by giving weekend herding lessons. He gained experience with most of the common herding breeds.

Eventually, with the help of his dogs, he was able to put himself through college and buy his own little farm. "That is what real working dogs are like. They help you shoulder the load," Mike comments.

Today, he still maintains a small flock of Border Leister sheep. He has six dogs, Aussies and Borders combined. Through the years, the dogs kept him connected to his rural heritage while they also introduced him to a lot of new experiences and people.

Chapter 22

KEEPING LIVESTOCK

BASIC NEEDS OF TRAINING ANIMALS

No matter what class or breed, all livestock need good management. This includes adequate nutrition, shelter, and care.

Stress and Injury Prevention in Training Animals

Recognizing and reducing stress is paramount in the management of training and trial animals. Clean corrals—so stock is not standing in deep manure—are paramount in reducing stress and sickness. Rough handling practices increase stress and injury in livestock. Transporting livestock—combined with the novelty of new environments, such as at a test or trial event—can be a major cause of stress in animals. Proper conditioning is a huge factor in minimizing worry and keeping animals healthy. Livestock that are tired, hungry, thirsty, and worried have anxiety. Signs of stress include lethargic appearance, poor grooming, sickness and disease, and reduced feed intake.

Stress caused by temperature extremes such as cold weather can be diminished by providing appropriate environmental modifications (shelter or some type of wind break), as well as by increasing the fiber and caloric density in the feed and providing a readily available source of clean water.

Fencing

Fencing required by sheep and goats should keep them in and predators out. Woven wire or multi-strand electrified high-tensile wire (with three hot wires and two grounded wires) at least 42 inches tall—with a wire close to the ground—should help with predator control and prevent sheep or goats from crawling under the fence. Goats are more likely to crawl under than jump over fences. Existing fences can be fortified with an electric strand positioned approximately six inches above the ground. Goats are also more likely to get their horns caught in field fences (woven wire). They like to climb and can easily traverse a diagonal brace (deadman) to climb out of pens.

Shelter

Training stock does not require elaborate housing, but they do need clean, dry, draft-free shelter with adequate ventilation to insure protection from inclement weather and predators.

Everyone should have at least one book on the general care and maintenance for the livestock they will be working with. You can also contact the local Agriculture Extension office for advice on livestock care and management.

Water

Animals should have access to an adequate supply of clean water. When unlimited access is not available, always give water before feeding animals and allow them to drink at least three times a day. Water needs will vary according to the feed they eat and the weather. Keep water troughs clean.

Feed

Training stock should have a year-round supply of roughage, such as pasture or hay. Nutrient-rich feed contains more energy than a poor quality feed. In order to get the most out of training animals, they need sufficient nutrients to stay healthy and have energy. Different types of grasses offer different levels of protein, minerals, and vitamins.

Green growing grass contains adequate nourishment, but in a dry season grass contains few nutrients. During these times it may be necessary to supplement with additional feed in order to maintain healthy weight. Cake (processed feed) or molasses/mineral blocks provide a supplemental source of additional nutrients for ruminants. A salt and mineral block should be available to the animals.

During the winter months, hay or silage is an important source of feed for ruminants. Hay is grass and legumes that have been cut and sun dried. The best hay is prepared from young grasses. Straw is a poor feed and very little use to animals. Do not allow animals to eat old or musty feed. Take special precautions when introducing fresh green feed in the spring and summer to avoid bloat. Change feed slowly.

Keep the livestock's housing and grazing areas free of debris. Wire, nails, tin cans, and broken glass can cut the mouth, feet, and legs. Additionally, wire and nails can be ingested, injure the rumen, and pass through the wall into the heart and kill the animal. Plastic bags can cause the animal to choke or can block the stomach. Hay should be fed in a feeder so the animals do not urinate or defecate on feed that hasn't been cleaned up.

Bloat

Cows, sheep, and goats are ruminants. Ruminants are animals that chew their cud (regurgitate and re-chew their food) and characteristically have four stomach compartments. Bloat, also called acidosis (ruminal tympany), occurs from increased gas production when fermentation builds up in the rumen. The animal's left flank balloons out as the gas builds up, which is one of the main signs of bloat. It is usually associated with lush forage (particularly if the pasture is wet). Fresh clover and alfalfa are especially dangerous.

Keep the animal on its feet, propped between hay bales if necessary. It is helpful to massage the distended rumen through the abdominal wall. It may be necessary to treat by relieving ruminal pressure with a stomach tube and defoaming agents such as vegetable or mineral oil, followed by baking soda dissolved in water, or with agents like Poloxalene or Therabloat. To prevent bloat, avoid turning animals out on lush wet pastures first thing in the morning. Offer hay or dry grass before putting hungry animals out to graze.

Parasite Control

All animals kept in small or confined quarters are at greater risk of parasitic infection. They do better in open pasture conditions to minimize infections among the herd. This is especially important with goats, that normally don't have a high resistance to parasites.

Poor condition such as a rough hair coat, is one of the outward signs of parasites. Loose stools and other signs such as pale mucous membranes can indicate the presence of parasites. A regular deworming program is an important part of maintaining healthy herding stock.

Examining Teeth

It is important to routinely check the flock's mouths. Worn teeth or missing teeth will interfere with the animal's ability to eat and chew its cud. Animals with missing teeth will require special feeding.

To examine the teeth, grasp the lower jaw with one hand and lift the lips by placing the other hand on top of the nose; lift the lips with the thumb and forefinger on opposite sides of the animal's mouth. Don't block the nostrils. To inspect the top and bottom molars, you need to open the mouth wide.

Hoof Care

Walking naturally wears down the hoof, but the hoof is like a toenail. It grows continuously. If the hooves become overgrown the animal won't be able to walk properly. This will have an effect on training. Also, when animals are kept in confinement or wet conditions their feet may become infected, a condition known as foot rot. Foot rot can be painful and lead to lameness.

Trimming Hooves

Use hoof or rose trimming shears for sheep and goats. Scoop out any visible dirt or manure. Trim the excess hoof growth by taking a little off at a time. The hoof walls should be level with the foot pad. Take more off the toes and less off the heels. Avoid cutting too deep. Pink tissue indicates you are near the blood supply. Stop before you draw blood. If you cut too deeply and blood appears, stop and treat the hoof with blood clotting powder. Before releasing the animal, paint some Betadine on the foot.

In order to trim cow's hooves they must either be cast or restrained in a tilt table—unless they are halter broke, and then the leg can be lifted and tied. Do not attempt to trim cow's hooves unless you are trained, because there is a greater risk of injury if you are not. You can contact a veterinarian or a cooperative extension office to find a hoof trimmer in your area.

Horns

Horns can be budded or dehorned at the appropriate time; however, since the horns are a part of the skull, it can cause brain damage if not done correctly at the appropriate time. Because of this we recommend you consult a veterinarian or a competent breeder to show you how.

Shearing

Hair sheep naturally lose their fleece in the warmer months, but wool sheep need to be sheared. Shearing is the complete removal of the fleece by using electric or hand shears. If the wool is not removed, the wool will be lost in patches. In order to collect cashmere from goats, they must be combed by hand in the spring. Angora goats must be sheared every six months.

Denver, a Belgian Tervuren owned by Mary Lou Hayden, herding sheep that are shedding their fleece. PHOTO BY LORI HERBEL OF XP RANCH PHOTOGRAPHY.

Contact local sheep breeders or the State Agricultural Extension office to find a shearer in your area. They may be able to tell you about shearing workshops where you can learn to shear your own sheep.

Crutching (Tagging)

Crutching is the trimming away of any dirty or wet fleece from around the crotch (tail and anus) of the sheep. The soiled wool attracts flies, especially blow flies. These flies lay their eggs on the wool, and in a day or two maggots hatch and burrow into the skin and feed on the sheep's flesh. The sheep will become odorous and nervous, wriggling its tail and stamping its feet.

Maggots must be removed from an infected individual. Part the wool and look for the small holes where the maggots have gained entry into the skin. You need to press around the wound to push out the maggots. Once they have emerged, the wound needs to be treated with Betadine.

Methods of Restraint

When you need to catch a sheep or goat to trim its hooves or to doctor it, you must work purposely, but quietly. In order to keep livestock disease resistant you should minimize handling stress as much as possible. It is easier to catch an individual when it is in a group in a small enclosure. Don't grab sheep by the wool, because you will bruise them. Instead, approach the animal from its blind spot (at the rear). Grasp the animal under the lower jaw with one hand. Lift the head upward, then clutch the rear flank or dock (tail) with the other hand for better control. Lifting the head shifts the animal's balance so you can control it more easily.

Once the animal is secured, turn its head away from you towards the outside flank, all the way to its shoulder. At the same time, press down on the animal's hip, then swing the animal towards you as you step backwards to set the animal on its rump.

Now that the animal's weight is on its rump, grasp the front legs and pull the animal into a sitting position. Make sure you position the animal on the rump, but off center so it is sitting on its hip rather than directly on its tail. Cradle its shoulders between your legs as you trim the feet.

If the animal struggles, grasp the brisket to move it into a more relaxed position (off center). The animal will be more comfortable when you enable its head to sag to the right and its body to slouch to the left to allow the rumen to expand.

Ducks and Geese

During the day ducks and geese can roam the farm yard free ranging. Otherwise they should be kept in a shaded fenced area. Either way, at night

Since ducks have no teeth, their food is swallowed whole and goes into the craw (or crop) where it is stored and mixed with saliva. The feed passes from the crop into the stomach, where it mixes with juices and is then passed to the gizzard, where it is ground up for digestion. Birds don't urinate. Waste from their kidneys mixes with their feces and is passed out through droppings. Duck droppings will be wetter than that of chickens, for example.

they should be enclosed in a covered pen to keep them from being victims of foxes and other predators. A four-by-ten foot ready-made kennel run may be adequate for a small flock of a half dozen or so ducks.

A pond is ideal for ducks and geese, but not necessary as long as they have a small wading pool. At the very least they need a water trough where they can dip their heads and necks into the water.

It is better to provide a small, clean bathing area than a large body of polluted, stagnant water. Most geese prefer shallow pools or a sloping ramp rather than steep banks for ease of getting out of the water. You may want to consider building an easily drained pond.

If ducks and geese are actively foraging for grasses and insects, then cracked corn or chicken scratch should be an adequate supplementation. They also enjoy fresh fruit and vegetable scraps. In the winter months when foraging is poor they'll require more supplementation. A mixture of hen scratch and laying feed may be adequate. Ducks and geese become weak and have difficulty walking properly when fed an insufficient diet.

Ducks and geese can get sore footed working on rough terrain. In the old droving days when driving them to markets, drovers would herd the geese through a mixture of soft tar and sand to protect their feet once the mixture hardened. A foot or pad conditioner containing tincture of Benzoin can be sprayed on the soles of ducks and geese to help protect them from injury.

Keep ducklings separate from adults (even if it is a hen with ducklings of her own) until they are older, because the adults may peck and kill them. Ducklings are easy prey for predator birds, hawks and owls, so provide adequate cover.

Wing Trimming

You can trim the feathers of one wing to prevent ducks from flying. Spread the wing and clip the tips of the flight feathers. Only trim about half the length on the last joint; be sure you don't trim the joint.

Introducing New Livestock to Dogs (Dog Breaking)

Whenever you obtain new stock, be sure to condition them to dogs over a period of several days in a controlled situation before turning them out to pasture. Feeding time is a good time to gentle your livestock. Once the animals have been fed, you can walk your dog around the perimeter of the feeding area. If the animals are nervous, they will be reluctant to eat, but when they realize that your dog isn't going to harm them, they will soon relax and become accustomed to having a dog around. If possible, work the new animals with a group of dog-broke stock. They will be much easier to handle later on.

Loida's Just Plain Charlie moving Brahma calves quietly to gentle them. PHOTO COURTESY CINDY LOIDA.

Livestock Guardians (Dogs, Donkeys, and Llamas)

Dogs, donkeys, and llamas have been successfully used to protect livestock from predators and livestock thieves. Dogs are considered the most successful method for livestock guarding. While the agile little stockdogs excel in herding, the larger guard dogs are ideally suited for protecting livestock. The guarding instincts, like the herding instincts, cannot be taught or instilled, only extracted and developed if they exist within each individual. These guardians have an independent nature and don't seek out human companionship.

Hugo, a Sharplaniac Livestock Guard Dog (LGD), watching over a flock.

Training or conditioning begins shortly after birth. Some guard dogs are raised on a ewe or nanny, which broadens their affinity for the sheep or goats they will be guarding. Since they eat and sleep among the stock, it is not surprising that they probably think of themselves as one of the flock and take a subordinate place in the group rather than a dominant one.

They live as members of the flock, staying with the animals day and night year-round. They are content to be among the grazing flock or herd, watching unconcernedly. If their charges get up and move, either during the day or night, the dogs follow. They don't try to stop them or "herd" them back. They simply accompany them and keep watch wherever they go. They become a member of the group and defend it from all threats.

Maternal instincts play an important role. Livestock guarding dogs protect their charges as most mothers would protect their young, therefore they will not leave the flock very far to apprehend an offender . . . even when the cunning coyote tries to lure the guardian away. A common tactic a coyote uses is to split the flock—and when the livestock guarding dog goes with one bunch, the coyotes attack the second unprotected group.

Disadvantages of using guard dogs are that they bark at anything they may perceive as an intruder, and some can be aggressive with other dogs and people, which can be a problem in areas with dense populations.

One fall on the Taylor ranch, when I was helping one of the herders move a large band of sheep (1,500 head) out of Utah to Colorado, we had two stockdogs to herd the sheep and three guard dogs, a Maremma and two Sharplaniac, to watch over them. When we were moving the flock, the guard dogs simply followed along.

These dogs remain placid until an outside influence disturbs the serenity. Their authoritative presence provides the initial protection; if that in itself fails to be effective, these dogs are capable of handling themselves in physical combat with an enemy.

We came across a small cow/calf herd on the canyon trail near Gateway. The guard dogs charged the cows. The mother cows fought the dogs to protect their calves. I'd never been in that situation before. There was no way we could call off the dogs, so the only thing I could do was to move the sheep. As soon as we moved the sheep a very short distance away from the cows, the dogs quietly followed along.

Just Jake hard at work herding the flock, while the Sharplaniac and Maremma livestock guard dogs follow along.

Donkeys

We've used donkeys to guard sheep on our family's ranch in Kiowa, Colorado. Although not all donkeys are good guardians, the ones we've used—wild ones we adopted from the BLM—have been fierce protectors of the flock. The instinct to protect is natural and cannot be trained.

They bond with the sheep and graze along side of them. If a coyote comes near the sheep, they bray, pin their ears back, drop their head, and run them off. They will bite, kick and stomp intruders. Some of the donkeys won't even tolerate the herding dogs, which can be a problem.

Donkeys don't require special feed. They eat what the sheep eat. They will need to have their hooves trimmed and require annual vaccinations for common equine diseases. Other than that, they are highly cost effective.

Intact males (jacks) can be too aggressive, so a gelded jack or a jenny is the best choice. A single donkey is more likely to bond with the sheep than two or more donkeys. They are most effective in pastures where the flock is cohesive.

Llamas

Our experience with llamas is limited. I once worked a flock of sheep guarded by two llamas, a mature one and a younger one. My dogs were able to outmaneuver them. The llamas were alert to their whereabouts and ran towards them. They alert the flock to danger and defend them by chasing, pawing or kicking at the predator. Positioning themselves between the sheep and dogs, they tried to herd the sheep away. Some sheep producers find llamas effective in protecting their sheep against predators.

Multiple guard llamas are not as effective as one llama. Problems associated with llamas include aggressiveness and attempted breeding of ewes (unless castrated). It is recommended to use females or gelded males. Llamas work best in fenced pastures of less than 300 acres and should be introduced to sheep or goats in a corral rather than in the open pastures. Also, they don't require any special feed.

Chapter 23

THE TRIAL DOG

Early sheepdog trials in Britain—heavily influenced by upper-class values concerning the nature of the shepherd's craft—were sponsored as an adjunct to the aristocratic kennel club-style dog shows. The first recorded sheepdog trial took place at Bala, Wales, in the fall of 1873, with 300 spectators braving the wet and the cold to watch the competition.

Herding trials were introduced to America during the 1880 Centennial Celebration in Philadelphia, but didn't become common until after the development of the International Sheep Dog Society in 1906, when farmers and shepherds who made practical use of dogs took over the direction of the sport, giving emphasis to the dog's ability to work both independently and as a partner to the shepherd.

The term "herding" was not commonly used to describe working dogs in the United States until 1983, when the American Kennel Club divided its Working Group classification. Until that time, herding dogs were known as working dogs, and farmers and ranchers commonly referred to them as sheepdogs, cowdogs, or stockdogs. Herding is what the dogs did. The term "herder" referred to the human part of a working team.

The Australian Shepherd Club of America (ASCA) Stockdog Program was drafted in the early 1970s out of a desire to preserve and maintain the working instincts in Australian Shepherds. With livestock increasingly being handled on large feedlots rather than ranches, fewer ranch jobs were available—and more Australian Shepherds were finding their way into suburbia, putting the breed at a fork in the road.

The ASCA's Stockdog Committee realized that the majority of owners at that time had no opportunity to work their dogs and no viable means to test the working instincts of their bloodlines. The program was initially organized to test and verify the breed's instinct and working ability. It was intended to be an evaluation program rather than a competitive activity and was meant to document herding characteristics and working style as a reference for breeders. Testing included all three categories of stock (cattle,

Las Rocosa Pecos, owned by Lisa Hartnagle, testing his skills working Barbados crosses at an ASCA trial in New Mexico. PHOTO BY DIANE DECKER.

sheep, and poultry), giving everyone, including the person who had only a small backyard and a few ducks, an equal opportunity to obtain certification.

In 1973, the Australian Shepherd Club in Colorado and the Stock Dog Fanciers of Colorado hosted the first-ever all-breed Cattle, Sheep, and Duck Trials, where dogs demonstrated their skills at gathering from a pasture, working in corrals, and loading chutes. One of the classes offered at these early trials was Sub-novice Poultry, for people who had never worked stock before. With this new activity now available, prospects looked better for fanciers who wanted to maintain the breed's identity as an outstanding stockdog.

In 1989 the AKC implemented a herding program to provide sanctioned events for AKC-recognized herding breeds (plus Rottweilers and Samoyeds); the program was based strongly on the success of the ASCA Stockdog Program. Until this time many of the herding breeds hadn't been used to work livestock in generations, being bred instead for show ring standards, but over the past two decades participation in herding events has grown by leaps and bounds.

Note: "Herding trials" usually refers to AKC Herding Events, and "stock-dog trials" is the preferred term of the ASCA Stockdog Program, but for the purpose of this discussion, the term "herding" will be used in its general sense (unless specifically referring to the AKC).

Until 1983, the AKC included herding breeds in the Working Group; the Herding Group was created when the Working Group's size became unwieldy. Breeds with a clear herding heritage, such as the Collie, Welsh Corgi, and Belgian Sheepdog were readily transferred to the Herding Group. Breeds such as the Giant Schnauzer and Rottweiler, which had been used for guarding, pulling carts and sleds and water rescue, remained in the Working Group. Australian Shepherds and Border Collies, primarily used as ranching and farm dogs, were not recognized by the AKC until the 1990s.

TRAITS THAT MAKE A GOOD TRIAL DOG

Competitive trialing is demanding. Not all dogs have what it takes to undergo trial training. Competing successfully requires a dog with desire and strong inner drive. The ideal trial prospect is a middle of the road dog (compliant, but responsive). This type of dog will learn quickly, and respond well to training. He is outgoing and adaptable, does fine with the novice trainer and excels with an experienced handler. When corrected he demonstrates good humor and readily bounces back by seeking his handler's attention. Even if this type of dog is somewhat reserved (but biddable) he will most likely exhibit a strong desire to please and will be fairly flexible in training.

When choosing a team of dogs for brace competition, consider the

The Border Collie, the king of open sheepdog trials, now dominates arena trials across North America. Conroy's Cato, a farm dog, driving sheep along a perimeter fence at a trial against the backdrop of a Minnesota landscape. PHOTO BY LORI HERBEL OF XP RANCH PHOTOGRAPHY.

Jeanne Joy working a team of dogs—WTCH Las Rocosa Bonny Kyle RDX and HOF Twin Oaks Tiara—in a brace competition at the 1989 Silver Bullet trial in Galt, California. PHOTO BY CEE HAMBO.

Eligible Herding Breeds

The AKC currently recognizes 22 dog breeds in the Herding Group, with others in the Miscellaneous Class (pending recognition) and about a dozen as Foundation Stock Service (FSS) breeds, which means that breed standards, bloodlines, and registries are in the development phase. In addition to the recognized herding breeds, other breeds are eligible for herding events—including general purpose dogs with herding backgrounds from the Working Group, such as the Rottweiler and Samoyed.

Other breeds eligible to compete in herding trials are not limited to dogs in the Working Group. The Spanish Water Dog, which retrieves waterfowl in marshy regions and works upland game, was assigned to the Sporting Group, but is primarily a herding breed. The plucky, long-legged Kerry Blue Terrier (used successfully in the nineteenth century to tend livestock) is also eligible to compete in herding events.

A lot of the breeds described in the profile section, while not recognized by the AKC, have long and distinguished histories in their country of origin; many are recognized by the Fédération Cynologique Internationale (FCI) and are eligible to compete in AHBA Trials, AKC Herding Events, and the ASCA Stock Dog Program, as well as FCI-sponsored traditional style tests and trials.

temperament of the dogs. A sensitive dog needing a lot of bolstering can be easily shut down when working with a strong, dominant dog requiring the handler's constant guidance.

STARTING OUT IN COMPETITION

While many people compete in trials sanctioned by national groups (as described in a following chapter), it is often easier and less nerve-wracking to begin competing in some of the numerous events hosted by local clubs, including fun trials, arena and field trials, and the popular point and time trials, where competitors receive points for each head of stock that completes an obstacle along the course in a set amount of time. Timed events have similar courses, but an obstacle time or course time is used to determine the winners instead of points per head per obstacle.

Each organization has its own course layouts, rules, and regulations. The American Herding Breed Association (AHBA), Australian Shepherd Club of America (ASCA), American Kennel Club (AKC), Canadian Kennel Club (CKC), and the United States Border Collie Handlers' Association (US-BCHA), as well as individual breed clubs, can all recommend local affiliate clubs, stockdog associations, and various herding groups where you can become acquainted with herding activities.

Instinct Testing
For many people, instinct tests are their first introduction to livestock and the world of herding. Tests can take place at a sanctioned event, a herding clinic, or a trainer's facility. Sanctioned events are officiated by a tester who is approved through the sponsoring association; otherwise, instinct tests are primarily informal tests, perhaps given as a dog is being introduced to stock while at a herding clinic or trainer's facility.

The objective is to determine whether or not the dog demonstrates the instincts appropriate for herding—to keep stock grouped. For example, if the stock gets split, the tester will watch to see if the dog attempts to head them off and regroup them. As to be expected, breed differences have to be taken into consideration.

Do not put a dog in a strange situation on an unfamiliar stock-instinct test when the dog is going through an insecure period of life; a bad encounter can have a lifetime effect. The ideal age for testing is at least one year of age, or when the dog has gone through puberty. A dog that shows a desire to herd or an interest in livestock isn't necessarily physically or mentally mature enough yet to outmaneuver the animals. Even at a year of age, some dogs are immature and just want to play instead of herd. Some pups don't show any desire at all at first, but it doesn't hurt to let them watch other dogs being tested or worked and then retest them at a later date.

The Test Itself. When a dog is instinct tested in AKC, he is brought into the arena on a 6-to-15-foot-long (1.8–4.6 m) line. The dog must demonstrate a stop (*down*, *sit*, or *stand*) and a recall before the line is dropped or removed. The elements for certification are described later in this chapter.

Generally, a circular pen is used to keep a soft, hesitant dog in contact with the livestock. If the dog is more direct and tries to chase the stock, the pen allows the tester to be in a better position to keep the dog from endangering the animals.

The person conducting the test needs to be adaptable to the dog's response and to act accordingly. When a dog is tentative or soft, the tester may instruct the handler to step in and encourage him. Or it may be necessary to back away to keep from inhibiting the dog. If the dog is forceful, the tester needs to protect the livestock without dispiriting him.

If the dog shows little or no interest, the tester may create awareness by moving the animals around or instructing you to do so. If the dog gets distracted, redirect his attention, if possible. Make an exciting noise (hand clapping, whistling, hissing, etc.) while walking toward the stock or moving the stock toward the dog.

Instinct testers must be adaptable to the dog's response and act accordingly. Jim Hartnagle working with Janet Cowan and her pup that shows strong herding drive.

The stock, which should be dog broke, can be an important element for instinct testing. Some dogs are turned on by one type of livestock but not another—maybe sheep or goats entice the dog when he won't even look at ducks. Others may be intimidated by sheep but motivated by ducks or cattle.

Assertiveness versus Predatory

While bite inhibition resistance to flock excitement must be developed through training, testers need to be able to recognize signs of true aggression. Confident, assertive dogs that intimidate the stock by the power of their presence should not be confused with dogs with detrimental predatory instincts. Sometimes the presence of a strong dog can be alarming to stock, even if he is merely standing at the owner's side. When the stock becomes disturbed, the dog may become anxious; this could further panic the animals and increase the potential for chasing and indiscriminate biting. The tester will have to be quick to protect the animals and may want to muzzle the dog to keep them from being injured.

A lamb reacting to the power and presence of Gabe, a confident Rottweiler. In a different circumstance, such as a small pen, this would cause an explosive situation. PHOTO BY BECKY PARKER OF DALLY UP PHOTOGRAPHY.

Some dogs are quite intense about livestock yet have little or no herding instincts. They may be very rough and bite severely and indiscriminately. This kind of dog will never be a trustworthy herding dog, regardless of the level of obedience attained. The type of bite and aggression needed for Ring Sport and police work is different from the grip desired for herding.

PROBLEM SOLVING:
Dog is belligerent with other dogs or people

Having a male neutered will not decrease territorial guarding, but it can reduce the tendency for aggression toward other male dogs. A dog with strong guarding instincts, bred to protect his master's flocks and herds from predators (coyotes, bears, wild dogs, and thieves), may not be sociable or want to play with strange dogs that run up to greet him. However, these dogs need to be trained well enough to be under their handler's control at all times.

About the fourth month, a dog is mentally mature and his character is largely shaped. However, his territorial instincts don't surface until sometime between 6 and 14 months. When that happens he can start becoming protective, and his level of aggression becomes more apparent. Fence fighting between dogs in adjacent pens or yards may occur at home.

Aggressive behavior can be made worse in public if the dog acts aggressive when he sees other dogs or people and is allowed to pull or keep tension on the leash. Don't let him do it. The tension on the leash triggers the dog's guarding behavior. Give him a sharp jerk and release. At the same time tell him, "Noooo" in a sharp, stern tone. Let him know in no unnecessary terms that this type of behavior is unacceptable. You must follow through consistently. Appropriate handling is necessary if your dog is to become reliable.

Teach him to sit or stand quietly on a relaxed lead. If you are experiencing behavior issues, don't invite (or let) the general public come up and pet your dog. Do not take a chance and allow someone to get nipped. Make sure you seek experienced dog people who are capable and willing to help you work through the problem. Conversely, even if your dog is friendly, you should not allow him to run up to other dogs or people uninvited. It is not always appreciated.

Chapter 24

TRIAL PROGRAMS

ORGANIZATIONS HOSTING TESTS AND TRIALS

Hundreds of trials are held year-round throughout the country, organized mainly by the AHBA, AKC, ASCA, CKC, and the USBCHA. Each of these associations has affiliate clubs at regional and local levels. A variety of classes at different training levels (from started to advanced) are available from a number of different associations. All dogs are required to perform the same work on the same course under the same scoring and rules, although requirements may vary slightly from one trial or organization to another.

AMERICAN KENNEL CLUB (AKC)

The American Kennel Club is the oldest purebred dog registry in the United States. AKC-sanctioned or licensed herding events are open to AKC registered dogs and dogs that hold Limited Exhibition Privilege (LEP) numbers. Herding dogs can earn titles at each level of the Herding Program: Herding Started (HS), Herding Intermediate (HI), and Herding Excellent (HX). The titles are distinguished by the type of stock or course.

Dogs qualify for the HS, HI, and HX titles by earning three qualifying scores under different judges at different trials. In order to qualify, dogs must receive at least 50 percent of the possible points in each category and a total score between 60 and a possible 100 on one of the three courses offered. Each course—A, B, or C—can be used for any level of testing, so that advanced dogs compete on the same general course as intermediate level or started dogs do, but as they progress up the ladder, they will have added requirements and increasing difficulty.

AKC Course A. This is an all-around farm or ranch course designed to demonstrate the versatility of a herding dog. It consists of an outrun, a lift, and a fetch or drive. After executing the gather and a turn around the first marker, the dog moves the stock through a series of chutes past different markers or posts indicating changes of direction. The course is completed when the stock are penned; the dog must hold the stock while the handler opens the gate. Dogs can earn qualifying scores on sheep, cattle, or ducks. The distance the dog must work from his handler increases with each level of difficulty.

AKC Course B. This is an open field trial demonstrating the dog's ability to control stock in an unfenced area. It consists of a 150- to 300-foot (45.7–91.4 m) outrun for sheep and cattle (60 to 100 feet [18.3–30.5 m] for ducks), a lift, a fetch, a turn around the handler's post, a fetch through two gates, and a pen and holding exercise for beginning dogs. The intermediate level includes a 250- to 600-foot (76.2–182.9 m) outrun for sheep and cattle (80 to 125 feet [24.4–38.1 m] for ducks) and adds a drive in the place of the second fetching exercise, followed by a hold and pen. Dogs at the advanced level must show their ability to make a 350-foot to 1,200-foot (106.7–365.8 m) outrun on sheep or cattle (100 to 150 feet [30.5–45.7 m] for ducks) in addition to the drive required in the intermediate level, and a cross-drive followed by a pen and shedding exercise.

Sadie, handled by Kent Herbel, negotiating a Maltese cross during the Herding Challenge at the 2005 BCSA National Specialty at Purina Farms. Steadiness is required by both dog and handler to keep the animals moving in one direction.
PHOTO BY LORI HERBEL OF XP RANCH PHOTOGRAPHY.

AKC Course C. This course is designed as a tending course. The dog moves a flock of no fewer than 20 sheep to different unfenced grazing areas, over a bridge and across a road, and then pauses and holds the flock in an open field. The sheep must be allowed to graze quietly while contained within boundaries and then must be safely moved on roads between those areas. The dog must keep sheep from trespassing onto prohibited fields and must be able to stop the flock for entrance onto a road with traffic.

The Beginner class on Course C is between 440 and 540 yards (402.3–493.8 m) long. Exercises include exit from a pen, a narrow road, and a bridge; a traffic pause, a wide graze, and a re-pen, all in a 30-minute time allotment. The Intermediate class adds placement before the flock (meaning that the handler positions the dog at the front of the flock) before the penning exercise, and allows 45 minutes on a course of 540 to 780 yards (493.8–713.2 m). Dogs in the Advanced class compete on a 780- to 880-yard (713.2–804.7 m) course with a 45-minute time allotment.

AKC Herding Champion Certificate

Once the dog has earned his HX title, he's eligible to compete for a Herding Champion certificate (HC). The Herding Championship is awarded to dogs that have been awarded an HX title and have earned a total of 15 points in advanced classes by finishing first through fourth place, with at least two first-place wins. Dogs that garner a Herding Championship can continue to compete in advanced classes.

AKC Instinct Tests. The AKC also offers two noncompetitive titles, Herding Tested (HT) and Pre-trial Tested (PT).

The Herding Test is scored on a pass or fail basis. In order to qualify for the HT title, dogs must pass the test on two separate occasions with two different judges. The test permits trainers to demonstrate the breed's natural herding instincts, as the dog is judged on its ability to control livestock and to move the stock in a set pattern. Handlers must demonstrate the dog's ability to stop or pause on command and make two changes of direction while controlling the movement of the stock. The test is completed with a stop, followed by a recall.

The Pre-trial title is also a noncompetitive test scored by two different judges. It allows novice handlers to gain experience in the trial arena and to show the dog's readiness (although not fully advanced by training) to herd stock under the control of his handler at a level just below the beginning trial level. The elements of the test are a controlled pause or stay, moving stock past four obstacles, a change of direction, and a stop on the course during the process of penning the stock. The test is completed when the stock are re-penned.

AUSTRALIAN SHEPHERD CLUB OF AMERICA (ASCA)

The Australian Shepherd Club of America is the largest single-breed registry in the country. Stockdog trials hosted by ASCA-affiliated clubs are open to Australian Shepherds and ASCA-approved herding breeds. To be eligible for certification, entrants other than ASCA-registered Aussies must have an ASCA tracking number. A dog is graded on the manner and efficiency that he displays as he herds a group of 3 to 10 head of livestock through a set of obstacles and back into a holding pen.

ASCA offers stock dog titles in three classes of stock (cattle, sheep or goats, and ducks or geese) at different levels: Started (Started Trial Dog—STD), Open (Open Trial Dog—OTD), Advanced (Advanced Trial Dog—ATD), and Post Advanced (Post Advanced Trial Dog—PATD). To title, the dog must receive two qualifying scores (at least 69 points out of a possible 100 for Started and 88 points out of a possible 125 for Open and Advanced) under two different judges. Each title indicates the class of stock it was earned on; for example, STDc (cattle), OTDs (sheep), or ATDd (ducks).

ASCA Started Division. Even though a Started Dog may have little or no trial experience, he should be able to "walk up" on command, exhibit a certain degree of control over livestock, and demonstrate a basic understanding of left- and right-side commands. Started dogs should respond to the control of their handler and should be able to demonstrate a reliable stop as necessary. Started dogs are not required to negotiate the center chute or center freestanding pen.

ASCA Open Division. When dogs move on to the Open level, they should be able to control and rate livestock. The side commands should be ingrained, and the handler should be able to command the dog to stop and change his pace while working at a greater distance from the handler. There is a handler's line, indicating where the handler may not cross (without penalty). Open dogs should be able to demonstrate a solid fetch, a cross-drive, and the beginning of a drive.

ASCA Advanced Division. An Advanced level dog should demonstrate good teamwork and be able to read, rate, and control livestock with minimum stress. He should respond appropriately to the handler's command from no less a distance than the Advanced Handler's line (the distance is determined by the size of the arena.) The outrun/gather, lift, fetch, drive, and cross-drive should be well established.

ASCA Post Advanced Division. Post Advanced is an optional division for sheep (or goats) and cattle that is run on a course of approximately six acres (2.4 hectares). The Post Advanced Trial Dog should be solid and capable of handling the class of livestock, regardless of flight zones and without the aid of a fence, at any distance on the trial course from his handler.

In addition, ASCA offers a **Ranch Trial Dog** (RTD) title through the Ranch Trial Program with sheep, goats, or cattle. Ranch courses can vary throughout the country, but the program was set up to simulate actual ranch work. To earn the RTD title, a dog has 20 minutes to handle no fewer than 10 head while performing the minimum requirements of pen work, sorting, and chute work, in a pasture situation of at least 5 acres (2 hectares). To qualify, he must earn 75 percent of the 100 points available.

An aerial view of Sherry Baker working with WTCH Twin Oaks Kit Carson RDX, RTDsc, competing at a Ranch Dog Trial in 1994. PHOTO BY CEE HAMBO.

ASCA introduced the **Farm Trial Dog** Program to provide a venue where Australian Shepherds and other breeds can display practical skills as all-around stockdogs. Dogs can earn titles in two divisions, Open Farm Trial Dog (OFTD) and Advanced Farm Trial Dog (AFTD) with cattle, sheep/goats, and fowl (ducks, geese, chickens, and turkeys). Dogs will be required to perform four mandatory tasks: pen work, sorting, chute work, and gathering, plus two additional tasks in the allotted 10 or 20 minutes. No two Farm Trial courses will be laid out exactly the same due to variances in different farm designs.

Dogs are judged on efficiency, attitude, and teamwork. Titles are earned when a dog receives two qualifying scores, with 70 percent of total points available (91 points), on two different farm courses under two different judges.

The ASCA Ranch Dog Inspection Program

The Ranch Dog program (RD) is only for owners who use their dogs in actual working situations on a ranch or farm, in the stockyards, at auctions, rodeos, and related-type work. It is not a competitive program, but rather an inspection designed to recognize stockdogs that help their masters do their jobs on a daily basis. While these dogs are not polished trial dogs, they are invaluable to their owners as they assist in real-world operations.

Dogs can earn the distinction of Ranch Dog on sheep, goats, or cattle from an ASCA-approved judge. The test should demonstrate the ultimate teamwork between dog and handler as they gather, sort, move, pen, and load livestock in chutes, corrals, and pastures in ranch work.

ASCA Working Trial Championship

The Working Trial Championship (WTCh) title is for dogs that have earned Advanced degrees in all three classes of livestock—cattle, ducks, and sheep.

ASCA Course A: The dog moves 3 to 10 head of sheep or cattle out of the "take" pen into the arena and then moves them in a drive or fetch counterclockwise around the perimeter of the arena (minimum size, 100 feet by 200 feet [30.5–61 m]), through the first panel at the top end. (*Note:* The layout for ducks in ASCA is the same for all courses, except that the minimum size is 60 feet by 90 feet [18.3 by 27.4 m], with a seven-minute time limit.) He continues in a cross-drive or fetch to a second set of panels on

The ASCA Ranch Dog Inspection Program tests the dog's ability to work in actual working situations on the ranch. COURTESY MINDY BOWER.

the left side of the top end, and then down through a Y-shaped center chute to re-pen the stock, with a 10-minute time limit.

ASCA Course B. Scoring begins when the dog is released to gather 3 to 10 head of sheep or cattle from the bottom of the arena. He then moves them clockwise to the opposite end of the arena, through the first set of panels, and to the second set of panels in a cross-drive or fetch to the right side. When the stock exits the second set of panels, the handler must move them into a freestanding pen in the middle of the arena. They are then re-penned at the bottom of the arena. There's a 10-minute time limit.

ASCA Course C. The course is laid out in an arena of a minimum size of 150 feet by 250 feet (45.7 by 76.2 m) for sheep or cattle. Handlers competing on Course C with a right-hand chute move stock up the middle of the arena until the stock are parallel to the opening of the first obstacle. They continue though the opening in a counterclockwise circle toward the second obstacle, moving toward the chute, which is reversed if the course has a left-hand chute. Once the chute is negotiated, stock is moved to the re-pen to complete the run.

AMERICAN HERDING BREED ASSOCIATION (AHBA)

The American Herding Breed Association offers herding instinct tests and a trial program—both of which are open to all herding breeds and breed mixes. The Herding Capability Tested (HCT) and the Junior Herding Dog (JHD) are instinct titles, judged on a pass or fail basis under two different testers. Tests may be held on sheep, goats, ducks, geese, or cattle. Unlike trial titles, legs earned on different types of stock may count toward a single title.

AHBA Herding Capability Test. The first leg of the HCT does not require formal training. The dog must demonstrate natural herding instincts and the desire to keep stock grouped together and manage their movement. The test takes place in a small arena; the tester may handle the dog instead of the dog's usual handler. The second leg of the HCT requires that the dog also move the stock in a controlled fashion from one end of a pen to the other and demonstrate a stop and a recall. In the second test the owner handles the dog.

AHBA Junior Herding Dog. The JHD test is held in a larger area. The owner handles his own dog. The dog collects and controls stock, moves stock in straight lines and turns, negotiates two corner panel obstacles and a free-standing pen in the center of the arena, and makes a reliable stop on command at the re-pen. The handler is allowed to accompany the dog and stock throughout the course.

AHBA Trial Program. There are four classes in the AHBA Trial Program, each with three levels of difficulty: Herding Trial Dog (HTD), Herding Ranch Dog (HRD), Ranch Large Flock (RLF), and Herding Trial Arena Dog (HTAD). All trial titles require two qualifying scores under two different judges. The dog can earn titles on cattle, ducks, sheep, goats, geese, or turkeys; the stock class is indicated after the title; e.g., HTD–cattle.

AHBA Herding Trial Dogs work on a course that includes an outrun, lift, fetch, wear and/or drive, and pen. The pen may be on the fence at the started level, but is freestanding for higher levels. At Level I the outrun is short, and the handler may accompany the dog and stock throughout the course. The outrun is longer for Level II, and the handler may accompany the dog and stock for only part of the course. In Level III the outrun is still longer, and the handler remains at the handler's post until penning. After the pen, there is a sorting exercise, in which the handler must remove a ribbon from a marked sheep to demonstrate the dog's ability to hold an animal to its handler. When cattle or ducks are used, one or more animals are separated and held apart briefly from the group to demonstrate the dog's ability to control livestock and work as a team with his handler.

The **AHBA Herding Ranch Dog** program offers work on various ranch- or farm-type courses. Tasks include a gather, fetch/drive, pen, sorting (in Level III only), and a variety of other elements such as chutes, bridges, and holding stock in a combination of pens, arenas, and open fields. The three levels are differentiated by the position of the handler and the variation in exercises or the addition of tasks.

The **AHBA Ranch Large Flock** program is similar to the HRD except that dogs work larger numbers of stock.

AHBA Herding Trial Champion Peaslee's Honey, an English Shepherd working on the AHBA RLF course. PHOTO BY ELSIE RHODES.

AHBA Herding Trial Championship

A dog earns a Herding Trial Championship (HTCh) by obtaining 10 additional qualifying scores in the advanced classes after a Level III title is earned. He may earn the HTCh on one type of stock or a combination of different types, including up to three scores allowed on ducks.

The **AHBA Herding Trial Arena Dog** program offers four basic courses designed for arenas with established minimum and maximum sizes. The foundation of each course includes either a gathering of stock from the arena or from a take pen, a variety of three different obstacles, a drive segment at Levels II and III, and some type of stock sorting.

Janet Cowan applauding her Aussie on a job well done! PHOTO BY DEB CONROY.

THE CANADIAN KENNEL CLUB (CKC)

USBCHA, AHBA, and ASCA trials are held throughout Canada, but the CKC herding program offers an all-breed set of courses specifically for CKC-registered dogs, as well as ones that have an event registration number or are in the miscellaneous-class list approved for herding trials. The program provides a test level (Herding Tested—HT) and three trial levels for dogs working with sheep, cattle, and ducks. Dogs can begin competing at any level, but once a dog earns a qualifying leg, he is no longer eligible to compete at a lower level.

The trial levels are Herding Started (HS), Herding Intermediate (HI), and Herding Advanced (HA), and all three levels are competitive. The dog must successfully complete each exercise and earn three qualifying scores (75 points, with no incomplete sections) under at least two different judges. Certain requirements are standard for each trial, although the course design may vary from trial to trial. Once the HA title is acquired and the dog has earned 15 championship points (according to a published point schedule) with at least two first-class placements under different judges in Advanced classes, the dog is awarded the Herding Champion (HC) title. The Herding Excellent title (HX) is earned by scoring 85 or above in the Advanced class under at least three different judges.

CKC also offers Stock Dog and Herding Tending titles. Stock Dog Started (SDS), Stock Dog Intermediate (SDI) and Stock Dog Advanced (SDA) are earned when the dog receives a qualifying score in three trials under a minimum of two judges. The Herding Tending titles are Herding Tested–Tending (HTT), Herding Started–Tending (HST), Herding Intermediate–Tending (HIT), and Herding Advanced–Tending (HAT). At the test level (Herding Tested–Tending which is noncompetitive), the dog must pass two tests under two different judges in a Tested level at tending trials. For herding Started–Tending (HST), Herding Intermediate–Tending (HIT) and Herding Advanced–Tending (HAT), the dog must pass in three tending trials under a minimum of two different judges at each particular level.

The CKC Herding Test (HT) is a noncompetitive program that requires two different judges to pass the dog. The dog picks up the stock in a calm, controlled manner and takes them to the handler, who is allowed to walk around each obstacle while the dog moves the stock. The dog must demonstrate a brief pause and a stop along the way and take the stock through fence-line obstacles. The stock is penned at the end of the course. The judge is in the arena and is allowed to walk with the handler or stand off to one side. Judges may make suggestions but may not handle the dog. The title available at the test level is the Herding Tested (HT).

CKC Herding Started. In the HS test dogs must take stock out of the take pen, control the stock (fetch or drive) on a fence line, and stop when asked, even if "off balance." The handler may not walk through any of the obstacles except for a chute. The dog must hold stock at the exhaust pen and then re-pen them. The exhaust pen is an enclosure, usually along the fence, where animals are deposited after the run. It may or may not be the same enclosure as the take pen, where the stock waits at the beginning of the run.

Faye Unrau's Aussie re-penning cattle at Tucker Creek Farms. PHOTO BY DEB CONROY.

CKC Herding Intermediate. The dog must be under good handler control. He must calmly take the stock from a pen. He is called off the stock to wait until the judge decides that they have sufficiently settled. The dog is positioned about 50 feet (15 m) from the stock to execute an outrun, lift, and fetch to the handler—and then moves the stock through the obstacles, drives them along a fence line and through a freestanding chute, holds them at the exhaust pen, and re-pens them.

CKC Herding Advanced. The dog negotiates a take pen, drive, settle, a 150-foot (45.7 m) outrun, lift, fetch, three obstacles along the fence, a freestanding obstacle, and an exhaust pen. The handler is required to stand at a line that runs through the center point of the arena as the dog works the obstacles at the far end. The handler is not allowed to walk through any obstacles when the dog is nearby. Dogs are expected to work under control and to leave the stock calmly when called off.

CKC Herding Course. On the Started course, the gather follows the drive (or fetch) from the take pen to a designated settling point (*the settle*). In the Intermediate class, the gather follows the drive from the take pen to the settle. On the Advanced course, the advanced handler's line runs through the center of the course, indicating the distance the handler is allowed to move during the run for maximum points. The entrances of two obstacles will be on the handler's side of the line; the entrances for the other two obstacles will be on the far side of the line. The gather follows the settle.

CKC Stock Dog Trial. The Stock Dog Trial is designed for the type of work that might be encountered on a farm or ranch. The course design for each level is decided by the course director (who also outlines the order for the optional-tasks chores [listed below]); approved by the judge; and posted before the trial. All levels (Started, Intermediate, and Advanced) must complete the seven basic chores: outrun/gather, lift, fetch, fetch and/or drive, take pen, a freestanding obstacle, and the exhaust pen.

CKC Stock Dog Course. In Started the dog is sent 60 feet (18.2m) to gather stock. During the gather the handler is allowed to work to a position between the dog and the stock but no closer than 15 feet (4.6 m) from the stock. The dog must fetch and/or drive stock for a distance of 120 feet (36.6 m).

In Intermediate the outrun is at least 100 feet (30.5 m) from the stock. The handler may move to within 50 feet (15.2 m) of the stock. The drive distance is a minimum of 75 feet (22.9 m), and the handler must be at least 115 feet (35.1 m) behind the dog during the drive.

In Advanced the outrun must be at least 220 feet (67 m) from the stock, while the handler stands at the post. The cross-drive is 30 feet (9.1 m), and the distance for the drive is 125 feet (38.1 m). The handler must remain stationary during the drive.

At all levels, competitors must complete three general chores and then optional chores or tasks required for each level of difficulty:

Started

- Load and unload chute
- Sort/gate work—Sort two or more head of stock into pens or stalls
- Gate work—At Started level, any stock may be sorted. Intermediate and Advanced dogs will need to sort predetermined marked stock.
- Bridge—Move stock over bridge
- Extra obstacles (trees, farm equipment, bales of hay, etc.)—Pass between, make turns around
- Hold—Keep stock from grain, a gate, a barn, or another group of stock
- Figure 8—Wear stock in a figure-8 pattern around cones, barrels, or natural objects

Intermediate/Advanced

- Sort—One or more head of marked stock
- Mock footbath—Move stock through footbath containing water
- Stock trailer—Load stock in trailer
- Graze—Settle and control stock in a boundary of no less than 60 feet (18.3 m) in diameter for two minutes

Advanced

- Shed—Sorting, split stock into two groups
- Freestanding pen with rope

CKC Tending Test. The Herding Tending Test involves six elements: a stay (controlled pause); controlled passage of the stock, which includes clearing three gates or obstacles; one stop on the course; containing the stock in a graze area; a stop while the handler opens the gate; and penning the stock. The dog is allotted 10 minutes.

CKC Tending Course. On the Tending Course the flock is moved along a narrow road to demonstrate the dog's ability to work both sides along a lane from front to back of the flock, keeping them from pending danger or preventing the animals from damaging crops. For the pause, the dog is positioned in front of the flock, facing them, to stop their forward movement. Then the handler guides the flock onto the road while the dog works the roadside boundary. The dog negotiates the flock across a bridge, pauses the animals along a traffic road, and travels along the road between a passing vehicle and the flock. In the Started class, the vehicle is parked but running. The handler then leads the flock to a wide grazing area, where they are allowed to spread out and graze while the dog works the boundary.

Gunther, a son of the well-known German Shepherd, Nicky, working the natural boundary of a wide graze on his master's farm in New York.
COURTESY ELLEN NICKELSBERG.

In all the divisions—Started, Intermediate, and Advanced—the dog works a minimum of 25 sheep. All courses at all levels begin with the exit from a freestanding pen; the handler leads the flock along a narrow road that connects all phases of work and across a bridge, demonstrates a pause for traffic, and then moves into a wide grazing area. In Advanced, dogs work a narrow graze. And finally, the flock is re-penned.

In Herding Started Tending (HST), the course is 400 to 500 meters (437.5 to 546.8 yd) long, with a 30-minute time limit. At the Herding Intermediate Tending (HIT) level an additional element is added. After the wide graze, the handler will position the dog (referred to as the Placement) before the flock to demonstrate the dog's ability to change the direction of the grazing sheep. The Intermediate course is 500 to 725 meters (546.8–792.9 yd) long with a 45-minute time limit. Finally, in Herding Advanced Tending (HAT), a narrow graze is added. The Advanced course is 725 to 820 meters (792.9–896.8 yd) long with a time allotment of 45 minutes.

UNITED STATES BORDER COLLIE HANDLERS' ASSOCIATION (USBCHA)

The United States Border Collie Handlers' Association is the sanctioning body for sheepdog and cattle dog trials throughout North America. USBCHA classes are open to all breeds and therefore referred to as *Open Trials*. The USBCHA and the American Border Collie Association sponsor the annual national finals to decide on the country's top working dogs. Titles are not awarded at USBCHA events, but members who qualify at Open trials throughout the year are qualified to compete in the national finals to determine the champion Open dog and handler for that year.

USBCHA trials follow the pattern of the International Sheep Dog Society (ISDS) trials. The names of classes and specific requirements may vary from trial to trial.

Novice—Entry level for inexperienced handlers and dogs. The course consists of a short outrun of perhaps 50 to 100 yards (45.7–91.4 m)—half the distance of the Open class— a lift, and a fetch. At this level the handler may move with the dog. Occasionally, the dog may be required to fetch sheep to the handler (wearing) through one or two sets of panels and a pen.

Pro-Novice is the next level for inexperienced dogs and handlers, although novice handlers working advanced dogs that have already competed at the Open level, or experienced Open handlers working a young inexperienced dog, are also eligible to compete in Pro-Novice. The course consists of a longer outrun—75 to 150 yards (68.6–137.2 m), two-thirds the distance of the Open Class—lift and fetch, a drive that can include one or more panels, and a pen.

Ranch Class is open to dogs that have graduated from the Pro-Novice class, inexperienced handlers with Open dogs, or experienced handlers with inexperienced dogs. The course requirements for dogs running in this class are the same as Open without the shedding segment, and the distance may be slightly less (150 to 200 yards [137.2–182.9 m]).

Nursery Class is the same as the Ranch Class except the outrun is the same distance as the Open. To be eligible to compete in this class, the dog's birthday must fall on or after July 1 of the year in which that Nursery Final will be held.

Open Class is the highest level for professional trainers and advanced dogs. It is a championship-level class in which points earned are accumulated toward the Purina Outstanding Field Trial Herding Dog Award. The outrun is 200 to 1,000 yards (182.9–914.4 m) long across flat or mountainous terrain. In this class the handler remains at the handler's post until shedding, penning, or singling. The eliminations, semifinals, and final runs have time limits determined by the judge.

USBCHA Semifinals—In the semifinal runs, the additional task of a single shed is commonly added. The handler goes to the shedding ring while the dog brings the flock from the pen to the ring, where he will sort off one sheep into the confines of the chalk circle and contain it, keeping it from returning to the other animals.

USBCHA National Finals—In the finals, a double lift replaces the single lift. The dog is required to collect two different flocks, each consisting of 10 head of sheep, at a distance of between 800 and 1,000 yards (731.5 and 914.4 m). Once the dog has gathered the first group, he leaves it to pick up the second one about the same distance away, but in a different part of the course, and brings them together, fetching them to the handler before the drive, which totals approximately 600 yards (548.6 m). Then, 15 unmarked sheep must be shed off, and the dog must pen the 5 marked sheep.

The fundamental work segments consist of outfield and infield work. Outfield work (outrun, lift, fetch) tests the dog's natural ability to locate, establish authority over, and move the sheep calmly and quietly. Infield work (drive, shed, pen) tests the dog's training and the efficiency between handler and dog.

Outrun: The dog may go left or right in an arc to a position behind the flock. Ideally, the arc is a pear shape, widening as the dog gets closer to the sheep's position. In order to get the highest number of available points, he must not cross the field between handler and sheep prior to the lift. Dogs receive the highest number of points if they don't stop, don't have to be redirected, and don't require additional commands to complete the outrun.

Lift: The dog must pick up the sheep from the drop point and move them in a quiet manner toward the handler. Any hesitation, instability, or multiple commands needed to encourage the dog are penalized. The lift turns into the fetch as the sheep melt away from the dog in the first few steps.

Fetch: The dog takes the sheep in as straight a line as possible through the designated panels to the handler. Ideally, the dog moves the sheep at an even pace as one group. Any deviations, zigzagging, or missed panels are penalized. The fetch ends when the sheep have turned around the handler at the handler's post.

Steve Waltenburg's Border Collie, XP Deuce, is wrapping the stock around the handler's post. PHOTO BY LORI HERBEL OF XP RANCH PHOTOGRAPHY.

Drive: The infield segment begins as the dog drives or moves the stock away from the handler at a steady pace on a diagonal to the right or left, depending on the judge's instructions. The dog takes the stock away from the handler through the first set of panels or gates in as direct a line as possible and then horizontally (cross-drive) through the second set. Dogs are allowed one attempt and scored accordingly. Points are deducted for missing a panel. The manner in which the work is accomplished also affects point deductions. The dog then brings the stock back to the handler, completing a triangle course pattern designated by the obstacles. The drive ends when the sheep enter the shedding ring and the handler enters the ring to assist the dog.

Shedding: Scoring for this test includes the manner in which the dog brings the sheep from the drive into the shedding ring. After assembling the sheep in the chalk circle, the dog sorts off and holds a designated number of sheep in the ring, keeping them apart from the other animals. After the shed is complete, the animals can leave the ring, but must be re-grouped prior to penning. Points are deducted if the dog fails to come in on command, does not adequately control the shed sheep, or has failed attempts or missed opportunities—and also if the handler interferes more than necessary.

Penning: For the final test, the handler opens the pen gate, and while holding it open instructs the dog to move the sheep into the pen. The dog works the sheep into the pen in a counterclockwise direction. The handler may assist and may block the sheep with her shepherd's cane or crook, but may not touch the sheep, which is a disqualification. Points are deducted for breakaway sheep, sheep that are milling around the pen opening, and for sheep circling the pen in the wrong direction.

▼

Open Trials sponsored by the USBCHA are open to all breeds; however, few breeds have the drive and ability to sprint out over a long distance to gather a few head of sheep and control them without the aid of fences.

▲

Chapter 25

WHAT JUDGES LOOK FOR

Inexperienced spectators are often impressed when there is a lot of action, whether it is necessary or not. When a dog has complete control and authority over his draw (the animals assigned to him) and moves the stock effortlessly from one point to another, a novice spectator may think that the dog "didn't do anything," as opposed to the entry that wildly takes his charges running from one point to another, racing them through each obstacle. While a novice may applaud this type of action, it takes a better and probably more experienced dog to keep the situation under control and to complete the course with ease.

In a nutshell, judges want to see the dog accomplishing the job in the most efficient way possible, and the dog working as a team with his handler for a winning trial run.

TIPS FOR COMPETING SUCCESSFULLY

Ideally, you should attend a trial or two as a spectator before competing. Even better, you may be able to participate in informal training trials that are designed to help the novice handler gain experience and confidence. If possible, have someone videotape your run(s). This is an excellent training and reference tool. Volunteer to be a timekeeper or scribe, or work in the back pens as a stock handler.

Well-trained trial dogs are the result of careful behind-the-scenes training and hard work. Trial dogs, like all athletes, spend more time training than competing. If you rush into competition before the dog is ready or work the dog on difficult stock in an area much larger than you are used to, he may develop bad habits that are difficult to correct. A trial situation offers many variables over which you have no control.

At home you have given the dog the opportunity to control the livestock in an environment you manage. If the dog tries to run straight at the stock and chase or scatter the animals at home, you are able to step in and reposition the dog. That is not always possible in a new situation. If things get out of hand during a competition, don't hesitate to stop the run, gain control of your dog, and retire from the arena until another day.

When you arrive at the trial grounds, you should check in and get particulars, such as the run order, when and where the judge's meeting will be held, appropriate places to exercise your dog, and where to set up away from the activities. Take your dog out and let him empty out and get a drink. Once you've taken care of your dog, it is a good idea to look over the trial course. Check the latching systems and movement of any gates you will be responsible to open and close during your run.

Prior to your turn:

1. Keep your dog relaxed and quiet until it is your turn.
2. Several runs away, walk him so that he can do his business and get a drink.
3. In open trials, let him observe a lift or two (so that he knows where to find the stock on the field course).

In the Arena or on the Hillside

Stock that are inclined to bolt when the dog makes contact require breathing room (more distance)—indicated by their heads and ears. They need time to settle. Nevertheless, the dog will have to work steadily and farther away to establish control and calm the animals. In the meantime, he will need to be positioned with appropriate flanking commands to continually point the stock toward the openings of the desired obstacles.

Stock is easier to control if moved at a walk, as demonstrated by Ruby, an Aussie owned by Conroy's Farm in Minnesota. PHOTO BY LORI HERBEL OF XP RANCH PHOTOGRAPHY.

Don't rush the stock. They will be easier to handle when they are calm and moving at a walk or trot. A lot of your success will depend on knowing when to move slowly and when to move quickly; you have to think ahead of the animals. If you are trying to stop a runaway, don't send the dog to where the animal already is, but to where it is heading—otherwise, the dog will be trying to catch up rather than outrun it. To stop the ewe or steer, move the dog ahead of it. To turn a runaway, put the dog opposite the side you want the animal to go, between its shoulder and its eye. To drive it forward, position the dog behind the animal's hips. (*See* Chapter 14, Stockmanship.)

Working Trial Champion Las Rocosa Western Legends RTDsc PATDs, a top winning trial dog and ASCA National Finals contender, is in position to block and turn this steer. PHOTO BY GARY R. ANDERSON.

In a trial it is not uncommon for livestock to be attracted to the stock in the exhaust area or holding pen and want to go to them. Once one animal has split, a second and third animal will often try to join it. It is important that the single animal's attention stay focused on the dog. When being moved away from the strong magnetism of the herd, stock will not move as easily and will require more pressure from the dog.

When you have the ewe's or steer's attention, you will be able to control it better because its attention won't be on the re-pen. Even if the animal is moving away, you'll know if it is paying attention to you or to the dog because it will drop an ear to the side and turn its head slightly toward you or the dog to keep you or him in its sight zone.

Mick, an Australian Shepherd, moving sheep away from the holding area.
PHOTO BY LORI HERBEL OF XP RANCH PHOTOGRAPHY.

Cowboy, an Australian Cattle Dog owned by Susan Crocker, is in control of the cattle. He has their attention and is moving them in the desired direction.
PHOTO BY LORI HERBEL OF XP RANCH PHOTOGRAPHY.

Although the stock may fan out, the dog must be positioned to funnel them through the various obstacles and panels—without spilling over the sides—for the maximum number of points. To do this, preparation begins when the animals are coming through the panel or obstacle preceding the current one you are attempting to negotiate.

As the sheep are being walked through the panel, Sadie—a Border Collie handled by Kent Herbel—is just beginning to flank slightly to her right to direct the sheep towards the next goal in her winning trial run. PHOTO BY LORI HERBEL OF XP RANCH PHOTOGRAPHY.

Applying Stock Sense

Bear in mind that the way the animals react will depend on their disposition, how much they have been handled, the weather, terrain, and even the wind direction. Livestock is generally more active in the morning and evening. Animals will not move as easily in hot, humid temperatures as they will when the weather is chilly, and they are more difficult to handle during a downpour of rain. Goats especially dislike rain—they will seek shelter and are hard to work. Sheep and goats are easier to drive uphill than downhill because there is a natural inclination for them to move uphill in the presence of danger—and because sheep usually bed down on high ground. Don't forget to use the animal's inclination to follow the leader to maneuver them (although sometimes in trial situations, the animal's natural pecking order is disrupted when they are sorted into small groups).

Each class of livestock offers a challenge of its own, and no two are the same. For example, heavy breeds of sheep such as the Hampshire, Shropshire, and Suffolk do not flock as tightly nor move as quickly as the light

Tips for a Winning Run

The lift sets the tone for the entire trial run. Don't be in a hurry. Take a deep breath and relax. Your ability to stay calm will greatly affect the dog's response. When livestock panic, they don't think clearly or react rationally. The best thing that you can do in that situation is to let them settle before continuing the run.

Keep in mind that even though the course diagram shows a dog picking up the livestock at 12:00, in a real situation the balance point for sending the dog to lift (pick up) the stock may not be exactly at 12:00. Watch the animals' heads to determine where to give the "there" command for the dog to turn in to lift and then fetch the stock. In other words, if you see the stock wanting to go (facing or heading) to the right, you may need the dog to pick them up at 1:00 to get them adequately lined out on the course.

In this scenario, the dog must be positioned toward one side of 12:00 to put pressure on the heavy side (direction sheep are inclined to go) in order to keep them lined out and heading in the desired direction.
PHOTO BY BECKY PARKER OF DALLY UP PHOTOGRAPHY.

To target the pen, ease the gate open as the stock is beginning to exit the previous panel. This will also attract their attention. Position your dog to head the animals to the entrance of the pen. They should be aimed somewhere between the gate's hinges and the back of the pen, which is gauged by the animals' flight zone. When the stock is contained in the opening, let the dog work his side of the pen while you work your side, exerting pressure to ease them in without causing them to explode.

hill breeds like the Cheviot or Montadale. They are slower and more likely to stand their ground and challenge a dog. You must learn to "read" the situation and respond accordingly.

Volunteer to handle stock at trials. You will gain valuable "hands on" stock experience and can watch the runs as well.

Linda Barhite and her dog, Spur, working together to pen sheep at a High Plains ASC trial in Colorado. PHOTO BY BECKY PARKER OF DALLY UP PHOTOGRAPHY.

PROBLEM SOLVING:
Dog works fine at home, but forgets his training or is out of control at trials
In this scenario, the dog may not yet be ready for competition. If this happens too often, he will become trial wise and be very difficult to correct. A young dog that has not been exposed to new areas with all the sights and sounds of barking dogs, unfamiliar stock, and new people can become excited and overwhelmed. Practice animals do not usually react to the dog (or trainer) with the same wariness as do unfamiliar stock in a trial. Working the dog away from home will often reveal areas that need more work. The dog needs to be hauled to many different situations, such as training and fun trials, where he can gain experience and, if necessary, you can correct him, so mistakes don't become habits.

PROBLEM SOLVING:
Handler anxiety at trials
Trialing can be stressful. Your dog can sense your anxiety. Be prepared as much as possible. The better prepared you are, the more confidence you should have. Expertise is gained with experience. Having your dog

well trained is the first and most important aspect of competing. The more practice you have, the more comfortable you will be.

Trials are not the place for training, unless they are training events. Training and fun trials are two of the best ways to prepare for competition, and provide excellent opportunities to gain practice.

Your attitude will make or break you. Set realistic goals. It is important to focus on creating an enjoyable experience for you and the dog. If your primary goal is gaining titles and winning, you may miss the joy of the journey. Titles and wins will come in their due time when the other aspects are in place.

PROBLEM SOLVING:
A male dog who lifts his leg (on fence posts, obstacles etc.) while competing

Dominant males will do this to establish territory, especially if there is a female in heat. It is more often a problem in males of loose-eyed breeds. It can also be a problem in dogs with moderate drive and herding instinct. Allow ample time prior to the trial to walk the dog around the trial grounds so he can mark his territory. Though the rules may not allow you to walk the dog in the trial arena prior to competition, you can walk him around the perimeter.

PROBLEM SOLVING:
A dog that is easily distracted while competing and wanders off to investigate things in the trial arena or on the sidelines

This type of dog may require more exposure. Haul the dog to work in as many different situations and locations as possible. The dog may also lack intensity. Work on developing the dog's focus, as described in "PROBLEM SOLVING: Dog lacks focus" in Chapter 6.

PROBLEM SOLVING:
Dog seems to have lost his enthusiasm

A dog can become sour from drilling on trial exercises. (*See* "Other Problems You Might Encounter in Advanced Training" in Chapter 12.) Keep in mind that older herding dogs may not have the speed and stamina they once did. They may also suffer from arthritis, so should be monitored for signs of discomfort. Buffered aspirin (regular strength, 325 mg) is tolerated well by most dogs and can be given for several days to reduce the swelling associated with bruises. The dog's diet should always be considered. A source of quality protein is essential for stamina.

Chapter 26

OTHER ELEMENTS OF WORKING STOCKDOGS

Conditioning is an important factor in successful training. Herding dogs should be lean, with an athletic physique. Dogs that are too heavy risk overheating, disease, injury, and stress on their musculoskeletal systems. If they are too thin, they lose stamina. Herding dogs must be maintained at the healthy weight for each dog.

Preparing for herding competitions should not be limited to weekend herding activities. It can also include general activities such as swimming and retrieving. Herding dogs must build up their aerobic condition and muscle strength for sufficient stamina. Stamina is also linked to metabolism—how efficiently a dog can convert food to energy.

The author and her dog, WTCH Las Rocosa Bonny Kyle RDX, putting on the miles to prepare for competition.

DOG CARE AND MAINTENANCE

Diet and Performance

Proper nutrition boosts performance levels, whether on the ranch or in the trial arena. Strong eyed dogs with intense concentration can exhaust more easily than dogs that are more nonchalant working in the same conditions. The demands of working can require much more energy than that provided by a maintenance diet.

Stockdogs like this Azores Cattle Dog loading cows on a transport truck need proper nutrition for the best performance. COURTESY SATU HUUSKO.

Determining the correct diet for a hardworking herding dog takes some extra thought. Fats and protein are the most important sources of energy for performance dogs. Dogs use fat to fuel athletic performance the way humans use complex carbohydrates. The fuel value of fat is 2.5 times more than the calories from carbohydrates or protein, so a high-fat diet offers more energy in a smaller amount of food. Fat is also said to aid in preventing heat exhaustion and dehydration in performance dogs, giving them a competitive edge. Essential fatty acids cannot be manufactured by the body; they must be obtained in the diet. Studies have shown that a high-carbohydrate diet actually lowers canine performance.

Research shows that dogs flourish on high-protein diets that are rich in fats with minimal carbohydrates. Good quality protein, such as that found in meat and eggs, is essential for the repair and maintenance of body tissue (muscles, ligaments, organs). In field tests, dogs fed diets high in protein (32–40 percent protein) were less prone to injuries than dogs fed lower-protein diets (16–24 percent). A diet lacking in good quality (digestible) protein contributes to a loss of condition and a lack of stamina.

The true test of any diet is the healthiness of the dog and the quality of his skin and hair coat. You should be able to feel the ribs through a layer of flesh, but not see them when looking at the dog. A heavy padding of fat over the ribs indicates an overweight dog.

Water and Stamina

The importance of water is often overlooked. Dogs lose water through breathing, even during winter, and need more water in hot climates to restore fluids lost through panting. Because every cell in the body is dependant on water, proper hydration can increase endurance by 75 percent. As water is lost during exercise, dehydration can impair the dog's stamina. Without sufficient fluid, the body cannot regulate its temperature properly. Water also affects the metabolic function necessary for digestion, which can affect stamina.

Provide shade for your dog in warm weather, and if necessary wet his head and belly and have a shallow pan of water for him to stand in. Guard your dog against heat stress; know the signs and watch for them.

Adequate hydration is necessary to boost stamina in hard-working ranch dogs.

Electrolytes

According to studies on electrolyte requirements in sled dogs, properly trained and conditioned working dogs maintained on high-quality diets and not affected by vomiting or diarrhea do not need electrolyte supplements.

Using such products as Nutri-Cal can be beneficial in times of extreme stress. Nutri-Cal is a highly palatable, concentrated source of calories with vitamins and minerals in a readily digestible paste. It is ideal for hard working stockdogs during extreme conditions.

Foot Care

Remember that old saying: "No feet, no dog?" Paying special attention to your dog's feet is of primary importance, because his feet probably endure the roughest treatment. Foot problems can be avoided if you are careful. The feet should be examined daily, and any time a foot seems tender. Toenails should be trimmed regularly to reduce the chance of injury.

Gravel and rocky surfaces wear the dog's pads thin, and hot surfaces can burn them. Dogs that are kept on soft carpeting, grass, or dirt will not have feet as tough as those that are gradually exposed to gravel surfaces. Pad-toughening agents such as tincture of benzoin are highly beneficial and may be necessary to help protect the feet in rugged terrain until they gradually toughen up from exposure. Booties are also beneficial to protect the feet. They should not be so tight as to hamper natural movements or cut off circulation. Remove them whenever the dog is not working and during rest periods.

Grooming the Herding Dog

Maintaining the working coat is somewhat different from preparing it for the show ring; however, grooming is important to the dog's comfort and basic health. A dog working in fields and pastures will probably pick up grass awns (cheat grass, foxtails, and wild oat seeds). These can work through the coat and into the skin, causing discomfort and injury. Regular brushing and bathing is imperative. A matted hair coat can keep you from seeing a problem until it has become difficult to treat.

Shelter and Containment

Even though stockdogs are used to working outdoors in all weather, they need a safe haven—a clean and comfortable place to rest in when they are not working.

The Importance of Whiskers in Stockdogs

The vibrissae are very different from other body hair. They're deeply rooted in erectile tissue that is served by sensory nerve fibers. They should never be trimmed, because they function as sensors, alerting to potential unseen danger and helping to gauge the precise distance from the dog's face to a point of contact with, for example, a pair of horns that the dog is dodging.

Stockdogs rely on their whiskers during close encounters with livestock. PHOTO BY GARY R. ANDERSON.

Basic Health Care

The fundamentals of good health are proper nutrition and adequate exercise. Without those factors in place, maintaining a healthy dog is difficult. Many common canine diseases can be avoided; prevention is the first line of defense. Immunization, deworming, strict sanitation, and parasite and rodent control are primary disease prevention measures.

COMMON PROBLEMS AND BASIC FIRST AID

Dogs don't work on stock without risk. They can be kicked, stepped on, run over, butted, rolled, horned, or otherwise injured. Dogs are highly vulnerable to heat stress when working hard to gain control of stubborn livestock in warm weather, especially when there is a lack of water.

Multi-drug Sensitivity in Herding Breeds

Individuals of several herding breeds including Australian Shepherds, Border Collies, English Shepherds, Rough and Smooth Collies (approximately three-quarters of Collies are affected), German Shepherd Dogs, Old English Sheepdogs, and Shetland Sheepdogs are affected by the MDR1 (Multiple Drug Resistant) gene. Some mixed breeds are also susceptible. They lack a key transport protein that protects the brain by helping to pump a variety of drugs out of the brain and back to the bloodstream where they can be safely metabolized rather than building to toxic levels in the brain and affecting the central nervous system. Toxicity is manifested by muscle tremors, seizures, ataxia, behavioral disturbances, and even death.

A simple test developed by Washington State University screens for the presence of this mutant gene. (You perform the test yourself and send it to the lab for results.) Testing your dog will help to determine the appropriate medications to be used if he proves to have MDR1. Unless your dog has been tested to be free from the MDR1 mutation, it is a good idea to print out a list of the drugs that have been documented or strongly suspected to cause problems and those that may potentially cause problems. (*See* the Washington State University Veterinary Medicine website, www.vetmed.wsu.edu). Make sure your vet is informed about MDR1 and its implications for the care of your dog.

Broken Teeth

In stock work, especially with cattle, a dog's teeth can become dislocated, chipped, broken, jarred loose, or even uprooted. They can get driven into the nasal cavity, lip, cheek, or tongue. Bleeding usually occurs and will be slow to clot due to the movement of the tongue.

If it is a minor injury and bleeding is minimal, apply an ice pack to control bleeding. You can also control bleeding from a single cavity by applying direct pressure to the wound. A veterinarian may have to suture large lacerations and may need to employ pinning and wiring to immobilize fractures to the teeth and jaw so they heal properly. In many cases a dislocated tooth with a root can be replaced in its cavity and remain functional with proper dentistry. If the tooth is not too dirty, rinse it with cold water. Preserve all gum fibers still clinging to the tooth. If the tooth is very

To work cattle effectively, dogs need to be athletic, sound, and healthy. PHOTO BY GARY R. ANDERSON.

soiled, rinse it in a cup (8 ounces/.24 L) of ice water mixed with 2 table-spoons (29.6 mL) of salt (saline solution). Seek veterinary care immediately.

Bruises

Bruises accompany many types of injuries. Tenderness, stiffness, and swelling indicate bruising. Apply a cold pack to minimize swelling of a new injury. Use a warm compress to improve circulation on an already swollen injury. Buffered aspirin is tolerated well by most dogs and can be given for several days to reduce the swelling associated with bruises.

▼

Beware! Do not give ibuprofen or acetaminophen
to your dog under any circumstance because they
are toxic to dogs.

▲

Eye Injury

Although nature's placement of a dog's eyes provides some protection from blows, scratches, and lacerations, his eye still may become injured. If injuries result in such symptoms as different pupil sizes between the right and left eye, pupils that are unresponsive to light, and/or graying of the cornea, these are emergency situations that require immediate veterinarian attention. These symptoms can indicate neurological issues.

A severe blow can cause the eye to become dislocated from the socket. This is a true emergency and requires immediate professional care. Do not attempt any cleansing or manipulation of the eye because you could further damage it.

If you see any material in the eye, try irrigating the eye with a gentle stream of lukewarm water or saline solution poured from a glass just above the inner corner of the eye. If a superficial foreign body is removed by irrigation, continue to observe the eye for irritation or pain, which will indicate that professional attention is required. Any foreign bodies in the eye that cannot be washed away should be treated by a veterinarian. Do not attempt any manipulation of an eye that has a penetrating foreign body in it.

Foot Injuries

Pad injuries are easily recognized, but injuries to the webbing between the toes and nail-bed injuries can also occur from rocks, granular snow, ice, and jagged or sharp objects. The skin between the toes can split or suffer blisters and friction burns. Cactus needles, thorns, grass spears, and barbs can puncture the pads and webbing between the toes, causing abscesses or even migrating to internal organs.

Problems with the base of the toenail can be difficult to resolve. Swelling of the tissue is usually associated with pus or serum around the nail bed; this is not easily recognized on long-haired dogs, so thorough inspection is a must. Rough terrain or breaking through snow or ice can tear the toenails. Wounds to the webbing can be as difficult to heal as nail-bed injuries.

Use a mild Betadine solution to treat the affected areas. Superglue or surgical glue can be used on the toenails, to mend cuts together, and to attach protective pieces of material to pads. Deep cuts may need to be sutured, and antibiotics are necessary if the feet become infected. All foot disorders heal more rapidly if the foot is kept clean and dry.

Heat Stress

Heat-related health risks for herding dogs include heatstroke, heat cramps, and heat exhaustion. Older working dogs and overweight dogs are more vulnerable to heat stress than dogs in good condition and excellent health,

Short-faced (brachycephalic) dogs such as Rottweilers have shortened and restricted air passages in the muzzle and are more prone to breathing problems and heat stress in hot, humid conditions than "normal" or medium-faced breeds.

but any dog that works hard in warm weather without adequate water or opportunities to rest is at risk. Make every attempt to avoid heat stress. Don't overwork dogs, and keep them in shaded, well-ventilated areas with constant access to fresh, cool water during sultry weather.

Heat exhaustion occurs when a dog has worked or exercised hard without adequate water and becomes dehydrated. It doesn't have to be hot for heat exhaustion to take place. Symptoms are heavy panting, fatigue, muscular weakness, inattentiveness, and dizziness, which may be indicated by a staggering gait. In heat exhaustion the pulse is fast and feeble, and the temperature is normal or slightly elevated. (Normal temperature for dogs ranges from 100.5 to 102.5ºF [38.1–39.2ºC], but may vary slightly.) This is an emergency situation that requires immediate action or it will lead to heatstroke.

Cool the dog off immediately. Move him to a cool, shaded area, and immerse him in cool, not cold, water or apply wet towels to his head, legs, and belly. A fan blowing air over the dog is helpful. Offer him limited sips of cool (but not cold) water, and get veterinary assistance immediately.

Heat cramps do not commonly occur in dogs, but can affect herding dogs working in intense heat. They are caused mainly by the loss of salt from the system and by extreme exertion and are the early warning signs of impending heat exhaustion. Heat cramps are painful; the main symptom is severe muscle spasms. Take the dog to a shaded area and give him small drinks of cool, not cold, water with 1 teaspoon (4.9 ml) of salt added to every 8 ounces (.24 L). Gently massage sore muscles to help relieve spasms. Give the dog several days of rest before working him again.

Nose Injury

Trauma or a blow to the nose can be painful and can cause bleeding and swelling. Apply an ice pack or cold compress to the nose to help curb swelling and bleeding; watch for breathing difficulty. Consult a vet if bleeding continues or if breathing is difficult.

Sprains

Sprains and other injuries to ligaments and muscles are often difficult to distinguish from fractures. In general, a dog willing to bear weight on an injured limb does not have a fracture. Sprains occur when there is torque on a joint that elongates the ligament; the affected area is swollen and tender. The most commonly injured ligament is the anterior cruciate ligament (ACL). Injury usually occurs when the dog twists on his hind leg making a sudden turn. The dog may appear lame and hold his foot off the ground.

Basic First-Aid Kit

No matter where you are working your dogs—a remote location or closer to home—you will usually be the first responder and should have a first-aid kit to deal quickly with minor injuries to your dogs. Here is a checklist of some items that should be in your trial kit:

List of drugs dangerous for dogs with MDR1 sensitivity
Veterinarian's number
Buffered aspirin (regular strength, 325 mg)
Povidone-iodine solution (a mild antiseptic antimicrobial
    germicide)
Topical triple-antibiotic ointment
Artificial tears (vial)
Thermometer
4x4 sterile gauze pads
Vet wrap or an Ace bandage
Muzzle or Gentle Leader
Towels—to cool a dog with water, to dry and warm—many uses
Forceps or needle-nose pliers
Cotton balls
Ear cleansing solution
Epsom salts
Saline solution
Antihistamine—diphenhydramine (Benadryl)
Styptic pencil
Ice pack
Vinyl gloves
Surgical skin glue
Nail trimmer
Small flashlight
Small container to hold water

Appendix

BREED PROFILES

HERDING BREEDS

When choosing a dog to fit your needs, study the breed profiles provided here, and determine which breed best suits your personality and situation. Keep in mind, individual dogs may display traits that differ from the general breed profile—and even other individuals in their lines. For example, Australian Cattle Dogs are described as low heelers, but sometimes you find one that bites high or will not heel at all. Every now and then you'll come across a loose-eyed Border Collie that won't go to the head—even though the breed is well-known for their eye and ability to block and gather livestock.

Most of the herding breeds—*providing they are from proven working bloodlines*—are candidates for recreational herding activities. Fewer breeds or bloodlines have the ability or the type of structure for ranch work. Working ranch dogs require strength, courage, and determination that is not easily put off by adversity.

Living arrangements and style of life weigh heavily in choosing a herding breed. For example, because of their size, dogs like Corgis, Shelties, and Swedish Vallhunds are adaptable to suburban or even apartment life and may be good choices for someone in pursuit of the herding sport who does not have acreage or a farm of their own.

Once you've narrowed down your choices, visit different owners and breeders. There can be noticeable variations in temperament, talent, drive, and trainability among bloodlines within a given breed. Many breeders administer standard puppy tests to help weed out individuals that may lack stability and spirit, that are too fearful or stubborn, or that may be too dull or too sensitive for herding.

Glossary of Breed Terms

Backs—Jumps on the backs of sheep crowded in chutes (sorting race) and alleys to move them

Body blocks—Uses their shoulder or body to physically block the animal

Furrow—Patrol a boundary such as when flocks are allowed to forage strips of grass between crops.

Guardian—Dog that barks to alert owner and will also defend owner's property against intruders

Loose eye—Dog that doesn't stalk his charges

Sharp—Quick to react to irritants (threshold stimulus)

Strong eye—Dog that uses predatory stare to stalk his charges

Territorial—Having a strong sense of boundary

Watchdog—Dog that barks to signal the arrival of a visitor or stranger but is not protective

Yard dog—A forceful dog with bark that will back sheep for paddock work

Alpine Shepherd
Origin: Alpine region of Europe
Character: Friendly, spirited, ready, willing, and eager
Overall working style: Upright, close, loose-eyed
In a nutshell: Their ancestors were used for tending flocks while they grazed in the mountains.

Altdeutsche Schaferhunde
The indigenous Old German Shepherds are a diverse group of rugged dogs selected for hardiness and stamina. They are classic large-flock dogs with power and presence still used in Germany today. Their overall working style is loose-eyed, upright, and close-working. They are easily trained to furrow. The temperament is wide ranging, from the spirited and friendly *Schafpudel* (Sheep Poodle) to the fairly sharp Tiger and the more independent Strobel to the moderately sharp Schwarzer, Gelbbacke and the Fuchs. They are alert and loyal guardians.

Australian Cattle Dog
Also known as: Queensland Blue Heeler
Origin: Australia
Character: Gutsy, rugged, independent, businesslike, stubborn, loyal guardian, reserved with strangers
Overall working style: Close, loose-eyed, hard, low heeler with gathering instinct; some will use force on the head to turn or stop cows; works silently, but may force bark or bite when heading.
In a nutshell: Developed for cattle, but some are adaptable and will work goats or sheep. Some still used in farm and ranch situations.

Australian Kelpie
Origin: Australia
Character: Independent, highly adaptable, reliable, good watchdog
Overall working style: Fast, strong gathering ability, medium- to strong-eyed; excels both in open spaces and yards, uses voice, backs; some strains forceful enough for cattle
In a nutshell: In the past, Kelpies with stamina and heat resistance were used to work large flocks over vast distances in unforgiving conditions of the arid Outback. They are one of the few breeds still used on ranches in the real world.

Australian Koolie
Also known as: German Koolie/Coolie, German Collie (Kuli)
Origin: Australia
Character: Devoted companion, highly attuned to master, eager to please; good watchdog, adaptable
Overall working style: Generally close, loose to medium eye; gentle and calm on ewes and lambs, knows when to use bite on cattle.
In a nutshell: Primarily a working dog, the Koolie was bred to meet a variety of needs. Station owners required hard-working paddock dogs; transport workers wanted small, agile dogs to back and outmaneuver livestock when working in chutes and cattle pots (large trailers with stackable decks); and stockmen handling semi-wild cattle needed dogs with strength and stamina.

Australian Shepherd
Also known as: Aussie
Origin: Western USA
Character: Sensible, dependable, attentive, quick thinking problem solver; easily trained, good guardian, reserved with strangers
Overall working style: Upright, close, loose to medium eye; strong gathering instincts, can head and heel
In a nutshell: Valued for their multiple uses—tough enough to turn a mother cow, yet gentle enough to nudge a lamb with their nose. Aussies from working bloodlines are still used as ranch dogs in the real world.

Azores Cattle Dog
Also known as: Fila De Sao Miguel, Fila
Origin: Portugal
Character: Sharp but biddable, easily trained, fiercely protective
Overall working style: Upright, close, loose-eyed, tough, highly instinctive; an aggressive, low, hard heeler
In a nutshell: Primarily a stockdog created to catch and gather difficult, feral cattle and goats in the dense vegetation, based on the Molosser (Mastiff) family of breeds.

Bearded Collie
Also known as: Highland Collie, Old Welsh Grey, Mountain Sheepdog
Origin: British Isles
Character: Effervescent, energetic, stable, self-confident, resourceful, determined, trainable; loyal, watchdog
Overall working style: Two styles, header (loose- to medium-eyed) or huntaway (upright and close, uses voice readily); circles naturally
In a nutshell: Beardies, one of Britain's oldest strains of droving dogs, developed for the climate and terrain in the Scottish Highlands. (Until about the late 1960s, it was not uncommon for Beardies to be crossed with Border Collies.)

Beauceron
Also known as: Berger de Beauce
Origin: France
Character: Calm, self-assured, gentle, fearless guardian; obedient, versatile, intelligent; can work independently
Overall working style: Upright, close, loose-eyed, high prey drive
In a nutshell: Primarily herding dogs, used mainly to work sheep, sometimes cattle. History suggests they are closely related to the Briard.

Belgian Shepherds (Laekenois, Malinois, Groenendael, Tervuren)
Origin: Belgium
Character: Energetic, enthusiastic, willing, affectionate with family but reserved with strangers; tend to be one-handler dogs, can be territorial or possessive
Overall working style: Aggressive, fast, upright, close, highly inclined to circle and bunch stock; strong prey drive, largely loose-eyed,
In a nutshell: Traditionally fearless workers used as herders and guardians on sheep and small cattle herds. Alertness, speed, and agility enabled them to become formidable police dogs.

In Europe the four different Belgian Shepherds—Belgian Laekenois, Belgian Malinois, Belgian Sheepdog (Groenendael) and Belgian Tervuren—are treated as different varieties of one breed. In the United States they are considered separate breeds. Consequently, there is a noticeable difference in herding ability and temperament of each breed, ranging from extremely hard to biddable.

Bergamasco
Also known as: Cane da Pastore Bergamasco
Origin: Northern Italy
Character: Energetic, tolerant, attentive, loyal, independent, reserved with strangers, good guardian
Overall working style: Agile, upright, close, loose-eyed
In a nutshell: Tended flocks grazing the mountainous terrain of the Italian Alps.

Bohemian Shepherd
Also known as: Chodsky Pes
Origin: Czech Republic
Character: Friendly, cheerful, fearless but not aggressive unless owner is threatened; energetic but not nervous; attentive, good watchdog, similar to German Shepherds but not as aloof.
Overall working style: Quick, upright, close, loose-eyed
In a nutshell: Was used for herding and guarding.

Blue Heeler
Also known as: McNiven Heeler, Dingo, Red Heeler, Queensland Blue Heeler
Origin: Australia
Character: Tough, hard dogs, rugged, independent, guardians, reserved with strangers, loyal and protective.
Overall working style: Close working, loose-eyed, silent, hard-hitting, low heelers.
In a nutshell: Tough, aggressive cowdogs with strong heeling ability and were used widely for loading cattle pots and for chute work.

Border Collie
Also known as: BC
Origin: British Isles
Character: Energetic, eager, alert, intelligent, focused, highly trainable, willing
Overall working style: Moderate- to wide-running, medium- to strong-eyed, very fast reflexes; strong gathering breed, mainly headers, though some have stronger driving instincts
In a nutshell: Border Collies are a premier stockdog. Their ability to sprint wide to gather sheep from far distances and control the flock with lightning quick reflexes and keen eye is their hallmark. They are well known for their willingness to follow instructions and respond to whistle commands given over a mile away. BCs excel in farm and ranch work, and as a trial dog. They are principally a sheepdog, but some bloodlines have been developed with the stamina and force to handle cattle.

Bouvier (Bouvier des Ardennes, Bouvier des Flanders, Roeselare Cowdog)
Also known as: Ardennes Cowdog, Roeselare Cowdog
Origin: Flanders (Belgium, the Netherlands, and northeastern France)
Character: Fearless, quiet, calm, steady; hardworking, obedient, playful, courageous, loyal guardian
Overall working style: Bold, loose-eyed, moves stock with power and presence, wearing, gathering, using shoulder or body to block.

In a nutshell: While generally thought of as cowdogs, the Bouvier—Bouvier des Flanders, the Roeselare Cowdog and Ardennes Cowdog (which is still used to drive milk cows on dairy farms)—also works sheep and other livestock. Bouvier were traditionally used to drive and guard large herds of cattle along the roads and through villages to market. As the era of unfenced pasture grazing began to disappear and Flanders became a battlefield, the Belgian cow dogs evolved into protection and draft or ambulance dogs for the military and police.

Briard
Also known as: Chien Berger de Brie
Origin: France
Character: Big-hearted, standoffish to strangers, dominant; stubborn but gentle and loving; good guardian
Overall working style: Upright, close, exhibiting power and presence; quiet, loose-eyed; tends to circle, gather, uses shoulder or nose to bump sheep.
In a nutshell: Used for tending as a herder and guardian and all around farm dog. As agricultural practices changed after the French Revolution and the land was divided into smaller parcels, they went from defending their charges against poachers and wolves to keeping sheep contained within the limits of unfenced pastures and grazing areas.

Canaan Dog
Also known as: Kelev K'naani
Origin: Israel
Character: Highly adaptable, exceptionally intelligent, attentive, vigilant, reserved with strangers, independent, territorial; extremely defensive (stays out of reach and barks) but not aggressive
Overall working style: Upright, close, loose- to medium-eyed, silent, and gathers, uses force-growl
In a nutshell: Used by Bedouins to herd their sheep and goats in the desert, protecting the flocks against predators and guarding the camp.

Carea Leones
Origin: Spain
Character: Sensible guardian, loyal, versatile
Overall working style: Upright, close, loose-eyed, capable, quick and agile
In a nutshell: Traditionally, Carea Leones tended Churra and Merino flocks in the mountain pastures where they have grazed since the Middle Ages. They do extremely well trailing sheep and cattle to pasture and handling them in cultivated areas as well.

Catahoula Leopard Dog
Origin: USA (State dog of Louisiana)

Character: Fiercely protective, territorial, independent, highly assertive, affectionate toward family

Overall working style: Tough, aggressive, upright, close, loose-eyed, strong heading and lead dogs

In a nutshell: Used to lead cattle, hold them bunched in a group, and keep recalcitrant stock from breaking away. Although they are not true hounds, they bay like coon dogs so that riders can locate them. Catahoulas have more prominent webbing between their toes than do most breeds; this is a benefit in swamp country.

Catalonian Sheepdog

Also known as: Gos d'Atura

Origin: Spain

Character: Pleasant, vigilant, highly devoted, suspicious of strangers; may appear unsociable

Overall working style: Upright, close, loose-eyed

In a nutshell: General purpose farm dogs in Catalonian Pyrenees used to tend sheep and cattle, keeping them out of yards and fields used for crops as well as guarding and defending them.

Collie (Rough and Smooth)

Origin: Great Britain

Character: Sweet, gentle, easygoing, easy to train, soft; watchdog

Overall working style: Nonaggressive, upright, close, loose-eyed, body blocks, occasionally grips, ranges from silent to use of voice

In a nutshell: Though a few have retained good herding instincts, many modern Collies have been bred primarily for looks and no longer exhibit strong working ability. Those who exhibit interest usually have adequate drive, requiring only clear direction and consistent handling to become capable herding dogs. Others with less drive tend to follow, pacing themselves to the stock, and may give up if a sheep balks or challenges them; they will require lots of encouragement, patience, and kind handling to develop a sustained interest in herding.

Croatian Sheepdog

Also known as: Hrvatski Ovcat, Kroatischer Schäferhund

Origin: Croatia

Character: Highly intelligent, quick learners, versatile, dependable, brave, loyal, devoted

Overall working style: Close, upright, loose-eyed, intense, fearless, strong dogs; will use voice and bite when working in yards, driving and gathering

In a nutshell: Traditionally used to drive herds of pigs to the oak forest in autumn. They are mainly cattle dogs but can be useful on sheep. Croatian Sheepdogs have been known to single out an individual cow on hearing its name.

Curs

Also known as: Florida Cur, Yellow Black Mouth Cur, Black Mouth Cur, Cow/
   Hog Dog
Origin: Southern USA
Character: Courageous, independent, strong-minded, territorial, guardian, sweet
   with family
Overall working style: Close working, loose-eyed, tough, aggressive, bay and
   catch dogs
In a nutshell: Curs are similar to the dog Fred Gibson wrote about in his classic
   book, *Old Yeller.* They were used by early settlers to herd livestock, hunt
   game, and for protection. Cow/hog dogs were developed to gather and pen
   difficult stock such as wild cattle and feral hogs in the dense brush country.

Dutch Shepherd

Also known as: Berger Hollandais
Origin: Netherlands, near Belgium's northern provinces
Character: Hard, courageous, territorial, strong guardians; independent thinkers,
   reliable, loyal; tend to be one-person dogs. The long-hair variety is considered more easygoing than the smooth coat.
Overall working style: Upright, close, loose-eyed, strong prey drive
In a nutshell: Although Dutch Shepherds are well-known by K-9 handlers as defense and service dogs, developed for police work, personal protection and
   military duty, in the past they tended flocks of sheep as guardians and
   herders.

English Shepherd

Also known as: Old-Fashioned Farm Collie, Old Shep
Origin: Eastern USA
Character: Calm, dutiful, honest, faithful, eager to please, a good guardian
Overall working style: Upright, close, loose-eyed; natural heelers, moderate grip
In a nutshell: All-American farm dog; excellent dairy dog used in general day-
   to-day chores around the barn, corrals, and pastures, able to trail lost or in-
   jured animals.

German Shepherd Dog

Origin: Germany
Character: Assertive, courageous, steady, attentive; tractable, watchful, reliable,
   protective
Overall working style: Upright, close, loose-eyed; primarily gathers but may display driving tendencies
In a nutshell: German Shepherds consistently rank among the most popular
   breeds in the country. Though perhaps better known for military, police,
   and protection work, they are still used to manage flocks in Germany,
   where livestock is commonly grazed in unfenced meadows next to culti-

vated fields. GSDs from HGH (Herding Utility Dog) bloodlines—a German breed performance test—are more likely to have natural instincts to furrow.
Breeds based on the GSD: White Shepherd Dogs and the White Swiss Shepherd (Berger Blanc)—generally possess similar temperaments and herding styles. The Shiloh Shepherd is considered more easygoing and gentle.

Hairy Mouth Heeler
Also known as: Wire Mouth Heeler
Origin: USA
Character: Calm, independent, strong minded, hard, tenacious
Overall working style: Tough, close, hard heelers
In a nutshell: They are a strain of cowdogs developed from working Airedale Terriers. In the early to mid-1900s, Airedales were commonly used to tend stock (sheep and cattle) on farms and ranches. They are excellent for tracking and finding cattle.

Hanging Tree Cowdog
Origin: USA
Character: Hard, tenacious
Overall working style: Close, loose-to medium-eyed, tough, bold and aggressive
In a nutshell: Not a true breed, but a composite of several breeds created to work cattle.

Icelandic Sheepdog
Origin: Iceland
Character: Intelligent, happy, friendly, playful, independent; strong-minded though subordinate; devoted watch dogs
Overall working style: Upright, close, loose-eyed, moderate prey drive, gathering instincts, circles to contain the sheep and uses bark, works with tail naturally curled over back.
In a nutshell: Icelandic Sheepdogs are very similar to the Norwegian Buhund. They are a tough and enduring breed. In the fall, they were used to find stray sheep in the hills and mountains and bring them to the valleys below. In addition, they watched over the flocks and guarded the farm at night. They could also track sheep that were covered with snow and dig them out. Some are still being used as herding dogs in their homeland. Refer also to Norwegian Buhund.

Kerry Blue Terrier
Origin: Ireland
Character: While gentle companions, they are scrappy, independent and protective.
Overall working style: Upright, close, loose-eyed, nip the hocks and noses of stock
In a nutshell: The spunky Irish Blue has served man as an all-purpose working

dog, able to herd livestock and guard the farmstead as well as hunt small game and birds, and retrieve from land and water.

Lancashire Heeler
Also known as: Ormskirk Terrier
Origin: Lancashire in northwestern England
Character: Lively, feisty terrier temperament; good ratter
Overall working style: Upright, close, loose-eyed; nips the hocks and noses of stock
In a nutshell: Originally used to nip the heels of laggard animals and keep the farmstead free of rodents. Butchers found them handy to move animals in the slaughterhouse. While a few, very rare original heelers can still be located on a farm herding dairy cows to the milking barn, modern Lancashire Heelers are mainly companion dogs.

Lapphunds (Finnish Lapphund, Swedish Lapphund, Lapponian Reindeer Dogs)
Origin: Lapland (Finland, Sweden, Norway and part of Russia)
Character: Stable, intelligent, quick learner; willing, energetic; faithful, friendly and affectionate companion. Natural alarm dog; not aggressive toward people, yet protective of the family
Overall Working Style: Upright, close with loose-eyed, natural gathering instincts, tendency to circle; uses voice readily.
In a nutshell: The courageous Lapphund originated as a reindeer herder. Determination, speed, and endurance are traits necessary for bringing domestic caribou or reindeer off the tundra to the forests to graze lichen. An effective reindeer dog can handle herds of as many as a thousand animals, keeping them on the move and together. They are sometimes sent out to collect the herd alone or fetch a stray animal back to the herd from a distance of more than a few miles. The instincts that were once used to herd reindeer are readily transferred to other classes of livestock.

Finnish Lapphunds have retained good herding instincts and are still being used on farms to manage the small herds kept nearby for milk and transportation. They love to run. Today, though some Swedish Lapphunds are still used for herding, more emphasis is placed on showing, companionship, and performance activities.

Lapponian Herders or Lapland Reindeer Dogs are reliable workers and territorial. They are calm yet energetic, with speed and stamina, and are still being used in Lapland to work herds of reindeer.

McNab
Origin: USA/California
Character: Sensible, willing to please, natural guardian, independent thinker
Overall working style: Upright, close, loose-to medium-eyed; moderate grip, may bark; capable of handling stock in open and confined areas

In a nutshell: Although originally a sheepdog, the McNab is an all-around stock-dog developed by herdsmen from a localized strain in the region around Mendocino, California.

Mudi
Also known as: Canis Ovilis Fenyesi
Origin: Hungary
Character: Highly versatile, alert, energetic, calm and steady; independent thinker, but not headstrong or stubborn; willing to please, loyal, reserved with strangers, good guardian
Overall working style: Determined, strong drive, upright, close, loose-eyed; uses moderate bark, characteristically works with tail held higher
In a nutshell: Rugged farm and ranch dogs, tough enough to hunt wild boar yet capable of tending sheep. Mudis are used for driving cattle or handling large flocks of sheep in vast open pastures.

Nenet Herding Laika
Also known as: Reindeer Herding Laika
Origin: Northern Siberia
Character: Happy dogs, easily trained, good watchdogs; bark to warn of strangers but are generally friendly; can be dog aggressive and will compete for dominance.
Overall working style: Close, loose-eyed herder that uses voice.
In a nutshell: The Russian Laika was developed by the ancient Nentsy people and is a close relative of the Samoyed. They are a tough, hardy breed. Laikas are fast, strong dogs with stamina, courage, and determination needed to work reindeer and keep the herds together in the harsh conditions of the Arctic.

New Zealand Huntaway
Also known as: Huntaway
Origin: New Zealand
Character: Highly intelligent, biddable, easygoing; good watchdog
Overall working style: Upright, close, loose-eyed; strong use of voice
In a nutshell: The New Zealand Sheepdog is used to hunt sheep hidden in vast, difficult, brush-covered terrain, and to force mobs of sheep into yards or paddocks.

North American Shepherd
Also known as: Mini Aussie
Origin: USA
Character: Intelligent, trainable, willing to please, may be reserved, barks to warn
Overall working style: Close, upright, loose-eyed, tendency to circle and fetch, uses voice or body blocks, may head or heel depending on bloodlines
In a nutshell: This breed is descended from the Australian Shepherd. The NAS is

considered primarily a companion and show dog, but some are good herders and excel in performance events.

Norwegian Buhund
Origin: Norway
Character: Strong willed, intelligent, learns quickly; devoted companion, guardian, less inclined to roam than other Nordic breeds in the Spitz family
Overall working style: Upright, close, loose-eyed, gathering instincts, uses voice
In a nutshell: Buhunds are hard workers but at the end of the day are content to lie at their master's feet. They are considered large enough to handle any variety of livestock, yet small enough for easy keeping. Traditionally, they were used in the fall to gather sheep that had been grazing in the mountains all summer. Buhunds rely on their natural hunting ability to find the sheep among the fallen boulders and rocky outcrops. Once the flock was assembled, the dogs drove them out of the hills and took them back to lower pastures where they watched over them. Nordic herding breeds, including the Buhund, were not bred to work in hot or humid climates.

Old English Sheepdog
Origin: Great Britain
Character: Sweet, independent, clownish, tough, stubborn, boisterous; not aggressive, shy, or nervous
Overall working style: Upright, close, loose-eyed
In a nutshell: One of the oldest droving breeds of record, used to take cattle and sheep to market in the rugged British terrain. Today, more commonly found as companion and show dogs rather than herding.

Ovelheiro Gaucho
Also known as: Garafian Shepherd
Origin: Southern Brazil
Character: Adaptable, cheerful, learns commands easily; willing to please, docile, natural guardian
Overall working style: Upright, close, loose-to medium-eyed
In a nutshell: Developed for cattle ranching, though traditionally used to work sheep. Gaucho Shepherds possess the top qualities of a sheepdog along with the more forceful nature demanded of hardworking cowdogs.

Pastor Garafiano
Origin: Canary Islands
Character: Confident, friendly, calm and quiet; watchdog, obedient and easily trained
Overall working style: Upright, close, loose-eyed
In a nutshell: Agriculture and livestock are the basis of the economy in the Canaries. The breed was used traditionally to manage goat herds in hard-to-

reach grazing grounds on the steep, rocky terrain of Las Palmas, but they are highly valued by cattle dealers. As a group, these dogs resemble the German Shepherd Dog but have a milder temperament.

Pastor Vasco (Gorbekoa and Iletsua)
Also known as: Basque Shepherd, Euskal Artzain Txacurra
Origin: Spain
Character: Alert, sensible, intelligent problem solver, ranges from the friendly, outgoing Gorbekoa to the more sensitive Iletsua that is more reserved with strangers.
Overall working style: Upright, close, loose-to moderate-eyed
In a nutshell: The indigenous Basque Shepherds were quick and agile in pursuing sheep on dangerous and windy crags and known for hardiness and longevity.

Patagonian Sheepdog (or Shepherd)
Origin: Argentina and Chile
Overall working style: Fairly upright, moderately close, strong gathering with good backing ability, loose- to medium-eyed
In a nutshell: Used to gather and move enormous flocks of sheep in the vast, open spaces of Patagonia.

Picardy Shepherd
Also known as: Berger Picard
Origin: France
Character: Reserved towards strangers, loyal, willful yet sensitive; alert guardian, clever and perceptive
Overall working style: Upright, close, loose-eyed, handles sheep as easily as cattle
In a nutshell: They tended dairy and beef cattle on farms in the plain north of Paris in the past.

Polish Lowland Sheepdog
Also known as: Polski Owczarek Nizinny, PON
Origin: Poland
Character: Good-natured, confident, dominant and strong-willed; somewhat aloof and suspicious of strangers; devoted, alert, a good watchdog
Overall working style: Upright, close, loose-eyed, tough; will use voice
In a nutshell: Bold, resilient working dogs, historically used for herding flocks on the plains of Poland.

Portuguese Sheepdog
Also known as: Serra, Cão da Serra de Aires
Origin: Portugal
Character: Spirited, happy, highly devoted, guardian, territorial

Overall working style: Keen, upright, close, loose-eyed, strong gathering instincts; quick and agile, proficient at bringing back strays

In a nutshell: All-purpose farm dog similar to the Spanish Water Dog. They are well adapted to tending sheep, cattle, and goats on the southern plain of Portugal.

Puli

Also known as: Magyar Puli

Origin: Hungary

Character: Bouncy, happy, fun

Overall working style: Upright, close, loose-eyed; uses voice

In a nutshell: In the past, Pulis were used for herding flocks on the vast rolling plains east of the Danube in all weather. They worked alongside the Komondor, a livestock guardian used to protect the flocks. Today, they are used mainly for recreational herding.

Pumi

Origin: Hungary

Character: Alert, sharp, lively, intelligent, biddable, spunky (terrier)

Overall working style: Upright, close, loose-eyed, tough, and aggressive; uses bite and bark

In a nutshell: Also known as Hungarian herding terriers, Pumis are valued by herdsman to handle Steppe Cattle in the Hungarian Lowland. They are general farm dogs, used not only for cattle but also for hogs, but not used as much with sheep because of their strong grip.

Pyrenean Shepherd

Also known as: Berger des Pyrenees

Origin: France

Character: Alert, intelligent, brave, energetic, loyal, aloof with strangers, resourceful; the smooth face (Face Race) is generally considered more reserved than the rough face (Museau Normal).

Overall working style: Upright, close, loose-eyed, works with voice

In a nutshell: Used to herd sheep among the windy crags in the Pyrenees Mountains. Two are considered adequate to handle flocks numbering a thousand head. In some areas, they are used to hold the sheep in place while the ewes are milked.

Rottweiler

Origin: Germany

Character: Assertive

Overall working style: Upright, close, forceful, loose-to moderate-eyed; will gather, use body blocks

In a nutshell: Butchers and livestock dealers needed robust drovers to take cattle to market and to keep their money safe from robbers. They wanted strong-minded dogs that wouldn't give up in the face of a threat. With this need in mind, livestock drovers developed the hard-working butcher's dog of Rottweil. When cattle were no longer driven along the road to market, the breed found a new role as a draught dog, and was later recruited for police and military work. Today, these powerful herders capably demonstrate their ability to gather and herd stock quite efficiently.

Samoyed
Origin: Siberia
Character: Cheerful, gentle, trustworthy, look to master for direction
Overall working style: Upright, close, loose-eyed, natural gathering instinct; circle and may use voice
In a nutshell: Well known as a sled dog, the Samoyed is treasured for his versatility as a shepherd, and a trusted guardian as well. They were selected for strength, courage, and the ability to trail and find lost reindeer and bring in lagging calves. If necessary they would not hesitate to swim across a river or lake to round up strays or follow their charges. Samis now test their ability on sheep and are being used to herd domestic farm animals just as they once drove herds of caribou.

Savoy Shepherd (Sheepdog)
Also known as: Berger de Savoie
Origin: France
Character: Trustworthy, quiet, inquisitive, loyal, loving, versatile
Overall working style: Upright, close, loose-eyed
In a nutshell: All-purpose farm dogs around Savoy. Used by dairymen grazing their Alpine goats, as well as for rounding up stray Abondance and Tarentaise cattle in the high mountain meadows.

Schapendoes
Also known as: Dutch Sheep Dog, Sheep Poodle
Origin: Netherlands
Character: Dynamic, attentive, clear thinking, headstrong, playful, affectionate, loyal
Overall working style: Upright, close, loose-eyed, uses voice
In a nutshell: Used by shepherds who depended on them to herd flocks of sheep grazing along roadsides and in unfenced meadows during the day, and then to bring them home to their enclosures at night.

Schnauzers (Giant and Standard)
Origin: Germany
Character: Alert, strong willed but tolerant and trainable; loyal family companion and guardian.
Overall Working Style: Upright, close, with loose to moderate eye. They have fairly strong prey drive and will use voice.

In a nutshell: Although they were not moved into the Herding Group when AKC divided the Working Group, Schnauzers were originally all-around farm dogs used by butchers and cattle dealers to bring the cows and goats in for milking, herd them to market, and to guard the homestead and control vermin. When modern transportation methods replaced cattle drives in Germany, the Giant Schnauzer remained a butcher's dog, stockyard helper, and guardian.

Shetland Sheepdog
Origin: Great Britain/Shetland Islands
Character: Sensitive, gentle, not headstrong; easily trained, willing to please, reserved with strangers, tends to be vocal
Overall working style: Upright, close, loose-eyed; inclined to circle, most use voice.
In a nutshell: These beautiful little dogs are highly successful in obedience and agility competitions and are proving their ability to work as herding dogs. Shelties were used on the small farms known as crofts. Crofters used them to keep sheep away from unfenced gardens, and in the summer months sheep were ferried to outlying islands. When autumn rolled around, the dogs helped gather the stock to be brought back to the mainland, where they were wintered.

Smithfield
Also known as: Smithy, Tasmanian Smithfield
Origin: Australia/Tasmania
Character: Sociable, exuberant, gentle, sensible, trustworthy, stable, confident, loyal, devoted
Overall working style: Forceful, upright, close; quick and eager, will bark or bite to move animals; some will catch and hold a ewe for inspection, some can be trained to cast wide for gathering
In a nutshell: Valued by pioneers for their versatility—herding, guarding, and hunting abilities. They are all-around dogs with good stock sense used in the stockyards and farms in temperate regions.

Soft Coated Wheaten Terrier
Origin: Ireland
Character: Self-confident, somewhat stubborn, gentle companions
Overall working style: Upright, close, loose-eyed
In a nutshell: Though related, the Soft Coated Wheaten Terrier is milder in disposition than the Kerry Blue. They were developed as an all-around farm and family dog to watch over the farm and to warn off trespassers. Capable of herding sheep and cattle in addition to being used as a hunting dog capable of tracking badgers or otters and keep down rats and mice.

Spanish Water Dog
Also known as: Perro de Agua Español

Origin: Southern Spain

Character: Adaptable, highly devoted, reserved but not shy; somewhat reactive

Overall working style: Loose-eyed, upright, close, authoritative stockdogs, able to head or low-heel, with strong gathering instincts.

In a nutshell: Spanish Water Dogs are primarily herding dogs with strong guarding and retrieving instincts. For centuries they were used to manage sheep and goats in the rocky terrain of Andalusia. Today, they are a multi-purpose farm dog used to gather, drive, and pen cattle as well as a fisherman's helper.

Water Dogs in Herding

The Portuguese Water Dog and the Barbet, a rare and very old French breed of water dog, are very similar in type to the Spanish Water Dog and believed to be related to Poodles, exceptionally intelligent and trainable.

They became known as a working man's dog, popular as a sailor's companion at sea as well as a shepherd dog for driving flocks. They were essentially a hunter's assistant for wild fowling, able to find, flush, and retrieve birds, as well as herd waterfowl lacking flight feathers (ducks or geese in molt) into traps. Likewise, the herding instincts of Portuguese Water Dogs have been used for herding fish into nets.

Stumpy Tail Cattle Dog

Also known as: Smithfield Heeler

Origin: Australia

Character: Loyal, courageous, tough, strong willed; inquisitive but suspicious of strangers

Overall working style: Silent, upright, close, driving dogs; will head and heel, loose to moderate eye

In a nutshell: Stumpy Tails were developed by cattle drovers to move untamed cattle across vast distances of rugged terrain. They are closely related to Australian Cattle Dogs, but generally considered faster and more agile, with a higher degree of stamina and heat tolerance than their cousins.

Swedish Vallhund

Also known as: Vastgotaspets, Swedish Cattledog, Viking dog

Origin: Sweden

Character: Typical Spitz personality; outgoing; a good guardian, yet gentle with children; devoted, eager to please, sense of humor, spontaneous

Overall working style: Upright, close, loose-eyed; low heeler, will head

In a nutshell: The Vallhund has long been valued as a cow dog, with the instinct to grip the heels of a slow-moving cow to prod it along. What they may lack in length of leg, they make up for in bravado.

Swiss Mountain Cattle Dogs (Appenzeller, Bernese Mountain Dog, Entlebucher, Greater Swiss Mountain Dog)

Also known as: Sennenhunds
Origin: Switzerland
Character: Friendly, even-tempered, well-behaved guardian; reserved with strangers, pleasant
Overall working style: Their ability ranges from quick, low heeling, hard-hitting cow dogs to gentle, easygoing herders.
In a nutshell: The Appenzeller, Bernese Mountain Dog, Entlebucher and the Greater Swiss Mountain Dog were used by butchers, dairymen, and cattle dealers to drive their herds to mountain meadows, and bring them home again. They were valued for their ability to keep the animals in the boundaries of their property, not allowing them to stray beyond. After harvest and haymaking they would drive the cattle to pasture in the valleys.

The sweet-natured Bernese has a mild herding style. They won't exhibit the more aggressive herding behaviors like the quicker, smaller Entlebucher or Appenzeller. History tells us they were used to seek lost cows and drive them to the milking place to be stabled. They will try to nudge a cow with their muzzle, but if necessary, may grip the cow's nose. On the other hand, the very capable Appenzeller and Entlebucher are self-confident and assertive. They are used to bring the cows off the mountain pastures and able to head or bite low on the hocks, then dodge a kick.

Terceira Island Cattledog

Also known as: Azorean Barbado Dog
Origin: Portugal/Azores in the North Atlantic
Character: Reserved with strangers, passive, happy, pleasant, loyal, clever, trainable yet willful guardian
Overall working style: Alert, upright, close, loose-eyed; rugged, agile cow dog
In a nutshell: Used for guarding and controlling cattle in the Azores, on Terceira Island.

Texas Blue Lacy

Also known as: Blue Lacy Hog Dog, Lacy
Origin: USA (state dog of Texas)
Character: Sensitive, friendly, fairly easy to handle
Overall working style: Tough, upright, close, loose-eyed, catch and bay dogs
In a nutshell: Rugged herding breed with speed, stamina; used for hunting and baying feral hogs and bunching wild cattle.

Texas Heeler
Origin: USA/Southwest
Character: Alert, reserved with strangers, clever, trainable guardian
Overall working style: Gutsy, rugged, upright, close, loose to moderate eye; low
    heelers
In a nutshell: Texas Heelers are popular cowdogs on western ranches. They are
    typically a cross between a Blue Heeler and an Australian Shepherd or a
    Border Collie.

Tibetan Terrier
Also known as: Dhokhi Apso
Origin: Tibet
Character: Friendly, but reserved around strangers; resourceful
Overall working style: Upright, close-and loose-eyed, circles and barks, inclina-
    tion to back
In a nutshell: Ancestors worked for nomadic tribes of the Himalayan valleys;
    today they are considered more of a companion and show dog than an
    actual working dog, but they are finding a niche in recreational herding ac-
    tivities.

Welsh Corgi (Cardigan and Pembroke)
Origin: Wales
Cardigan Corgi — Character: The Cardigan has been described as "a German
    Shepherd Dog with short legs." Big attitude, even tempered, devoted, af-
    fectionate
Pembroke Corgi — Character: Kindly, spirited, loyal, affectionate, intelligent,
    alert
In a nutshell: Corgis were used for centuries as drovers' dogs in Wales. Their
    short legs enable them to nip the heels of cattle—to keep them moving
    along the road or to push them through chutes or a gate—as well as to
    perform other jobs, such as keeping sheep off the feeders while hay is being
    put in. To some extent, the Cardigan has an advantage over the Pembroke,
    due to slightly longer legs to outmaneuver stock.

Welsh Sheepdog
Origin: Wales
Character: Courageous, devoted, highly adaptable; good watchdog, generally
    good with children, reserved with strangers
Overall working style: Upright, close, loose-eyed; uses voice strongly if neces-
    sary; a strong dog can catch and hold a ewe on command; most will catch
    a ewe or lamb for treatment. Some will run across the backs of sheep if
    they become jammed.
In a nutshell: Tempered by the environment of the high, stony slopes of their
    native country, Welsh Sheepdogs are a highly capable farm dog. They are
    prized for their stamina and the power to move large numbers of sheep, as

well as face stubborn rams and angry cows. They will spring to flush sheep from rocks or undergrowth and have tremendous agility and stamina.

Westerwälder Cowdog
Origin: Germany
Character: Audacious, hard and protective
Overall working style: Upright, close, loose-eyed, low-heeler; will furrow, but has less tendency to furrow than other types of Altdeutsche Schaferhunde.
In a nutshell: The Westerwälder Cowdog is highly regarded by herdsmen for its ability to easily manage a herd numbering 500 head, keeping them from straying from unfenced pastures to adjacent fields with crops and protecting their master from bull attacks.

Dogs Not Suitable for Herding

Although the FCI standard lists the Romanian Shepherd Dogs (Carpathian Herder and the Mioritic Shepherd) as herding breeds, they are livestock guardians. They don't control the movement of the flock, but follow the herding dogs in their work.

There are several breeds or types of dog that erroneously appear in certain books and on some Internet sources as herding dogs, such as the Hovawart, a re-creation of a very old type of German estate and flock guardian dog that has not in fact been bred to have the instinctive behavior that makes for a successful herder. In the same way, the Czechoslovakian Wolfdog (Czechoslovakian Vlcak) classified as currently destined for the AKC Herding Group in the Foundation Stock Service (FSS) Registry, has not been selected for qualities that make for a good herding prospect. They were developed strictly behind the Iron Curtain as service dogs for the army, but not for herding ability. Some texts describe the South Russian Sheepdog as a livestock guardian and herder. However, they were primarily developed to be highly protective guardians against wolves and other predators. Their character is fierce, courageous, independent, willful, and dominant.

Index

About the Authors

Jeanne Joy Hartnagle-Taylor and Ty Taylor

Jeanne Joy Hartnagle-Taylor is the third of four generations to enjoy a lifetime association with working stockdogs. Her experience has taken her on assignment with the Department of Interior to work wild bison bulls with her Aussies as well as with the United States Department of Agriculture to gather livestock for various inspections. She has titled Australian Shepherds in all areas of competition and has been in the top ten at the ASCA National Stockdog Finals. Success in training and competitions eventually led to invitations to exhibit her fine dogs at various livestock events, fairs, and rodeos. Jeanne Joy performed at the Livestock Expo in Tepatitlan, Guadalajara, by special invitation from the Governor of Jalisco, Mexico. She has judged the European Championships at the Continental Sheepdog Trials in Germany as well as presented training seminars all across North America and Europe. She was one of the original AKC Herding Judges and is one of only a few ASCA Stockdog judges qualified to judge conformation as an ASCA Senior Breeder Judge.

Jeanne is uniquely qualified to talk about stockdogs and has written for numerous publications such as *Western Horseman, American Cowboy* and *The Cattleman*. She has authored several books, including *All About Aussies: The Australian Shepherd from A to Z, Stockdog Savvy*, and *Greasepaint Matadors: The Unsung Heroes of Rodeo. All About Aussies*, currently in its third edition, was nominated for a Dog Writer's Award, and now we have *Stockdog Savvy*. Additionally, Jeanne is featured in the highly acclaimed stockdog training series, Herding I, II, III by Canine Training Systems.

Her co-author and husband, Ty Taylor, is a cowboy who has handled stockdogs from the ranch to the sales yard. He was first introduced to using working dogs while riding for a major cutting horse operation. Besides being a cowboy, Ty is a professional auctioneer, and also a country singer, songwriter, and producer who has performed on the Grand Ole Opry numerous times and on Austin City Limits while working for country legend Loretta Lynn and Doug Stone, respectively.

Acknowledgments

The authors would like to acknowledge the following contributors for their outstanding photographs:

Australian National Travel Association
Gary R. Anderson
Mindy Bower
Deb Conroy
Judy Cummings
Diane Decker
Joel Finch
Jim and Sue Foster
Cee Hambo
Carol Ann Hartnagle
Lori Herbel
Satu Huusko
Jeff Jaquish
Silja Jonsson
Cindy Loida
Doug MacSpadden
Hildy Morgan
Pat Morgan
Ellen Nickelsberg
Becky Parker
Mary Peaslee
Adriana Plum
Michael M. Trafford
Christine Renna
Elsie Rhodes
An Vanhoof
Tanya Wheeler

We would also like to thank Katy Lynn Taylor and Tyler Justin Taylor for their terrific illustrations, as well as Deb Conroy, Sheila Dolan, Carol Ann Hartnagle, Jim Hartnagle, Matt Mason DVM, Chris Renna, Chris Rolf DVM, Mike Ryan and Tanya Wheeler for their comments that helped improve the manuscript.

FOR MORE INSTRUCTION ON HERDING . . .

Herding I, II and III on DVD

A well-trained stockdog is among the most disciplined of all working dogs. An Australian Shepherd driving steers across the wide-open plains, a Kelpie jumping over the backs of tightly packed sheep in a chute to get them moving again, or a Border Collie rounding up a flock of ducks at a show are impressive sights – graceful, single-minded, and in complete control.

Herding dogs need jobs to do or they will become anxious and unhappy. When acquired as companions, herding dogs require skilled owners who understand how to draw out their best traits and satisfy their herding instincts. When acquired as true stockdogs for the farm or ranch or as competitive trial dogs, they require careful and consistent training. Put a working dog in charge of a flock of sheep set out to pasture, have him drive a herd of cattle into pens, or let him excel at competitive events. **Herding I, II and III** provides tips for selecting a puppy, and delves deeply into the training necessary to prepare a dog for trial competitions or herding on the farm and ranch in the real world.

For more information about **Herding I, II and III**, the companion series to **Stockdog Savvy** on DVD, contact:

Hartnagle
32160 Private Road 55
Kiowa, Colorado 80117
Phone: (303) 621-2880
Fax: (303) 621-9624
Website: http://www.lasrocosa.com/education.html
E-mail: hartnagle@aol.com